27.50/22.

Privatization and Provincial Social Services in Canada

Privatization and Provincial Social Services in Canada

Policy, Administration and Service Delivery

EDITED BY
JACQUELINE S. ISMAEL
YVES VAILLANCOURT

 THE UNIVERSITY OF ALBERTA PRESS

First published by
The University of Alberta Press
Athabasca Hall
Edmonton, Alberta
Canada T6G 2E8

Copyright © The University of Alberta Press 1988

ISBN 0-88864-132-X cloth
    0-88864-133-8 paper

Canadian Cataloguing in Publication Data

Main entry under title:

Privatization and provincial social services in Canada : policy, administration and service delivery

Includes bibliographical references.
ISBN 0-88864-132-X (bound). — ISBN 0-88864-133-8 (pbk.)

1. Social service - Canada. 2. Social service - Government policy - Canada. 3. Privatization - Canada. I. Ismael, Jacqueline S. II. Vaillancourt, Yves.
HV108.P75 1988   361.6'15'0971   C88-091075-5

All rights reserved.
No part of this publication may be produced, stored in a retrieval system, or transmitted in any forms or by any means, electronic, mechanical, photocopying, recording, or otherwise, without the prior permission of the copyright owner.

Typesetting by Pièce de Résistance Ltée., Edmonton, Alberta, Canada
Printed by Gagne Printing Ltd., Louiseville, Quebec, Canada

Contents

Preface vii

Contributors xi

1 Privatization of Social Services: A Heuristic Approach 1
JACQUELINE S. ISMAEL

2 British Columbia 13
MARILYN CALLAHAN
CHRIS McNIVEN

3 Alberta 41
JOSEPH P. HORNICK
R.J. THOMLISON
LYNNE NESBITT

4 Saskatchewan 75
MICHAEL O'SULLIVAN
SANDRA SORENSEN

5 Manitoba 95
DENIS C. BRACKEN
PETER HUDSON

6 Ontario 119
RAMESH MISHRA
GLENDA LAWS
PRISCILLA HARDING

7   Quebec   141
    YVES VAILLANCOURT

8   New Brunswick   171
    ROBERT MULLALY
    NÉRÉ ST-AMAND

9   Federal Policy and the Privatization of Provincial Social Services   197
    ANDREW F. JOHNSON

10 Conclusion: Privatization in Comparative Provincial Perspective   219
    JACQUELINE S. ISMAEL
    YVES VAILLANCOURT

Preface

Privatization of social services has been both heralded and decried as the most significant provincial social policy trend in the eighties. While privatization advocates have aggressively advanced it as the solution to public social service fiscal, administrative and political dilemmas, its antagonists have as aggressively attacked it as an erosion of the principles of universality and equity in the social service delivery system. The debate has been fundamentally ideological, however, and there is little systematic or comparative information available on the scope or nature of federal or provincial policies with regard to privatization.

This polemical debate about privatization of social services in Canada stimulated the initiation of this project. It represents an effort to examine both the scope and significance of privatization of social services in the Canadian provinces. Given the limited amount of systematically comparative research available on provincial social policies and social services, a case study approach was adopted to bring forward as an initial overview provincial trends in privatization.

The objective of each case study is to identify provincial policies directly bearing upon the phenomenon of privatization and to examine their impact upon the provincial social service delivery system. The first chapter sets forward a general perspective on privatization from the available literature, and identifies significant dimensions of the process. The subsequent case studies explore provincial policies in the framework of this perspective, with attention to the dimensions identified. Federal policy, which can act as a significant stimulus or hindrance to provincial policies, is also examined. The final chapter considers the findings of the case studies from a comparative perspective.

In 1945, Harry M. Cassidy published his seminal survey of provincial health and social services in Canada, entitled *Public Health and Welfare Reorganization: The Post-War Problem in the Canadian Provinces*. The volume represented something of a milestone in Canadian social policy and administration studies, highlighting as it did the importance of comparative interprovincial research of Canadian human services. Unfortunately, however, the way pointed by Cassidy over forty years ago has remained tangential to the mainstream of Canadian social policy and administration studies.

Indeed, since World War Two, most Canadian writing in the domain of Canadian social policy has focussed either on the role of the federal state, or on the role of some provincial states. There has been very little effort at systematic comparison across provinces of social policy issues, development or administration. As well, the concept of Canadian is often misused in Canadian social policy research and literature. From a Quebec perspective, for example, it is astounding to see that many social policy writers in English Canada do not hesitate to label Canadian some social policy books and papers in which we find almost no reference to Quebec social policy experience or literature. But in Quebec social policy literature, it is easier to come across references to European countries such as France, Belgium, Germany and Sweden rather than to other Canadian provinces. It could also be observed that much social policy research in Canada shows a better knowledge of American, British or French social welfare programs than of provincial Canadian programs.

Just as international comparisons are essential to understanding the welfare state phenomena, so too interprovincial comparisons are necessary to grasp the evolution and current situation of Canadian social policy practice and theory. In examining the issue of privatization, this book could be considered an attempt to follow the path of comparative analysis of provincial social policy and administration pioneered by Harry Cassidy. It is only a beginning, of course, and like Cassidy's study, confines itself to a case study approach to explore the parameters of descriptive comparison. Hopefully, it will demonstrate the theoretical significance and empirical utility of interprovincial comparisons in the study of the Canadian welfare state, and lead to more rigorous analytic comparisons of social policy and social administration issues generally and privatization particularly.

This project has proceeded through several stages of development. Initiated in the summer of 1985, there was an effort to include every Canadian province in the study. However, this proved impossible. Seven of the ten Canadian provinces are included, providing sufficient coverage to overview the direction of any trend in Canada.

In March 1986, a workshop for the project participants was held in the Faculty of Social Welfare at The University of Calgary for the purpose of refining the general framework, presenting initial findings on the case studies, and developing guidelines for completion of the project. And in June 1986, a three-hour panel was organized at the Learned Societies meetings held at The University of Manitoba. Through these meetings and through correspondence, the project participants attempted to develop and maintain a common perspective on the project. A more rigorous comparative approach was considered premature at this exploratory juncture.

We wish to thank the project participants for their role in this endeavor. It has been a great pleasure to work together as a team, and we hope we will have further opportunities for such fruitful collaboration. We also wish to acknowledge the role of Dean Ray Thomlison, Faculty of Social Welfare, The University of Calgary, in making the March 1986 workshop possible. It was a most significant meeting in the project's progress, and without his assistance it would not have been possible.

Contributors

DENIS C. BRACKEN is an Assistant Professor and Director of the Inner City Social Work Program at the University of Manitoba. His major interests are in the area of criminal justice policy and social welfare. He has authored reports on Native people and probation, and the private sector and criminal justice policy.

MARILYN CALLAHAN is an Associate Professor and Director at the School of Social Work at the University of Victoria. She is currently involved in research in women's work environments, social services for family and children, and national child welfare trends. She is an active member of the social work profession and a past president of the British Columbia Association of Social Workers.

PRISCILLA HARDING is a doctoral student in the Faculty of Social Work, University of Toronto.

JOSEPH P. HORNICK is the former Director of Research of the Faculty of Social Welfare, The University of Calgary. He is currently Executive Director of the Canadian Research Institute for Law and the Family. Among his recent publications is a special issue of the *Journal of Comparative Family Studies* entitled "Children and Family Law: An International Perspective," XVIII, No. 2 (Summer 1987), co-edited with Barbara A. Burrows.

PETER HUDSON is an Associate Professor and Director of the School of Social Work, University of Manitoba. He has recently completed an evaluation of the Canada-Manitoba-Northern Indian Child Welfare Agreement, and has authored or coauthored several articles on the subject of native child welfare.

JACQUELINE S. ISMAEL is a Professor of Social Welfare at The University of Calgary. She is the author of numerous books and articles on international and Canadian social policy. Her recent publications include *PDR Yemen: The Politics of Socialist Transformation*, *Canadian Social Welfare Policy: Federal and Provincial Dimensions* and *The Canadian Welfare State: Evolution and Transition*.

ANDREW F. JOHNSON is an Associate Professor of Political Science, Bishop's University. He has published various articles on Canadian social welfare policy and has recently edited a collection of articles on "Labour Leadership in Comparative Perspective" for the journal *Studies in History and Politics*.

GLENDA LAWS teaches in the Department of Geography, York University.

CHRIS R. McNIVEN is an Associate Professor of Social Welfare, University of British Columbia. Her current research interests include a study of factors that influence support for different types of welfare programs among various segments of the Canadian public.

RAMESH MISHRA teaches in the School of Social Work, McMaster University. He is the author of *Society and Social Policy* and *The Welfare State in Crisis*.

ROBERT MULLALY has a doctorate in social work from the University of Toronto. Founding member of social work studies at the St.-Thomas University, he has chaired this department from July 1983 to June 1987. His interest and publications are in social policies and programs for minorities, self-help groups, and citizen participation. He was recently on sabbatical leave and studying social policies in Sweden.

LYNNE NESBITT has a MA in Sociology from the University of Manitoba and was a research assistant for Policy Planning and Applied Research in Calgary.

NÉRÉ ST-AMAND has a doctorate in sociology, University of Nice, France. He has been the Director of the Université de Moncton's School of Social Work since 1983. As well as many articles on mental health and professional burnout, he is the author of "Folie et Oppression" and co-author of "Multidisciplinarity, an innovative new approach?"

MICHAEL W. O'SULLIVAN is the former Director of Education for the Saskatchewan Human Rights Commission and was, at the time of writing, lecturing in the School of Human Justice and Department of Political Science at the University of Regina. He is presently the Regional Field Officer for the Latin American Program of CUSO and is living in San Jose, Costa Rica.

SANDRA G. SORENSEN was at the time of writing the Communications Director for the Saskatchewan Government Employees Union (SGEU). Previously she has worked as an educational programmer for special needs groups in Manitoba and Saskatchewan. She is founder of The Women's Press, a feminist publishing house in Toronto.

RAY J. THOMLISON is Professor and Dean of the Faculty of Social Welfare, The University of Calgary. He has published numerous articles, has contributed chapters to books, is a co-editor of *Perspectives on Social Services and Social Issues*, and is the editor of *Perspectives on Industrial Social Work Practice*.

YVES VAILLANCOURT is Professor in the Department of Social Work at the University of Quebec in Montreal. He has done extensive writing on Quebec social policy in recent years, and has participated in two forthcoming publications—*L'evolution des politiques sociales au Québec 1940-1960*, and *La privatization des services sociaux*. His Ph.D. thesis is entitled "Canada Assistance Plan: A Quebec Perspective."

1 Privatization of Social Services
A Heuristic Approach

JACQUELINE S. ISMAEL

Privatization of the welfare state has been identified as a major trend changing the process and structure of social service delivery in capitalist society.[1] As a process, it has been identified by a broad range of state policies aimed at rolling back either the rate of growth or the absolute amount of state activity in the social service delivery system.[2] As a trend—a general tendency in the course of events and conditions that indicates a particular direction or movement of change in the structure of the welfare state—privatization may be identified as part of a broader process of devolution of responsibility for social provision to the needy from the public to the private sector. Insofar as this broader trend represents a return to a more residual model of welfare provision—where the market, the family and organized philanthropy are the primary providers—privatization reflects the promotion of this trend through public policy.[3]

Because there has been little systematic examination of privatization in Canada, this volume presents an overview of privatization of personal social services in seven provinces as well as at the federal level. A common framework has been adopted to allow some general comparisons across political jurisdictions about privatization as a process, and to provide an empirical basis for speculation about it as part of a broader trend. While there are other dimensions to privatization,[4] this study focuses primarily on the reduction of direct state provision of social services. The framework, set forth in the following pages, provides a focus on the division of labour between public and private provision in the social service delivery system.

Domains in the Delivery System

In their seminal work on domain theory, Kouzes and Mico[5] argued that human service organizations are comprised of three distinct domains—policy, administration and service provision. They maintain that each domain operates by different and contrasting principles, success measures, structural arrangements and work modes. This construct can be used to differentiate levels of action or domains in the division of labour within the service delivery system.

Policy Domain

Provincial authority over social welfare, established by the BNA Act and reaffirmed by the Constitution Act, 1982, has made provincial policy the principal arbiter in the evolution of social services within each province. Because the province has almost unrestricted legal authority (though not fiscal power) over social services, provincial policy sets the conditions for events in the other domains. And as a result there is wide variation among provincial social service delivery systems.

Within the policy domain, we are focussing on the reduction of direct state provision of social services, attempting to identify if a province has adopted explicitly or implicitly policies that reduce state responsibility for social provision to the needy. While overt cutbacks in services or benefits constitute an explicit policy and an absolute reduction, it is important in terms of identifying the trend toward devolution of responsibility to identify policies that have this implicit effect—incentive mechanisms to stimulate private sector provision and restraint mechanisms to cut back the rate of growth of the public sector.

Viewed as part of a process of devolution of responsibility for service provision from the public to the private sector, privatization relates to the division of labour between public and private sectors. Generally, the development of the Canadian welfare state is correlated with the evolution of responsibility to higher levels of authority—from private charitable organizations to municipal authorities, then to provincial and federal levels of public authority. This evolution has been the pattern of development over the century—a patchquilt pattern no doubt, but in broad historical view still a pattern.[6] The process of devolution is in strong contrast to this. The demise of the comprehensive social security review in the seventies serves as a benchmark for it.

The political debates over social security reform, so prominent in the early seventies, were displaced by the end of the decade by debates over the contingencies of federal-provincial relations and the exigencies of fiscal restraint.[7] The momentum of devolution has picked up since that benchmark and is evident in the restraint programs adopted across all political jurisdictions to forestall the rate of growth of the public sector. As one of the fastest growing components of the public budget, social expenditures have come under particular scrutiny. Privatization is a means of rationalizing social spending in a market economy and restraining the rate of growth of the public social service sector in a period of increasing demand for services. The shift of responsibility for service provision from public servants to private markets provides a political buffer against public discontent in an era of fiscal restraint and economic restructuring, and an administrative buffer against service accountability.

Many services delivered through a pluralist market type delivery model rather than the state bureaucratic model may well be more efficient, effective, and responsive, as its advocates claim; and many may not, as its critics claim.[8] This is not the issue we are addressing, however. The issue of responsibility for social provision to the needy is at the core of the ideological debate about the welfare state. An assessment of the scope and magnitude of privatization policies across provinces—a central task of this project—will contribute to an understanding of the trajectory of change on this issue within the Canadian welfare mosaic.

Administration Domain
The administration domain is the level at which policies are operationalized into programs of service. The domain includes programs in the public sector, the private nonprofit sector and the proprietary sector. It is, in other words, the hodgepodge of agencies that constitute the social service delivery system. The issue we are addressing is whether the fiscal, regulatory and subsidy policies that constitute a provincial privatization package are changing the power and accountability structure between policy and administration domains and the division of labour within the administration domain.[9]

Traditionally, the distinctions between statutory and nonstatutory programs and sources of funding (public or private) have been the basis for the division of labour between public social services and private nonprofit social services funded philanthropically (the voluntary sector). Privately marketed services (proprietary sector) have for the most part fallen outside of the welfare state framework. In some provinces, a symbiotic relationship developed between the public and voluntary sectors with some statutory services delivered through philanthropic agencies, but generally this has been confined to specific areas as in children's aid societies. However, with the rapid expansion of the welfare state through the sixties and early seventies, public subsidy to private nonprofit agencies—primarily in the form of program or project grants—became a vehicle for the expansion of community based social services and a focus for volunteer mobilization.[10] A study by the Canadian Council on Social Development documents the extent of provincial fiscal support for volunteer programs.[11]

Public fiscal policy in the social services area during this period effectively stimulated the growth of a dynamic voluntary sector engaged in crisis intervention, advocacy, self-help, public education, information and referral—a plethora of social services activities to fill in the interstices of the public safety net.[12] This autonomous voluntary sector has played an important advocacy role in promoting public recognition of unmet needs and public accountability to community standards of welfare and human rights. The development of crisis centres and women's shelters are examples of the social action function of mobilized volunteerism. Ralph Kramer has summarized the role of the voluntary sector accordingly:

> Most discussions of the character, goals and functions of voluntary agencies imply the performance of four organizational *roles*.
> (1) As *vanguard*, the purpose of the voluntary agency is to innovate, pioneer, experiment, and demonstrate programs, some of which may eventually be taken over by the government.
> (2) As *improver* or *advocate*, the agency is expected to serve as a critic, watchdog, or gadfly as it pressures a governmental body to extend, improve, or establish needed services.
> (3) As *value guardian* of voluntaristic, particularistic, and sectarian values, a voluntary agency is expected to promote citizen participation, to develop leadership, and to protect the special interests of social, religious, cultural, or other minority groups.
> (4) As *service provider* the voluntary agency delivers certain services it has selected, some of which may be a public responsibility that government is unable, is unwilling, or prefers not to assume.[13]

But the traditional distinctions between public and voluntary services disappeared in the process of expansion of the welfare state. The voluntary sector has become increasingly dependent upon public funds; purchase of service contracts are used to provide statutory and ancillary services through the voluntary sector; and proprietary firms have entered the competition for service contracts. Thus, the division of labour in social service provision is no longer demarcated by publicly funded and provided statutory programs and privately funded and provided nonstatutory programs. Public funding permeates the voluntary sector and is the primary incentive for the emerging proprietary sector.

These are general trends manifested differently in each province. The division of labour varies from province to province, dependent as it is on the financial constraints on social spending within a province, the ideological context within which public policy on the social services is determined, as well as the historical, social, and demographic forces that have variously shaped patterns of service delivery within a province. Nevertheless, the general pattern of increasing public provision of social services through the private sectors appears to be a general trend in Canada as well as other welfare states.[14]

These trends were stimulated by the rapid expansion of state social spending and generally reflected expansion in the scope of state social responsibility for provision to the needy. The assumption of state responsibility was certainly at the core of the welfare state concept. The rhetoric of privatization is in strong contrast to this. It is stimulated by the objective of limiting both public social spending and the scope of public responsibility for social provision to the needy, and legitimated by a market ethos of efficiency, effectiveness, and responsiveness[15] (rather than the social action ethos of community empowerment, accessibility, and equity that constituted the dominant themes of welfare state expansion). The introduction of the proprietary sector as a competitor in the provision of publicly funded services in effect formalizes the market framework of service delivery.

The essence of the privatization of the administration domain is the transformation of private nonprofit agencies into business enterprises. Their customers are government bodies, not service consumers. This fundamentally changes the power and accountability structure and imposes bureaucratic patterns of coordination and control on the private sector. These changes are manifested in the imposition of rules and regulations governing task performance and the necessity of maintaining detailed records of financial accounting as the essence of accountability in the expenditure of public funds and the delivery of public services. A vision of this is presented by Candace P. Mueller in reviewing the problem of accountability and purchase of service contracts in the American context:

In connection with pricing the service, the provider agencies must be accountable for the use of public funds. A system should be established to require this . . . . Such a system should include use of uniform cost accounting and reporting methods, availability of complete fiscal records to the state for review, development of methods and criteria for evaluating the efficiency and effectiveness of services provided, and use of licensing standards and cooperation with the public agency in strengthening those standards.[16]

Rather than fostering the debureaucratization and deregulation that is the essence of the privatization vision, it is more likely that these noxious features of the welfare state will devolve unto the private sector. This is because the state itself is the principle customer. Furthermore, within this structural framework, the position of clients as objects of service rather than the subjects of service will be formalized. Neil Gilbert aptly summarized this accordingly:

With this type of third-party payment the entire transaction is perceived by neither the customer, who does not pay for the service, nor the purchaser, who does not receive the service. Under these arrangements the service provider is more accountable to the public body purchasing services than to the customer . . . this indirect line of accountability often travels through two or three layers of government; the information costs are quite high; and the degree of accountability thus achieved is often limited.[17]

The devolution of responsibility for service provision from the public to the private sectors will impact upon the administration domain in profound ways. While the pattern is still emerging, we may deduce some initial changes in the administration domain that indicate the broad outlines of the pattern. However, these are more hypotheses about outcomes based upon particular events and conditions rather than conclusions from representative samples. Nevertheless, the outline is compelling and should draw our attention to some important issues in the changing service delivery system:

1. The erosion of private sector autonomy in the setting of service priorities, the definition of service tasks and/or the mode of delivery. By buying services which meet priorities established in the public sector and tying grants to the question of the complementarity of

services with public services, the policy domain may effectively reduce the autonomy of the private sector in its outreach and advocacy roles, in effect depoliticizing it as agencies increasingly compete to service specific funder needs rather than diffuse client needs.[18]

2. The devolution of residual provision onto the private sector. The division of labour organized in the public sphere around the functionally specific categorical approach to service delivery is devolving unto the private sphere.[19] This division of labour evolved to control social problems and contrasts sharply with the functionally diffuse division of labour organized around the needs of population sub-groups or communities that has characterized the voluntary sector. What this means is that in the competition for contracts and grants agencies are tending to become organized around the delivery of treatment services which in effect define the needs and rights of clients, rather than around clients whose needs and rights define the services. In other words, the funded services define the services available to clients rather than the clients' needs defining the services. In the market framework of services as commodities—services bought and sold—it is not surprising that the least valued services and the least traded are those that are most intangible—the developmental services that are more a product of creative problem solving and affective interaction than the performance of specific tasks. Developmental, preventative, outreach and advocacy services will be cut back in favour of treatment services as the state shifts residual provision onto the private sector.[20]

Service Provision Domain

The service provision domain relates to the frontline of service delivery—the point at which social programs are operationalized into client services. As a labour intensive area, service provision relies on human skills applied to human relationships. This is the central domain of the social work profession which provides that the most dependable standard of quality available to assess service provision is the professional qualifications of the providers. The issue we are addressing in this domain relates to how privatization is affecting the interface between social service delivery and social work practice.

One impact of contracting out public services to the private sector has been identified as the deprofessionalization of the public sector.[21] A consequence of this may be the dilution of the impact of professionalism as a challenge to administrative authority in the public policy and public administration domains. As a professional body heavily concentrated in public sector services, social work has played a central role in Canada in promoting the assumption of public responsibility for provision to the needy.[22] In response to privatization policies, new career opportunities are opening up for social workers in the private sector at the same time that restraint policies are diminishing opportunities in the public sector. While private practice may enhance the prestige and status of the social work profession, it also reinforces the market framework of social service delivery, contributing to the devolution of responsibility for social provision to the needy from the public to the private sector. In effect, the social work profession is developing a vested interest in privatization at the same time its role in the public sector is weakening.

In addition, there appears to be an increasing tendency to rely on nonprofessionals as service providers at the front-line of service. As social work itself is becoming more professionalized, social service provision may be becoming more deprofessionalized. This is indicated in the increasing use of volunteers in public services and in community services.[23] Most grants in the social services are directly tied to volunteer programs.[24] Obviously, this is a significant cost-saving device. Furthermore, purchase of service contracts with both the voluntary and proprietary sectors result in the tendency of agencies to rely on nonprofessionals or nonunionized professionals as service providers to cut costs.[25] We do not know how pervasive this actually is. The information is of an ad hoc nature. But the implications are profound for the relationship between social policy and social work.

Conclusion

The perspective on privatization developed in this chapter is meant to provide only a heuristic guideline for the following case studies rather than a methodological or analytic approach. While the domain framework provides a common focus on the role of the policy level in the service delivery system, each case study pursues its own logic in addressing the implications of privatization on other domains against the perspective developed here. In this sense, the perspective provides a common starting point. Given the variability of policies and delivery systems across provinces, and the lack of comparative information on them, it is feasible to start at a common point, but not to constrict the individual studies within preconceived parameters.

The common focus addresses the question of provincial policies that have the direct and indirect effect of reducing public sector provision of social services: to identify these policies and assess their impact upon both the rate of growth and the absolute amount of public sector provision; and to examine the implications of these policies on at least one sector in the administration domain. The underlying question is the extent to which privatization is related to a trend of devolution of responsibility for social provision to the needy from the public to the private sector.

Notes

1. Neil Gilbert, *Capitalism and the Welfare State: Dilemmas of Social Benevolence* (New Haven: Yale University Press, 1983).
2. Julian LeGrand and Ray Robinson, eds., *Privatization and the Welfare State* (London: George Allen & Unwin, 1984).
3. For a concise and systematic overview of the rationale and scope of privatization of the Canadian welfare state being advanced, see Thomas J. Courchene, *Social Policy in the 1990s: Agenda for Reform* (Toronto: C.D. Howe Institute, 1987).
4. For a discussion of these dimensions, see LeGrand and Robinson, *Privatization and the Welfare State*, pp. 3-6.
5. James M. Kouzes and Paul R. Mico, "Domain Theory: An Introduction to Organizational Behavior in Human Service Organizations," *Journal of Applied Behavioral Service* 15, no. 4 (1979), pp. 449-69.
6. See Dennis Guest, *The Emergence of Social Security in Canada* (Vancouver: University of British Columbia, 1980); also, Frank Strain and Derek Hum, "Canadian Federalism and the Welfare State: Shifting Responsibilities and Sharing Costs," in Jacqueline S. Ismael, ed., *The Canadian Welfare State: Evolution and Transition* (Edmonton: University of Alberta Press, 1986), pp. 349-71.
7. Jacqueline S. Ismael, ed., *Canadian Social Welfare Policy: Federal and Provincial Dimensions* (Toronto: McGill-Queen's University Press, 1985).
8. For a summary of main positions on both sides, see Social Planning Council of Metropolitan Toronto, *Caring for Profit: The Commercialization of Human Services in Ontario* (October, 1984).
9. Alfred J. Kahn, "A Framework for Public-Voluntary Collaboration in Social Services," *The Social Welfare Forum, 1976* (New York: Columbia University Press, 1977) identified three models in the division of labour for personal social service delivery: the extension ladder model, the parallel bars model and the public agent model.
10. See, for example, John W. Langford, "The Question of Quangos: Quasi-Public Service Agencies in British Columbia," *Canadian Public Administration* 26, no. 4 (Winter, 1983), pp. 563-76.

11. Jean-Bernard Robichaud, *Voluntary Action: Provincial Policies and Practices* (Ottawa: Canadian Council on Social Development, 1985).
12. Ibid., for an inventory of provincial programs.
13. Ralph M. Kramer, *Voluntary Agencies in the Welfare State* (Berkeley: University of California Press, 1981), p. 9.
14. The trend in the U.S. and Britain is much better documented than in Canada. On the U.S. case, for example, see E.L. Brilliant, "Private or Public: A Model of Ambiquities," *Social Service Review* 47 (b) (1973): pp. 384-96; Paul Terrell, "Private Alternatives to Public Human Service Administration," *Social Service Review* 53(i) (1979), pp. 56-73; Robert Morrise, "Government and Voluntary Agency Relationships," *Social Service Review* 56, no. 3 (Sept. 1982), pp. 333-45. On the British case, see *The Future of Voluntary Organizations: Report of the Wolfenden Committee* (London: Croom Helm, 1978); Maria Brenton, *The Voluntary Sector in British Social Services* (London: Longman, 1985). Kramer, *Voluntary Agencies in the Welfare State* provides a comparative study of the voluntary sector and the welfare state in four countries.
15. See, for example, E.V. Savas, *How to Shrink Government: Privatizing the Public Sector* (Chatham, N.J.: Publishing, 1982); and A.R. Bailey and D.G. Hull, *The Way Out* (Montreal: The Institute for Research on Public Policy, 1980).
16. Candace P. Mueller, "Purchase of Service Contracting from the Viewpoint of the Provider," in Kenneth R. Wedel, et al., eds., *Social Services by Government Contract: A Policy Analysis* (New York: Praeger, 1979), pp. 50-51.
17. Gilbert, *Capitalism and the Welfare State*, p. 15.
18. See, for example, Langford, "The Question of Quangoes: Quasi-Public Service Agencies in British Columbia." For an insightful analysis of voluntarism and politics, see Ron Labonte, "Politics: The Darker Side of Volunteerism," *Perception* 8, no. 2 (Nov./Dec., 1984) pp. 11-13.
19. See, Alfred J. Kahn and Sheila B. Kamerman, *Social Services in International Perspective* (Washington, D.C.; Government Printing Office for the Department of Health, Education, and Welfare, 1977) for a comparison of the categorical approach to service delivery with other approaches.
20. The proliferation of food banks is an example of the shift of residual provision onto the private sector. See Graham Riches, "Feeding Canada's Poor: The Rise of the Food Banks and the Collapse of the Public Safety Net." in Ismael, ed., *The Canadian Welfare State*, pp. 126-48. For an example of cutbacks in developmental, preventative, advocacy and outreach services, see John A. MacDonald, "Privatization and Social Services in British Columbia: An Examination of the Issues in Legal and Historical Perspective," a paper presented at the Privatization and the Public Trust Conference in Vancouver, May 31 - June 2, 1984. Also see Marilyn Callahan, "The Human Costs of 'Restraint'," in Warren Magnusson, et al., *The New Reality: The Politics of Restraint in British Columbia* (Vancouver: New Star Books, 1984), pp. 227-41.
21. Arthur J. Katz, "Quality of Service, Professionalism, and the Purchase of Service Factor," in Kenneth R. Wedel, et al., *Social Services by Government Contract: A Policy Analysis*, pp. 92-106.
22. For examination of the role of the social work profession and professionalism

in the development of Canadian public standards of welfare see Richard B. Splane, "Social Welfare Development in Alberta: The Federal-Provincial Interplay," pp. 173-87, in Ismael, ed., *Canadian Social Welfare Policy*; and James Struthers, "Shadows from the Thirties: The Federal Government and Unemployment Assistance, 1941-1956," in Ismael, ed., *The Canadian Welfare State*, pp. 3-32.

23. This is documented by the Canadian Council on Social Development survey of provincial policies, Robichaud, *Voluntary Action: Provincial Policies and Practices*. For a case study of public service use of volunteers, see E.W. Harrison and M.G. Gosse, "Privatization: A Restraint Initiative," *Canadian Journal of Criminology* 28, no. 2 (April 1986), pp. 183-93. The British Association of Social Workers undertook a comprehensive study of the relationship of social workers and volunteers in the public services, concluding, "Clearly volunteers should not be used to do what paid workers are normally supposed to do, and professional workers should not support practices which might undermine standards." Anthea Holme and Joan Maizels, *Social Workers and Volunteers* (London: George Allen & Unwin, 1978), p. 184.

24. See Robichaud, *Voluntary Action: Provincial Policies and Practices*, for an inventory of these programs. As this survey documents, the Saskatchewan Ministry of Social Services initiated a grant program to voluntary sector agencies in 1975. Grants for 1984 amounted to $5.6 million. In response to restraint, however, public social services have been cut back significantly, in effect debilitating the public safety net while strengthening private provision. See Sandra Sorenson, "Are We All Being Short Sighted?", *Perception* 8, no. 3 (Jan./Feb., 1985), pp. 23-25.

25. See, for example, Lorna Hurl, "Privatized Social Service Systems: Lessons from Ontario Children's Services," *Canadian Public Policy* 10 (1984), pp. 395-405; Langford, "The Question of Quangoes"; Lorna Hurl and Christa Freiler, "Privatized Social Services: The Ontario Experience," paper presented at the Second Conference on Provincial Social Welfare Policy, The University of Calgary, May 1-3, 1985.

2 British Columbia

MARILYN CALLAHAN
CHRIS MCNIVEN

Announcements from the Government of British Columbia regarding the privatization of social services have provoked a great deal of public controversy. Government has proposed that privatization is a way of maintaining public commitment to services in times of restraint. Further, advocates argue that private delivery ensures more community involvement and reduces the alienation of consumers. Opponents have identified the ideological and practical drawbacks of privatization, particularly when for-profit agencies are involved.[1] All of this debate has created confusion about the meaning of privatization and commanded a great deal of attention by media, where government and community organizations are often portrayed as adversaries in the provision of services.

In British Columbia in the last two decades both the New Democratic Party (NDP) government (1972-75) and the Social Credit government (1975 to date) have favoured a policy of public/private delivery of social services—a mixed economy. However, the ideological arguments for voluntary and government services and the subsequent models of delivery differed substantially between the two governments. In addition, the NDP undertook a much more vigorous role in policy making and funding, while in recent years particularly, the Social Credit government has attempted to reduce its overall responsibilities for social services. The purpose of this paper is to examine the nature and scope of recent privatization measures in one area of personal social services, family and children's services, and begin to assess overall the impact of these trends. The authors have attempted to find answers to several key questions. Firstly, to what extent has government actually reduced its commitment to family and children's services? In downsizing, have most of these services been contracted to the formal private sector of voluntary and proprietary agencies (privatization), or turned over to the informal sector of self-help groups, individuals and families (divestment)? What are the mechanisms that government has utilized to implement privatization and/or divestment policies? Finally, what has been the impact of these changes on policy makers, administrators, service providers and consumers? The analysis will be limited to data from the provincial ministry primarily responsible for these services, Social Services and Housing, but will include trends from the Attorney General and Health. Additional data has been obtained from several other studies and a preliminary study of voluntary and proprietary agencies carried out by the authors, although only broad trends can be noted at this point.[2]

The Government Record in Social Services in B.C. in the Last Two Decades

Although family and children's services emerged originally from voluntary efforts, there has been a general recognition in the twentieth century that government must assume some responsibility. Kahn has proposed three models to describe the relationship between public and private sectors in social services which are a useful reminder of a long-standing partnership.[3] In the extension ladder model, the public sector is responsible for a minimum level of provision for all, while the private sector raises the funds to offer supplementary services. Although the definition of an acceptable minimum level has changed over time, the development of personal social services in Canada until the fifties was largely based on an extension ladder concept. In the second model, parallel bars, public and private agencies carry out essentially the same tasks, with private agencies doing more in the area of innovation, standard setting, monitoring and advocacy, primarily from their own funding efforts. Much of the developments in family counselling in the fifties and sixties followed the parallel bars model, with alternative family service agencies and women's organizations forming the vanguard of developments in family work. In the third model, public agent, a substantial amount of public funds is channeled through purchase of services contracts or direct grants into the private sector to carry out public social services. In this case voluntary organizations rely as much or more on public funds as their own sources.

In British Columbia in the sixties, under a long-reigning Social Credit government, the relationship between provincial government and private agencies was primarily one of an extension ladder and parallel bars nature, although the Children's Aid Societies in Vancouver and Victoria were quasi-governmental agencies and served as public agents of government. In general, the two sectors remained separate from one another in planning, funding and delivery and often relationships were strained. The voluntary sector was considered by many professionals as the preferred vehicle for delivering quality services and as the source of innovation and advocacy. In Vancouver, new graduates from the School of Social Work coveted positions in the Family Service Agency or United Way community development programs. The YWCA pioneered multicultural outreach programs in the inner city and alternate voluntary services such as crisis centres, transition houses and youth hostels emerged. The poor began to organize, often with the help of federal government grants. The target of their criticism was frequently provincial social services. These groups were joined by professionals such as the British Columbia Association of Social Workers (BCASW) which publicly criticized the low welfare rates on several occasions, and in one celebrated case, several public welfare workers resigned because of inadequate resources. There were few forums where public and voluntary service providers or policy makers met to consider mutual concerns, although the local area councils funded by the United Way in Vancouver and the social planning groups organized by the Social Planning and Review Council of British Columbia throughout the province emerged near the end of the sixties.

The gulf between public and voluntary sectors was exacerbated by the rural-urban differences in service delivery systems which existed at the time, and still do to some extent. Essentially, the vast rural areas of the province had few formal voluntary services and depended upon self help and government resources. The more densely populated lower mainland, with its temperate climate and urban lifestyle, attracted professionally trained social workers and supported the development of a wide range of voluntary services. In British Columbia in the sixties, employment with government was negatively associated with "working in the sticks" as well as working in a less progressive agency. This attitude was by no means shared amongst all workers, managers and policy makers but furthered the wedge between the two sectors. One exception to this rule was government mental health services which required a master's level degree for social workers even in rural areas and through various other measures promoted an image of high quality services.

Two very different but influential politicians furthered the notion of inadequate government or quasi-government services. In the sixties, the Socred minister of the social services department frequently alluded to the indolence of those on welfare and the debilitating effect of welfare benefits. Prior to his election as the NDP minister of Human Resources in 1972, Norm Levi was a social activist in Vancouver and was instrumental in promoting changes in the boards of the powerful Children's Aid Societies. In Mr. Levi's view, government funded services were too bureaucratized, centralized and professionalized to meet the needs of their clientele.

He set about to change this after his election. The Community Resource Board Act created or intended to create a system of locally controlled boards throughout the province, similar to school and hospital boards. Funding for social services increased rapidly and was provided on a global basis to the locally elected boards which, in turn, allocated money to nonprofit organizations through sustaining and project grants and service contracts. The community grants budget of government increased enormously from $242,678 in 1971 to $9.3 million in 1974-75 to implement this policy.

The era of the voluntary sector as public agent had begun in earnest and certainly these initiatives by the NDP could be viewed as one model of privatization. Although the government maintained some involvement in providing income and social services, it substantially increased its subsidy to the voluntary sector for a wide range of preventive, advocacy and planning functions as well as direct client services. The aim was to breakup large government monopolies on service delivery, equalize opportunities for rural and urban citizens and increase community control. Ironically, some of these measures seemed to contradict left wing ideologies concerned with government delivery but, in other ways, appealed to the community based, populist values of the left. Although resource boards created their own set of opponents and controversial issues, the concept was generally supported by activists and professionals because government expanded its vision of social services and funding for these services, at the same time as it encouraged more involvement of the voluntary sector in their delivery.[4]

After the election of the Social Credit government in 1975 the model of service delivery changed substantially although funding continued to expand. Initially government increased its responsibility for providing services by dismantling resource boards and assuming the delivery of at least some of these services, primarily in the Vancouver area. Government also added a range of family and children's services including the family support worker program, child abuse teams, and community based preventive and alternative programs for juvenile offenders. This was a period of expansion in government service delivery and subsidy to voluntary agencies, at least in the delivery of direct client services. It was buoyed in part by increased government revenues, in part by the federal-provincial social services review which was underway at the time. However, government support for advocacy, planning and prevention services in the voluntary sector gradually declined during this same period. Most of these trends appeared contrary to conservative ideology on one hand, but were packaged to appeal to conservatives on the other. Accordingly, the dismantling of the Resource Boards was viewed as a move to streamline government decision making and control costs. Moreover it was argued that these boards delegated too much decision making to community members who were, in turn, subject to influence by self-serving professionals and special interest groups.

The revocation of the Community Resource Board Act provoked serious disputes between public officials and the voluntary sector. Opposing groups developed across political parties to some extent. Those favouring resource boards were mainly elected members of the boards, academics, professional and voluntary organizations' professionals and even some consumers. Although they had varying commitments to resource boards, all felt left out of the decision-making process. The public debate was fractious and in the end futile. This event seriously damaged relationships between the public and voluntary sector which had begun to improve during the NDP and had continued cordial to this point.[5]

During this period, the Social Credit government also introduced a new Family and Child Services Act which did not enshrine its new family support services in legislation. The act was a modest one in scope, basically updating the language of the former Protection of Children's Act and adding some improvements in administrative and court processes. It made no mention of the government's role in family and children's services beyond the basic one of protection of children. Homemaker and general family support services were authorized under the income maintenance legislation, the Guaranteed Available Income for Need Act, enacted August 19, 1976. According to this act, social services to children and their families were to be authorized only "when the child is at risk of being removed from his or her home or community because of exceptional physical, social, or behavioural needs." The restrictive nature of these two pieces of legislation was crucial to the privatization and divesting policies subsequently introduced.

The development of the Family and Child Services Act which began during the NDP government was a misadventure from beginning to end. The NDP initiated the process with a Royal Commission into many aspects of family law and the commission undertook to maximize public involvement in the process. The draft Children's Act produced by the commission recommended an expanded role for government in supporting family life and ensuring respect for child and family rights. This act was discarded by the Socreds who introduced another public input process. However, the final product reflected few of the Royal Commission's recommendations or subsequent public submissions. The whole process further soured relationships between voluntary and public officials.[6]

In many jurisdictions the two decades of growth in the concept of the welfare state, 1960-80, paralleled an increase in the presence and power of professional social workers. This was not true in British Columbia. Although social service expenditures grew substantially during this period, both parties of the left and right remained inherently suspicious of professional help and were convinced, in the last analysis, that family, friends, and volunteers provided effective support and care for many in need. Although they differed in how social services should be planned and administered—the NDP favouring decentralized community control and the Socreds centralized bureaucratic systems—they shared a common skepticism of human service professionals. Even the NDP minister of the Social Services department, himself a social worker, was convinced that many professionals were afraid to take risks and were more committed to preserving their own power and position than making favourable changes for their clientele. Both parties have strong connections to grassroots movements and to populist approaches to problem solving. Whether this situation is unique to British Columbia or typical of large, sparsely populated regions with frontier values and a concomitant lack of liberal, middle-of-the-road political strength is not known. In any event, it left British Columbia with a legacy of voluntary and ad hoc services and a modest complement of professionally trained social workers.[7] The privatization policies of the 1980s in some ways fit with this history.

Relationships between the public and voluntary sector further deteriorated in the early 1980s when the Social Credit government developed policies to divest itself of providing the services it created in the 1970s and to reduce subsidies to the voluntary sector for services developed during the NDP era. Initially, these policies were not explicit but were considered a part of the general government hiring and spending freeze of the early 1980s. However, in July 1983, shortly after an election victory, the

Social Credit government introduced its budget with 26 bills aimed at severely restricting the number of civil servants and the power of their unions, reducing regulatory bodies and expenditures on human services, centralizing decision making and increasing taxes for the middle class. Privatization was declared as a major policy direction for government and, in social services, several mechanisms were adopted to reduce public provision and subsidy.[8]

The introduction of these policies was both logical and illogical, depending upon one's point of view. During the early 1980s, government revenues from natural resources fell dramatically from approximately $1,319 million in 1979/80 to $544 million in 1982/83. Overall revenues from other sources such as income and sales tax fell markedly during the same period. However, demands on government coffers increased. Unemployment doubled between 1980 and 1982, from 6.5% to 13% and numbers on welfare increased from 66,277 cases in March, 1981 to 146,021 cases in March 1984.[9] Between 1980 and 1983, the numbers of British Columbia families in poverty increased by 52.8%, the highest rate in the nation.[10] For some the recession provided the opportunity for government to reduce its ill-founded commitment to social services. For others attempts to reduce government expenditures through cutbacks in social services, while regrettable, was a necessary measure. And for others, it seemed like punishing those in need twice: increasing stress through unemployment and uncertainty and decreasing support and benefits at the same time. Moreover, many considered the restraint measures as self-defeating in terms of rejuvenating the economy. The debate erupted during the rise of Operation Solidarity in the summer of 1983 and has persisted albeit in less visible and audible terms since then.

Privatization Mechanisms

Although privatization policies were introduced hurriedly, the government implemented several different approaches. Specifically, these measures included:
1. *Cancelling the provision of nonstatutory services*
   Services such as the family support worker program, the child abuse teams, family service coordinators and outreach services to street adolescents were cancelled, thereby eliminating approximately 500 public service positions.[11] There was no expectation that these services would be assumed by the voluntary sector, although other government

workers, primarily field social workers and school teachers were expected to deliver some of these. The Special Services to Children Program, a government contracting program for many of these needs, was left intact and might have picked up some of these cancelled services. However, the budget for this program has remained flat and in fact decreased in recent years from $6,679,354 in 82-83, to $6,370,362 in 84-85.[12]

2. *Reducing the provision of some statutory services through bureaucratic disentitlement*[13]

    This approach involves the development of policies which exclude certain clientele or increase the barriers to obtaining services. It is sometimes more difficult to monitor because the exclusions are mandated through the modifications in internal policy while leaving the legislative framework intact. Although most of disentitlement occurred in income services, the change in the Planned Life Placement policy for children in care is one child welfare example. Originally, this policy attempted to create life plans for permanent wards, either through adoption or permanent foster homes. However, after some uneven application of this policy at the regional and local level, it was changed in 1985 and thereafter all permanent wards were to be referred to central headquarters for possible adoption. One reason for centralizing decision making and excluding foster parents and permanent foster homes as a suitable life plan was to attempt to reduce government responsibility for the long term care of children.

    Another more informal approach to disentitlement occurred after the substantial reduction of field staff in 1983. Fewer workers can provide less service and must make daily decisions about priorities. Workers in Human Resources report that they have had to eliminate most family service cases unless there is clear evidence that children are at risk. Thus parents who are having problems coping with their children are usually unable to obtain service from government workers unless the child is clearly abused, neglected or commits an offence under the Young Offenders Act.

3. *Contracting existing and new statutory services to nonprofit and for-profit organizations*

    In the initial privatization in 1983, this contracting amounted to a small number of Vancouver-based services, approximately 22, which had been assumed by government during the resource board takeover. Throughout the rest of the province these services were already offered by private sector organizations. International adoptions have also been put out to tender, although these still represent a small number of adoptions (428 regular in 1984-85, 36 international).

Although few existing government services have been transferred to the private sphere, there has been a rapid increase in the development of new contracted services, primarily in the juvenile justice field, in response to the requirements of the Young Offenders Act. (See Table 2-2.) In addition, the deinstitutionalizing and normalizing trend in services to the handicapped has had a major impact on contracted services. One large institution has been closed and most residents have been relocated to small community based facilities, contracted to proprietary and nonprofits. Overall, proprietary organizations have dominated these in care services (283 in 1983-84, 91 nonprofits in the same year) and tend to provide care to the more severely handicapped. There has been a modest expansion of special care homes, designed to assist severely disturbed or handicapped children in family homes. Funding for community based services for the handicapped, primarily the Chance program for normalization in public schools, has also increased. (See Table 2-1.)

4. *Transferring government services to other jurisdictions*

This approach is similar to the preceeding mechanism but really includes a more fundamental shift of responsibility. In recent years, several Native bands have assumed control over their own child welfare matters, with and without provincial government approval. This action was taken not as a result of provincial policy but in spite of it, at least in the case of the first band, the Spalumcheens, in 1981.[14] Latterly the ministry has developed a policy of transfer of authority with several other bands, with the federal government assuming full and direct responsibility for funding. This shift will have significant implications for government services as approximately 35% of the children in care in British Columbia are Native Indians.[15] Although status Indians are the only ones affected by these measures, there will be some considerable reduction in provincial government responsibility for child welfare.

In education, this transfer has occurred from the provincial government to local school boards and municipal governments which are now required to raise school taxes to meet shortfalls in school operating budgets. Although the numbers are unknown at the time of this writing, several jurisdictions have been required to take this measure.

Table 2-1 Funding of Contracted Family and Children's Services in Ministry of Human Resources, 1981–85

Family and Children's Services	1981–82	1982–83	1983–84	1984–85
Day Care (b)	16,684,275	19,986,295	19,287,794	18,665,316
Community Projects Funding (b)	6,628,428	6,786,647	6,004,385	5,195,469
Special Services (b)	5,587,642	6,679,354	6,437,266	6,370,362
Homemakers (b)	4,489,412	4,532,843a	4,043,765a	3,665,092
Rehabilitation Resources (b)	3,983,946	4,566,560a	4,712,683a	4,694,682
Chance (b)	3,738,536	4,765,753	4,865,244	5,219,186
Total in Home Services	41,112,239	47,317,452	45,351,137	43,810,107
Foster Care & C.I.C. (c)	18,998,301	21,591,431	21,693,758	23,006,269
Child Care Resources (c)	41,909,072	42,930,515	49,724,126a	75,582,065
Grand Total: Family & Children's Services	102,019,612	111,839,398	116,796,020	125,873,316
Overall Ministry Expenditures	822,843,045	1,092,391,265	1,298,965,019	1,417,000,000
% of Total Ministry Expenditures on Family and Children's Services	12.3%	10.2%	8.9%	8.8%

a) figures may not be comparable with previous years
b) primarily in home services
c) primarily in care services

Definitions

Day Care—income tested subsidies to parents for a full range of day care options provided by proprietary and nonprofit agencies.
Community Projects Funding—provided to nonprofit societies for the delivery of community based family support services such as crisis centres, youth projects, counselling and information centres, etc.
Special Services to Children—counselling and support services provided by contracted child care workers to families and children at risk. All workers employed by nonprofits.
Family Support Homemakers—provided to mentally handicapped adults, parents of handicapped children and families experiencing difficulties, nonprofit and proprietary agencies involved.
Rehabilitation Resources—provided to children experiencing difficulty in school or who have dropped out by contracted child care workers, primarily employed by nonprofits.
Chance—provided to children with handicaps who are "mainstreamed" and require personal attendants. Services are purchased by contract from school districts.
Foster Care and Children in Care—support and maintenance provided by government workers and foster parents to children who are wards of government.
Child Care Resources—contracted special services for children with special needs who cannot be cared for in foster homes. These include Respite Resources for handicapped children, Receiving and Assessment homes, Group homes, Special Care homes, Specialized Residential and Nonresidential resources and Intensive Child Care Resources.

Table 2–2 Numbers of Contracted Family and Children's Services in Ministry of Human Resources, 1981–85

	1981–82	1982–83	1983–84	1984–85
Day Care – number of subsidies—				
half time (2)	2,041	2,547	1,985	2,878
full time	8,194	7,956	8,170	8,514
Community Projects	240	194	185	167
Special Services to Children (children and families served per month)	not available	1,220	1,416	1,397
Homemakers				
nonprofit agencies funded	not	88	90	86
proprietary funded	available	15	15	17
families and individuals served per month		1,137	1,264	1,093
Rehabilitation Resources				
number of contracted programs	not	121	120	139
number of government programs	available	24	25	
Chance				
number of personal attendants (4)	not	356	371	414
number of children served	available	1,332	1,339	1,511
number of contracts		70	76	77
Foster Care & C.I.C.				
number of children in care (5)	8,454	8,132	7,688	7,535
number of C.I.C. in foster care as of March 31	not available	4,507	4,181	4,061
Child Care Resources (facilities contracted)				
respite homes	8	29	37	41
receiving and assessment	54	50	73	89
group homes	124	156	132	124
special care homes	298	355	331	376
specialized residential resources	74	70	65	72
specialized nonresidential resources	38	44	41	45
intensive child care (6)	not in			
residential resources	existence	17	21	24

5. *Reducing subsidy to the private sector for nonstatutory preventive type services*

As noted, government support for these services grew rapidly during the NDP period primarily in funding for Day Care, Community Projects, Special Services, Homemakers, and latterly under the Social Credit government with programs for the handicapped. These services then declined in the recent years. Total government funding for these programs decreased from $47,317,452 in 1982-83 to $43,810,107 in 1984-85. (See Table 2-1.) Government expectation about who will deliver these preventive services or how the voluntary sector will make up the shortfall has not been made explicit although it does not appear that private fund-raising efforts can compensate.[16] For instance in a 1985 survey of voluntary agencies in British Columbia, 69% of agency directors said they would not have sufficient funding this year to cover operating and service costs at a 1982 level in spite of an increased demand on their service, both in terms of quantity and complexity. Government cutbacks in funding were cited as the major reason for the shortfall with modest but inadequate increases coming from donations, local governments and the United Way.[17] These agencies reported a substantial shift in their activities towards more treatment oriented, client service work and fund-raising from client support, education and advocacy activities. Interestingly agencies also reported an increase in their referral activities in response to the demand. The use of referral in government services with reduced mandates and voluntary services with reduced resources may mean that many clients, particularly those with complex problems, are in perpetual motion between unresponsive services.

6. *Increasing user fees*

Fee for service has not been a significant mechanism in family and children services in British Columbia except in child day care. In other services, low income, nonvoluntary clients make poor prospects for collection. There has, however, been a slight increase in payments from parents whose children are under voluntary care orders.

In child day care, user fees are the responsibility of the voluntary and proprietary sector, however, the government does play a significant role in establishing fee levels. According to a recent national report on child day care, the cost of providing licenced and unlicenced care for infants and preschoolers is higher for providers and consumers in British Columbia than other provinces.[18] The report suggests that one reason for this is that British Columbia is one of three provinces where the government does not offer substantial operating grants to providers who, in turn, charge higher fees for service. However, overall government expenditures on subsidies to low income families to assist with these high fees have declined in recent years, although the actual number of subsidies has increased. (See Table 2-1 & Table 2-2.) This suggests that, although more families are obtaining subsidies, those that do have higher incomes as the subsidies are income tested. Clearly some poorer families are unable to pay the shortfall between the government subsidy and the fee charged by the caretaker and have given up using formal child care services. Thus, in day care, fee for service has had the impact of reducing consumption of those who cannot pay while generating revenues from those who can.

7. *Reframing the nature of family and children's problems so that their solution lies mainly outside of the government ministry responsible for social services or outside of government entirely*

This mechanism has been widely used in British Columbia to narrow government's overall responsibilities. For instance, recent policies on wife assault and family maintenance view the government's role in these matters as primarily one of legal enforcement rather than social service. While these are valuable and necessary policy initiatives, they have not been accompanied by a regular increase in social assistance rates to ensure that women and children have minimally adequate incomes if maintenance is not forthcoming. In addition, there has been a shift towards defining family problems as mental health problems and a projected growth in these services within the health ministry. This view of social problems as legal or health problems reinforces a "private troubles" perspective, with government intervening only to get tough with those who do not meet their obligations.

Government has repeatedly declared that it is not in the business of providing social services and has commended the capacity of the voluntary sector and individuals to manage on their own. This has had the effect of discouraging approaches to government for funding and service, thereby confirming that such intervention was unnecessary in the first place. Kierans has suggested that the debate on privatization, even if it leads to little action, will create an atmosphere "where the public is less prone to appeal unthinkingly to government initiatives or, in the case of the social services, an environment where government inaction is expected."[19] The rise in privately arranged adoptions is one indicator of the success of this approach. While waiting periods for a government adoption are often five years, well connected individuals can obtain a child much sooner without government assistance. Private adoptions in British Columbia have increased 16% in two years, although they are still a small number compared to government adoptions. Government still provides home studies for private adoptions but does not make placement arrangements or offer natural parent services.

Social services are not on the current policy agenda. They are rarely, if ever, mentioned in policy discussions or new government initiatives.

In a recent throne speech the government indicated recovery measures for health and education but did not include social services. Without a strong consumer or professional constituency social services have little chance of gaining public attention, except on a sensational case-by-case basis.

Outcomes and Emerging Trends

The British Columbia government approached the issue of privatization and divestment of social services with a wide range of strategies, applied in earnest, although often with little apparent planning. While all of the strategies aimed to decrease government involvement in services, only some were directly related to privatization. Programs which were transferred to other jurisdictions or contracted out were continued, albeit in different forms. But where government subsidies were cut and programs cancelled, there was no such outcome, except on an ad hoc basis and unless families, individuals and informal groups are considered a part of the service delivery sphere.

The following discussion is primarily speculative as clear trends are only now emerging. Moreover there are few studies which document recent developments in social services in British Columbia. Those that do exist focus on the voluntary sector[20] while the transformation of the public sector has been recorded mainly in the media as well as annual reports of government, professional associations and union reports.[21]

Overall there has been no agreement on the privatization debate. The professional association, British Columbia Association of Social Workers (BCASW), and the government union, British Columbia Government Employees Union (BCGEU), have spoken vigorously against wholesale privatization but, within the profession and amongst clients, a significant number remain committed to the notion that nongovernment agencies (NGOs) are more hospitable to social work practice than large bureaucracies. There is also no consistent preference for voluntary organizations over proprietary ones in the delivery of service. Some argue that "Mom and Pop" type proprietary operations bear more similarity to the small non-profits than with their larger counterparts: established voluntary and for-profit organizations. However, there is general agreement that the extent of the overall privatization and divestment policies and the abruptness of their introduction has had a negative impact on delivery of social services in the province and has impeded much needed improvements. Several outcomes are apparent and, although interrelated, can be identified as follows.

Rise in Regulation

While an increasing number of family and children's services are delivered by the voluntary and private sector, government still owns overall responsibility for child protection by virtue of its legislative mandate, The Family and Child Service Act, enacted June 1, 1981. In an atmosphere of growing concern about its performance,[22] government has had two choices: to further reduce its legislative mandate or increase controls on those providing the service.

Paring down the child welfare legislation would have enormous political ramifications in the present context and the Young Offenders Act (1982) is outside provincial jurisdiction in any event. Instead the government has increased its activity in administrative regulation, both in public and private service delivery. For instance, the position of superintendent of Child Welfare, originally occupied by the deputy minister, has been separated and the new occupant has as her mandate the monitoring of government care of children. A new inspections and standards division has been created within Social Services and Housing to further monitor field service delivery. The operational policy manual has been refined and now includes a practice manual for child welfare workers which outlines the steps to be taken in investigation, case preparation and case monitoring, all of which are subject to inspection. Moreover, field workers have reported to the authors that they have to spend more of their time on accountability activities to ensure that their professional practice is protected during inspections and consequently have less time for day-to-day client work.

There are also indications that government regulation of voluntary services is increasing. The government's reduction of grants and increasing use of contracts to fund the voluntary sector is in fact a regulatory measure. Contracts are accompanied by more stipulations about the kind and amount of service that must be provided than global and project grants. In addition a new policy directive requires that all government staff and contractors must pass a police check for previous offences. The minister of Social Services and Housing recently announced an interministerial inquiry of all sexual abuse cases in the last five years with the objective of eliminating offenders from positions of trust in both the public and nongovernmental sectors. Standards of practice for government and contracted services exist within the Attorney General's ministry and are emerging in Social Services and Housing, albeit slowly.

This rise of regulation may lead to improvements in service delivery. However, regulatory activity which is increasing is more of a mechanical and controlling nature, closely related to centralized organizational structures and traditional management approaches. Thus there is an increase in rules to control individual providers and clients, and inspections to ensure these rules are maintained. There has also been an increase in staff to carry out these inspections and assist with the development of regulatory policies. The more comprehensive approaches to regulation such as legislated rights, ombudsman-type services, service standards, and program evaluation are less evident and, in some cases, nonexistent. There is growing cynicism about the effectiveness of these latter approaches in a climate where there is little money to ensure that standards are met or evaluation recommendations implemented in practice.

Centralization of Policy and Practice Decisions
The structure of organizations to carry out privatization policies has increasingly become a hierarchial one with decision making concentrated in centralized headquarters. Within government, Treasury Board, inner cabinet and nonelected officials in the premier's office have taken charge of major financial decisions, partly because of distrust of the service ministries' ability to do so. Since most government social service workers disagreed with the scope of the privatization and divestment mechanisms and the swiftness of their passage, decisions have also become more and more centralized within this ministry as senior management first tried to sell the new policy and then monitor its implementation. A review of policy directives since 1983 supports this contention.[23] Field staff participation in policy decisions has occurred mainly in those areas considered relatively inconsequential in policy and financial terms, e.g. foster home discipline, interministerial protocols in child abuse, and foster parent insurance. Decisions with financial implications, such as the elimination of some prevention programs, privatization itself, permanency planning and the reduction of staff training were carried out by politicians and senior staff. Moreover, as the privatization and divestment policies have created media problems for the ministry, decisions have had to follow quickly to quell news stories, further discouraging consultation with field staff or social services groups. As well as centralization of decision making within the bureaucracy, worker's casework decisions are increasingly influenced or made by the court because of the residual mandate of government workers. Workers have reported to the authors that much of their work has shifted to reflect the demands of proper evidence, court schedules and case preparation, a more adversarial than conciliatory model.

In the voluntary and proprietary sector a similar pattern of centralization is occurring. In response to the increase in contracting services, a new form of agency is emerging, one almost solely dependent upon government contracts.[24] The board of such agencies, if one exists, has little raison d'être as policy is essentially made by government. Staff usually consists of a band of temporary contract workers. In such circumstances the executive director, or contractor, is one of the few or only full time workers and is in a powerful position with little accountability to staff, board or a constituency of members and consumers.

Any brief discussion of centralization and decentralization can be misleading as there are arguments supporting both positions in research and practice. These authors agree with organizational analysts, particularly Mintzburg and others, who have proposed models for the professional bureaucracy.[25] Accordingly, it makes sense to decentralize service delivery units and practice and administrative decisions affecting these units, while maintaining central control over major policy directions, regulation and evaluation. Maintaining mechanisms for ensuring feedback between the policy, administration and service domains is an equally important assignment for the central authority. Both the NDP and Social Credit government have had difficulty maintaining this balance; initially the NDP decentralized overall decision making and monitoring and was forced to retreat. In turn, the Social Credit government has been too parsimonious in its decentralization of authority, particularly in recent years. Privatization policies and their ramifications have exacerbated this trend.

Specialization and Deskilling
A further factor contributing to separation of the domains within the public sector and an increased gap between public and private is the development of specialized and less challenging functions for each. In the policy domain, the narrowing of the public mandate to remedial action on behalf of families and children and the subsequent reaction to that shift, has changed the public policy making role from one which contained some measure of problem solving to one that is primarily defensive and ideological. Within senior management in the social service ministry, there is little financial room to manoeuver and few arguments to do so. Given the burgeoning nature of child welfare complaints,[26] the diminished staff and resources, and the distrust created between management and field staff, management's job has increasingly become one of developing and implementing regulatory systems. Although there have been few changes of personnel in senior and middle level management, there is diminished value placed on administration skills emanating from a social work tradition and more on public management approaches which are relatively free from social policy

commitments. Managers eager to survive in such an atmosphere have maintained a careful distance from professional associations and other social welfare forums.

New categories of specialists are emerging at the field level: case managers, investigators, clinicians, caretakers, entrepreneurs and marginal workers. Case managers diagnose, mobilize resources, deal with crisis and carry out referrals; investigators conduct adoption and foster home studies, and deal with cases of suspected fraud, neglect, abuse and delinquencies; clinicians provide various forms of therapeutic interventions; caretakers staff group homes, residential centers, and day care services; entrepreneurs take advantage of opportunities to set up, operate or manage new programs, projects and services; and marginal workers take any job that is available and try to perform it, often for low wages and for temporary periods of time.

The first two categories are employed mostly in the public sector, while the rest are sometimes finding employment in the voluntary sector or private practice. Not surprisingly, a majority of caretakers and marginals are women, although women continue to work in the public sector as protection workers.

The results of this new assignment of tasks are only beginning to emerge. Although the social service ministry has maintained a preference for trained social work staff, many social workers in the public sector find themselves reluctant to carry out investigative and referral work only. However, employment opportunities with comparable salaries are few in voluntary agencies or in private practice which has not increased in recent years.[27]

The equally difficult tasks of providing support and therapy to troubled families where a clear case of neglect and abuse cannot be made and caring for children after court are now the responsibility of a cadre of natural helpers and marginally employed semi-professionals. While both groups are essential to these services, they are ill equipped to provide the only resource. A preliminary review of the data from a current study on contracting agencies indicates that academic qualifications for program staff are grade 12 or a community college certificate, although several respondents indicated that as employers, they take what they can get for wages of $8 or $9 per hour.[28]

In both sectors many workers have experienced a mismatch between their skills and work assignments but with few other choices for employment. The results have been an unprecedented expression of low morale, anxiety and stress, particularly as accountability systems are in place to monitor performance and media coverage of poor quality service has greatly increased.

Similarly, there is also an air of increasing tension between voluntary agencies which view their mandate as a multi-purpose one (research, advocacy, innovation, community involvement and service) and government which is willing to purchase only a narrow range of remedial services. Many voluntary agencies particularly regret that their long standing specializations, innovation and advocacy, are being eliminated through the purchase of government defined services. However, most of the antagonism between the sectors is related to funding. Many of the long established agencies are demanding adequate funding for a comprehensive service and can afford to turn down contracts when this is not forthcoming, leaving the field open to less experienced service providers.

Individualization

The reduction of nonstatutory services, the increase in contracting and the rise of regulation have had a particular impact on collective action. The provision of specific services to an established number of individuals has replaced most group and community approaches. This trend has had a more substantial impact on the voluntary sector than government where casework has always been the favoured approach.

Within voluntary and for-profit services, there is pressure to serve clients individually in order to maintain sufficient statistics to justify further funds and government contracts tend to be designed on individual service units. This places inordinate faith on one technology for a wide range of client problems, only some of which are amenable to individual counselling and support. Staff and volunteers of these agencies are frequently ill equipped to provide individual therapies. They are often on contract themselves with little job security or collective agreements. There are few advocacy groups remaining and those that do risk retribution in the highly charged political atmosphere.

Contracting particularly has the potential to create the divisions between agencies and make service coordination an even more difficult task. Agencies are often widely scattered geographically, separated by government program categories or pitted against one another in their quest for contract success. There are several interorganizational forums for these agencies in British Columbia including professional and service associations. Thus far, established organizations for nonprofits have not noted a decline in membership, although proprietary agencies usually remain outside these organizations. However, these interorganizational structures are increasingly concerned with the relationship between their individual members and government, particularly regarding funding and standards of service, and have limited time and few resources for the broader issues of advocacy and program development in family and child welfare.

Shifts in Funding Patterns
One clear outcome of government policies has been the consistent rise in government funding for in care and treatment services and an apparent increasing reliance of voluntary organizations on government contract funding. In one sense the reverse may have been expected as it was hoped that privatizing would save money overall and encourage the voluntary sector to search for other sources of funding.

In government services, it is clear that while expenditures for in home services have remained flat (from $41M to $43M in FY 81-82 to FY 84-85) they have increased rapidly during the same period for in care services (from $60M-$75M). This has occurred during a period when the actual numbers of children in care was declining because of an overall reduction in the child population (from 8132 in 82-83 to 7535 in 84-85). It has also occurred during the period when government was implementing privatizing and divestment policies. Some have indicated that this increase could be related to reduction in preventive, in home services and the need to apprehend severely damaged children who require specialized care. Others point to deinstitutionalization which certainly accounts for some but not all of the increase. There may be a further explanation related to the nature of contracting itself. Some contractors, by virtue of their specialized service or geographical location are "the only game in town" and they can command increasing costs for their services. Moreover, there may be a built in status quo element to contracting. Administrators in the public sector make cordial connections with those in the private and voluntary sector, particularly in decentralized locations. Tendering contracts on a regular basis can also create more administrative work. Furthermore practitioners may be reluctant to change contractors because of the importance of continuity of care for children. Thus the notion that contracting increases competition and decreases costs may not be true in many social service situations.

The results of a preliminary study of voluntary family and children's services throughout the province during this period indicates that their dependence upon provincial government contracts has increased during this period from 44% of their budget in FY 81-82 to 47% in FY 85-86. At the same time provincial government grants have declined from 12% to 7% and United Way funding has also decreased from 10% to 8%. The transformation of the voluntary sector into one of public agent appears to be continuing.[29]

Politicization and Undermining of Services

Although privatization and divestment policies promise a great deal to different political constituencies, the appeal of these arguments has been tarnished by ill conceived policies in recent years. The attempts by the federal government to tamper with old age pensions caused many to reflect on the need for such services at a time of uncertainty and the benefits of Canadian altruism, particularly for the deserving. There has also been an increased public awareness of the problems of child abuse and neglect. The release of major Canadian reports on the subject,[30] an unprecedented coverage of child abuse cases in the media, and the rise in soup kitchens and foodbanks, coincides with the cutbacks in family and children's services in British Columbia. The British Columbia government has responded by defending its policies and those who challenge this view have been regarded as political rather than professional critics. As indicated in the opening section of this chapter, this politicization of social services has occurred before in British Columbia. However, it has been particularly evident in this instance since privatization was a part of overall government policy closely connected with a controversial budget and political philosophy. Moreover, as the British Columbia experiment in modern residualism was introduced with such fanfare, there has been little political room for reassessment or retreat.

Managers and policy makers have also learned a painful lesson about the longer term implications of cutbacks. By eliminating prevention programs, contracting caretaking services and transferring some treatment programs to another ministry, management has left its family and children's services with a narrow and unstimulating mandate: investigation and referral. This year, more funding has become available for education and health services which had been mainly cut across-the-board rather than program by program. However, the same was not true for social services. Management in social services may have a difficult task mounting a case for further funding, not only because of the slim remaining mandate, but also because these services are included in a ministry whose budget has already increased rapidly through rising income maintenance payments.[31]

The impact on clients in receipt of these services is less clear. Certainly demands for service have increased while services have been cut. There has been an unprecedented number of complaints from parents about investigations by social service officials and a fledgling organization for parents who feel wronged by this ministry has been formed. Because of the politicization of services and the volatile nature of child welfare services at any time, there has also been a blizzard of media stories. It is difficult to determine from these reports whether clients are receiving a poorer quality of service overall or whether they have better access to the media to report longstanding concerns or both.

Unemployment, particularly amongst youth and in northern and rural areas have remained at record high levels. One result is the growing number of young people migrating to central urban areas where homelessness, unemployment, poverty and hustling are daily fare. In the longer term, the outcome may be similar to the experience in Britain where similar policies were enacted several years previously.[32] There has been a gradual shift in community expectations and tolerance for the plight of such young people. The facts that some will never find work, have their own homes or achieve other expected milestones, while not embraced, have slowly become the norm.

For women, particularly middle-aged ones, the prospects of kinkeeping may well be increasing. While women have always served as family caretakers, the numbers of family members requiring care are expanding with few alternate resources for elderly parents, older children who remain at home longer, and preschool children and grandchildren. All of this is occurring at a time when women are participating most actively in the workforce, increasingly as sole support breadwinners. As Rosenthal states:

> When politicians talk about the family's time honored responsibility . . . we know that women are already doing it and all the rhetoric simply increases their guilt because they don't think they are doing enough.[33]

Conclusion

The British Columbia experiment in privatizing and dismantling social services has produced similar results to experiments in other jurisdictions.[34] The process of policy making, characterized by swift decisions and unpropitious timing, was likely as significant to the outcomes as the substance of the policy itself. Probably the most difficult problem to contend with now is that there is no alternate vision in British Columbia to replace either the government version of social services or that ascribed to the left, namely more services and more community control. At the same time, the significant actors in the policy, administration and service domains of public and private services have never been as far apart, as untrusting of one another and as beleaguered in day-to-day problems. The prospects for moving forward are unlikely without some significant initiatives on the part of key actors in each domain.

Whether or not the British Columbia experience in privatizing social services has been a successful one to date depends entirely on preferred outcomes. For some, it has meant a much needed reassessment of the role of government in family life and a formalizing of the relationship between government and the voluntary sector through contracting out. Others, particularly those in the service domain, both private and public, have voiced serious concerns about the impact of these measures on service quality, flexibility, comprehensiveness and cost.

This chapter is being written at a time when government has announced that it will proceed with fundamental changes in government structures and undertake major new initiatives in privatization. Few details are known. However, one question which is foremost in the minds of those in the social service community, regardless of their views on the success of the privatization ventures to date, is the degree to which government will disengage further from responsibilities for vulnerable members of society and the services to empower them. The questions do not concern who delivers the service, or the role of the proprietary sector or even the value of community and preventive services, but whether government will provide sufficient resources for planning, funding and evaluating services to enable them to survive in any meaningful way. Instead will further privatization and divestment measures result in a return to the extension ladder situation of the 1950s whereby government maintained responsibility for the most remedial efforts and the voluntary sector provided all other services, primarily from its own resources? It is feared that the current trends in contracting may be the first step in "off loading" — a process in which government first transfers services to the private sector and then gradually withdraws funding altogether.

The prospects of influencing privatization policies in social services are slim as they are tied to overall government initiatives. However, it is tempting to offer some prescriptions which could be implemented within government and voluntary services. Two initiatives are essential: the depoliticization of services and interdomain development.

It is important to reassess services according to their effectiveness and efficiency rather than their ideological origins. In addition, it is essential to renew professional autonomy and expand the range of professional functions for government social workers. There is some evidence that ministry officials recognize these needs. A plan for restructuring district offices to hire casework supervisors, reward professional degrees and provide for further training for staff is currently in circulation. A newly appointed deputy minister has identified the importance of evaluation and professional standards in meetings with staff, professional associations and community groups.

The present relationship between the voluntary and government sector is similar to one between long disputing spouses after their marriage is finally dissolved. In the typical scenario, the wife is left to care for the family on what to her is an inadequate allowance. The husband resents her continued pressure for funds and is certain he could hire a housekeeper more cheaply in the long haul. Within their families are disagreements about who was really to blame and who should pay. Somehow the real issues about the care of the children and the repair of the spouses is lost in the fray. So it is between the voluntary and government sectors in British Columbia. It is timely for both sectors to take some initiatives through joint research, work exchanges, conferences, and joint planning vehicles. This requires a redefinition of the problems, not as the failure of one another to perform adequately, but as the ongoing provision of quality services.

Notes

1. For an excellent review of these arguments see *Caring for Profit. The Commercialization of Human Services in Ontario* (Toronto: Social Planning Council of Metropolitan Toronto, 1984), pp. 5-22.
2. J. Butcher, "Restraint Economics and the Social Safety Net in British Columbia" (Vancouver: U.B.C., Department of Geography, October 1985). J. Rekart, "Voluntary Sector Social Services in the 1980s. A Preliminary Study of the Impacts of Economic Changes and Shifts in Government Policy in British Columbia" (Vancouver: Social Planning and Research Council of British Columbia, September 1987). M. Callahan and C. McNiven, "Contracting Services in B.C.—A Five Year Study," in progress (University of Victoria and British Columbia Schools of Social Work, 1985).
3. A.J. Kahn, "A Framework for Public-Voluntary Collaboration in the Social Services," *The Social Welfare Forum, 1976* (New York: Columbia University Press, 1977).
4. For a fuller account of the history of public-private provision of social services in B.C. and present directions see: J.A. MacDonald, "Privatization and Social Services in British Columbia—An Examination of the Issues in Legal and Historical Perspective." Paper presented to the Canadian Council of Social Development and Social Planning and Review Council of B.C. Conference, *Privatization and the Public Trust* (Vancouver: June, 1984). M. Clague, R.

Dill, R. Seebaran and B. Wharf, *Reforming Human Services: The Experience of the Community Resource Boards in B.C.* (Vancouver: University of British Columbia Press, 1984).
5. Ibid.
6. M. Callahan and B. Wharf, *Demystifying the Policy Process: The Case Study of the Development of the Family and Child Services Act in B.C.* (Victoria: Evergreen Press, 1983).
7. Recent figures from the Ministry of Social Services and Housing indicate that approximately 36% of social workers employed with that ministry in a direct service position have a B.S.W. or M.S.W. In the North, only 18% of workers are professionally qualified.
8. R. Dobell, "What's the B.C. Spirit?" unpublished paper (Victoria: Institute for Research on Public Policy, 1983). "Privatization Budget Applauded," *Province*, July 8, 1983, C5. "Government Gets Jump on Privatization," *Province*, July 10, 1983, B1.
9. J. Schofield, "Recovery Through Restraint? The Budgets of 1983/84 and 1984/85" in W. Magnusson et al., eds., *The New Reality* (Vancouver: New Star Books, 1984), p. 41-55.
10. National Council of Welfare, *Poverty on the Increase* (Ottawa: 1986).
11. In a recent letter from H. Saville, an assistant deputy minister of Social Services and Housing, he provides figures on field staff within the ministry in the past five years. Prior to the cutbacks the ministry had 837 social workers and 284 family support workers (1981-82). In 1985-86 there were 876 social workers and 3 childcare counsellors resulting in a loss of 242 direct field staff.
12. For a review of these cutbacks see: M. Callahan, "The Human Cost of Restraint," in Magnusson et al., eds., *The New Reality*.
13. For a detailed discussion of this mechanism, see M. Lipsky, "Bureaucratic Disentitlement in Social Welfare Programs," *Social Service Review* 68, no. 1 (March 1984), pp. 3-27.
14. J. MacDonald, "The Child Welfare Program of the Spallumcheen Indian Band in British Columbia," in K. Levitt and B. Wharf, eds., *The Challenge of Child Welfare* (Vancouver: University of British Columbia Press, 1985), pp. 253-65.
15. B. Wharf, *Native Indian Child Welfare in B.C.*, study in progress (University of Victoria, School of Social Work, 1986).
16. The increasing shortfall between fund-raising efforts and the financial needs of voluntary agencies has been well documented. Morris estimates that voluntary social service organizations in the United States have experienced an 18 billion dollar decline in government funding at a time when corporate and individual donations has also decreased. See Robert Morris, "Government and Voluntary Agency Relationships," *Social Services Review* 56, no. 3 (September, 1982), pp. 333-45. See also: *A Report of Family Service Agencies in Victoria* (Victoria: Community Council of Greater Victoria, February 1985); *Report on Provincial Restraint Program Cutbacks: Community Projects Funding Cuts* (Vancouver: Social Planning Department, City of Vancouver, October 1983).
17. Butcher, "Restraint Economics and the Social Safety Net."
18. *Report of the Task Force on Child Care* (Ottawa: Status of Women, Canada, 1986), p. 196.

19. T.E. Kierans, "Privatization If Necessary But Not Necessarily Privatization," *Choices*, a publication of the Institute for Research on Public Policy (November, 1984).
20. J. Butcher, "Restraint Economics and the Social Safety Net"; "Survey of the Impact of Restraint, Federation of Private Child Care Agencies," preliminary report in SPARC News (June 1986), p. 3; "1981-85: What Has It Meant to the Social Services of Kelowna, B.C.," report prepared by the Central Okanagan Social Planning Society (1985); "Social Need and Social Services Provision in Greater Victoria," report prepared by the Community Council of Greater Victoria (1985).
21. J. MacDonald and J. Karpoff, "Privatization and Child Welfare Services in B.C. A Proposed Policy for the B.C. Association of Social Workers" (Vancouver: 1984); B.C. Government Employees Union, *A Promise Broken* (Vancouver: September 1985).
22. "Social Workers Warned Before Tot Dies," *Vancouver Sun*, January 17, 1985, p. 1; "Youth Worker Has Sex Record," *Vancouver Sun*, February 26, 1985, p. 1; "Husband Accused of Day Care Sex Assaults," *Vancouver Sun*, March 2, 1985, p. 1; "Curbs Cut M.H.R. Probe Trial Told," *Vancouver Sun*, April 3, 1985, p. B1; "Abuse One Child's Short Life and Long, Slow Death," *Vancouver Sun*, May 9, 1985, p. B 1; "Michael Jack's Death," *Vancouver Sun*, May 12, 1985, p. 4; "Judge Blasts M.H.R.—Again," *Victoria Times-Colonist*, C.P. Story, July 24, 1985.
23. B. Wharf and M. Callahan, "The Implementation of the Family and Child Services Act, 1981-85," unpublished paper (Victoria: University of Victoria School of Social Work, 1986).
24. Callahan and McNiven, "Contracting Services in B.C."
25. H. Mintzberg, *Structure in Fives: Defining Effective Organizations* (Englewood Cliffs: Prentice-Hall, 1983).
26. Cases of substantiated child abuse complaints rose from 604 in 1978 to 1751 in 1983-84 and have continued to increase.
27. The number of social workers registering with the Board of Registration of Social Workers as private practitioners has not risen much in recent years. There may be more private practitioners who have not registered because of inadequate qualifications or other reasons but their numbers are unknown.
28. Callahan and McNiven, "Contracting Services in B.C."
29. Rekart, "Voluntary Sector Social Services."
30. See particularly: *Report of the Committee on Sexual Offences Against Children and Youth* (Ottawa: Government of Canada, 1985); *Pornography and Prostitution in Canada*: Report of the Special Committee on Pornography and Prostitution (Ottawa: Government of Canada, 1985).
31. Expenditures on income assistance have increased from $227,145,681 in 1979-80 to $815,379,309 in 1984-85. The ratio between these expenditures and those spent on all other government programs has changed dramatically in the last five years as the following table indicates.

Percentage Change in Expenditure by Program: Ministry of Social Services and Housing, B.C. 1980/81 to 1984/85

Year	Total Ministry Expenditure	Income Assistance & GAIN for Handicapped	Other Programs
1980-81			
1981-82	+ 9.1	+26.5	− 3.4
1982-83	+32.8	+53.5	+13.5
1983-84	+18.9	+28.3	+ 7.1
1984-85	+ 9.1	+ 9.4	+ 8.5

SOURCE: Province of B.C., *Supplement to the Annual Report 1984-85* (Victoria: Ministry of Social Services and Housing, B.C., 1985).

32. Figures recently released in Britain by government reveal that the number of people claiming state handouts rose from 5.9 million in 1979 to 8.8 million in 1983 with a population of about 56 million. The Child Poverty Action Group claimed nearly one in every three Britons now lives in poverty or on its edge. See "Poverty Figures Paint Grim Picture," *Times Colonist*, Sunday, July 27, 1986, p. A6.
33. C. Rosenthal, "A Perspective on the Lives of Middle Aged Women" (Toronto: University of Toronto, Department of Behavioral Studies, 1986).
34. See particularly: L. Hurl and C. Freiler, "Privatized Social Services: The Ontario Experience," paper presented at the Interprovincial Conference on Social Welfare, Calgary, May 1985; M. Fabricant, "The Industrialization of Social Work Practice," *Social Work*, National Association of Social Work, 30, no. 5 (September 1985).

3 Alberta

JOSEPH P. HORNICK

R.J. THOMLISON

LYNNE NESBITT

Historical Development of Social Services

The Development of Government Departments in Alberta: 1905-1918
When Alberta achieved provincial status in 1905, a Liberal government was elected and several acts were passed creating two ministries: the Ministry of the Attorney General and the Ministry of Agriculture. These two ministries shared responsibility for those in need over the next two decades. The Attorney General was responsible for custody and confinement of the mentally ill and matters concerning children and juveniles, while the minister of Agriculture was responsible for public health and relief for the poor.

Also at this time the development of a system of municipal government led to increased activity in public health and relief for the poor. Beginning in 1907, by-laws regarding public health, relief for the poor, the establishment of hospitals and the provision of care for the sick were included in the Village and Town Acts[1] and various other acts incorporating the cities of Alberta. According to Krewski, the period between 1905 and 1918 was characterized by four major health and welfare issues: (1) public health; (2) care of the insane and the mentally defective; (3) relief of the poor; and (4) programs for neglected and dependent children.[2]

PUBLIC HEALTH: As the population grew and sanitary conditions worsened, public health reports began to document a rapid increase in diseases such as tuberculosis and typhoid fever. This caused much public concern and resulted in calls for compulsory vaccination and enforcement of by-laws in order to control the spread of infectious and contagious diseases.

In 1917, the province enacted the Municipal Hospitals Act under the Municipal Affairs minister. This act empowered a municipal jurisdiction to appoint a board and collect tax in order to fund the construction and operation of hospitals. Patients paid one dollar per day in these municipal hospitals and the remainder of the costs were borne by municipalities, using property tax revenues.

The flu epidemic of 1918/19 highlighted the importance of public health. More significantly, the epidemic indirectly resulted in the establishment of the federal Department of Health and its provincial counterpart in Alberta, an improved system of vital statistics, and increased public attention to the shortcomings of the sanitation system. It also confirmed the power of local boards of health in a time of crisis.

THE INSANE AND MENTALLY DEFECTIVE: Maintenance expenses pertaining to care of the insane and mentally defective were borne by the individual, his/her relatives or his/her estate. Management of the estate became the responsibility of the Attorney General in 1907, but by 1918 this responsibility had been transferred to the Provincial Treasurer.

Throughout this period in Alberta, the mentally ill were confined to an asylum built by the provincial government in Ponoka in 1911. Then, in 1918, the first home for mentally defective children was established in Edmonton by the Department of Education.[3]

RELIEF OF THE POOR: In the early 1900s, most direct services for the poor were provided by religious orders, volunteers, and the North-West Mounted Police. Formal arrangements also existed for many years between the municipalities, the federal and provincial governments and charitable organizations to provide emergency assistance to those in need. For example, during the 1915 drought, the first arrangement for emergency assistance was made between Alberta and the federal government. In response to the widespread drought, the federal government supplied seed grain for distribution to those in need. Traditionally, municipalities provided some form of relief to the poor. However, after 1905, municipalities became incorporated within the provincial structure and councils were formally established. One of the first examples of such municipal legislation is found in the Act of 1907 which incorporated the city of Strathcona.[4] This act granted council power to create by-laws to provide assistance to needy residents.

NEGLECTED AND DEPENDENT CHILDREN: The Attorney General was responsible for matters involving neglected and dependent children in need of care. Such children were usually placed in homes where they worked for board or wages, institutions, or industrial training schools.

In the early 1900s, many of these children were affected by the Juvenile Delinquents Act passed by the federal government in 1908. This act specified procedures to protect, rather than incarcerate, juveniles under the age of 16. In response to this legislation the Alberta government also passed an act to protect children, namely the Children's Protection Act of 1909, which marked the newly emerging trend away from indenture. Under the provisions of this act a superintendent of neglected and dependent children could be appointed, Children's Aid Societies could be organized and children's shelters could be built. Also under the act, municipalities could be ordered to pay maintenance for children and they could then seek reimbursement from the parents.

In 1913, the province, again responding to federal legislation, passed the Juvenile Court Act.[5] This act authorized the establishment of juvenile courts and the appointment of commissioners under the Children's Protection Act in every town with a population greater than 500.

Near the end of World War I, the role of the Ministries of Agriculture and the Attorney General regarding health and social welfare matters started to change. A change in ministries was marked by a shift in responsibility for public health to the Provincial Secretary in January 1918 and then to the minister of Municipal Affairs in August 1918. Also significant was the growth in expenditures for public health, relief, care of the insane and the protection of children. For example, in 1906 the expenditures for hospitals, charities and public health totalled $33,500 and by 1918 had increased to $211,817.[6] Similar increases were evident in expenditures for relief, caring for the insane and children's protection.

The Origins of the Department of Public Health: 1919-1935
By the end of World War I, the political and social climate of Alberta had changed considerably. The creation of the Department of Public Health in 1919 and its steady growth over the next two decades diminished the role of the ministers of Agriculture and the Attorney General in health and welfare issues. The need for health and social services increased as the

population grew from 73,022 in 1901 to 588,454 in 1921.[7] Moreover, a major political shift occurred in 1921 when the United Farmers of Alberta (UFA) party was elected to replace the Liberals.

The range of activities and the number of branches within the Department of Public Health grew as its responsibility for relief of the poor increased. In addition, responsibility for the provision of care for neglected and dependent children was transferred to the minister of Public Health by 1930.

PUBLIC HEALTH: Following World War I, numerous programs were initiated by the Department of Public Health in response to health problems caused by poor social conditions and widespread poverty. In addition to this growth in the Department of Public Health, more health units were established in local areas. Revisions to the Municipal Hospitals Act in 1919 resulted in increased grants to hospitals and closer monitoring of the municipal hospitals by the Department of Public Health. Also, the minister was granted power to establish health districts in municipalities which requested them, as a result of an amendment to the Public Health Act passed in 1929.[8]

THE INSANE AND MENTALLY DEFECTIVE: Following World War I, "mentally defective" adults were placed in large institutional settings in isolated or semi-isolated areas. In 1920, an amendment to the Mentally Defective Persons Act of 1919 [9] guaranteed that the municipal district in which these people had previously resided assumed the cost of their institutional care.

A number of major changes began to occur in 1922. Responsibility for "mentally defective" children was transferred from the Department of Education to the Department of Public Health, and responsibility for provincial insane asylums was also transferred from the Department of Public Works to the Department of Public Health. The amendment to the Insanity Act in 1924 was monumental in that it changed the term "insanity" to "mental disease" and referred to "hospital" rather than "asylum."[10]

RELIEF OF THE POOR: During the 1920s, municipalities assumed greater responsibility for providing relief to poor families. The provincial government's role was to assist only in exceptional circumstances. However, legislative authority was required to assist municipalities in borrowing funds, given the difficulty often experienced by municipalities in mainaining a strong financial base for providing relief.[11]

Before the war, direct relief was provided to a limited number of families. Later on, however, relief for the poor developed into a complex funding system which involved the municipal, provincial and federal governments. The provincial and federal governments provided most of the funding and the municipalities tended to be responsible for distribution of services. In the words of Krewski, "Relief arrangements during the 1930s were far more complicated due to the number who were suffering from economic hardship and unemployment, and the inexperience of government in coping with a problem of this magnitude."[12]

In short, the federal government made financial contributions to the province, and the provincial government then assisted the municipalities with the costs of relief.

NEGLECTED AND DEPENDENT CHILDREN: The Children's Protection Act of 1909 was revised during the 1920s to expand the powers of the superintendent of Child Welfare. For example, beginning in 1920, children under six years of age could not be surrendered for adoption without consent of the superintendent. In 1925, a major revision of the Child Welfare Act further increased the superintendent's powers and also increased agency and municipal responsibilities for child welfare. Then in 1930, the responsibility for all child welfare matters was transferred from the Attorney General to the Department of Public Health.[13]

The Origins of the Department of Public Welfare: 1935-1951
By 1935, the Department of Public Health had become a major government department with a budget of more than eight million dollars and responsibility for a population of approximately 750,000 people. As a result of the economic crisis during the 1930s however, reform advocates began to raise fundamental questions about the role of the state in health care and social welfare, as well as the balance of federal and provincial responsibilities. In addition, there was growing concern and criticism regarding privately-owned health programs and municipally-based relief and public health services. These issues were important and they became a topic of debate during the 1935 provincial election, which was subsequently won by the Social Credit party.[14]

PUBLIC HEALTH: The province, recognizing that more intensive programs were required, took steps to develop a plan for financing the increasing demand for a wide range of social services. One step taken by the new government was to make local authorities responsible for both the hospitalization of their impoverished sick residents and for developing specialized health programs and services. Development of these special health services, as well as hospital services in the province, continued to expand slowly.

Developments in public health were not dramatic during this time, but by 1951 it was increasingly evident that public health programs were needed throughout the province. The Health Unit Act of 1951 divided the province into geographic areas to be served by local health units. Each unit had its own board and administrative system and received up to 60% of its budget from the province.

PUBLIC WELFARE: In 1935 the Social Credit government established the Bureau of Relief and Public Welfare under the direction of the minister of Public Health, and reorganized relief and welfare programs within the Department of Public Health.

With the Social Credit party in power, Alberta prospered from the 1940s through the 1960s and made substantial social, educational, and cultural progress. Public welfare programs grew so dramatically that the Department of Public Welfare was established as a separate government department in 1944. The new department was responsible for all forms of relief, child welfare and children of unmarried parents, the Metis population, part of the Domestic Relations Act, the Juvenile Court Act, and by 1945, old age pensions and mother's allowance.[15]

Public welfare issues received significant public attention, especially those specifically related to child welfare programs. In the mid-1940s, criticism and scandal arose from a publicized inquiry by Charlotte Whitton regarding the administration of child welfare programs and the handling of child welfare cases.[16] Unfortunately, this public scrutiny had little positive effect on Alberta government policy which remained out of harmony with other provinces' approaches towards social welfare through the 1960s.[17]

In 1949 a number of changes took place involving the Department of Public Welfare's financial responsibility. According to the Public Welfare Assistance Act of 1949, 60% of the municipal costs for child welfare services were to be paid by the Department of Public Welfare. The legislation extended this arrangement to social assistance services.[18] In addition, changes to the federal Old Age Pensions Act in 1949 resulted in some of the Department of Public Welfare's financial responsibility being shared with the federal government. The provincial government, however, retained its administrative responsibility for old age security.

The Separation of Public Health and Public Welfare: 1952-1970
In 1952, Public Health and Public Welfare became separate ministries. These programs continued to become increasingly complex and diverse, and the federal contribution towards provincial social welfare programs became more significant. Also at this time, the financial role of the federal government was clarified, and the concepts of insurance plans and allowances were introduced.[19]

DEPARTMENT OF HEALTH: On April 1, 1958 the first hospital insurance program was introduced and federal contributions amounted to approximately 35% of program costs. This was probably the most dramatic improvement in the Department of Health at this time.

Programs continued to diversify from 1959 to 1966, and significant changes occurred between 1967 and 1971. The Department of Public Health became the Department of Health in 1967.[20] The new department was subdivided into Hospital Services and Health Services Commissions, with each headed by a commissioner. The Alberta Health Care Plan was also introduced in 1967, and an administrative unit responsible for this program was established under the Health Care Insurance Act of 1969.[21]

Between the mid-1950s and early 1960s, the province cost-shared some Department of Health programs with the federal government, such as the programs for the blind and the Widow's Pensions. Other programs, such as income support, were totally supported by the federal government. Still others, such as the Mother's Allowance Program, were not sharable but received increased funding from the province.

In 1947, municipalities were delegated primarily responsible for child welfare. However, by 1958 the province assumed all costs for care of Crown wards and by 1969 the transfer of responsibility for children's protection services from the municipality to the province was complete.

In the area of public welfare, the most significant occurrences during the next two decades included the appointment of the first social worker by the department in 1952, the creation of the Social Planning and Development branch of the department in 1962 by the Social Credit government, and the subsequent introduction of Alberta's Preventive Social Service Program in 1966. The introduction of this preventive program reflected a fundamentally new and innovative approach to program planning and service delivery. It marked an attempt to change the underlying philosophy of social welfare programs from custody and maintenance to focus on prevention and the social development of the individual. According to Bella,[22] the goals of the policy makers who introduced the Preventive Social

Service Program included: preventive welfare; improved general well-being; municipal autonomy; municipal social planning; involvement of volunteers; stimulating self-help; the development of social programs; and federal cost-sharing. This program provided for the province to fund 80% of the costs for social welfare preventive service to municipal and local governments.[23]

In 1970, the Department of Public Health became the Department of Social Development and the Public Welfare Act was replaced by the Social Development Act.

Alberta Social Services and Community Health: 1971-1979
In 1971, two major events occurred. First, the Progressive Conservative government under the leadership of Peter Lougheed won the provincial election. Second, the public health and public welfare mandates which were separated in 1952 were amalgamated under one minister by the passing of the Health and Social Development Act. In 1971, the department served a population of 1,627,874 people.[24]

During the years prior to the election, Peter Lougheed, as leader of the Opposition, expressed concerns about mental health services and services for retarded persons. Thus, in the early 1970s, the department began to develop noninstitutional services for handicapped children and the mentally ill. In addition, extended health benefits were developed.[25]

In March 1975, the priorities of the Progressive Conservative government were confirmed when the name of the department was changed to Social Services and Community Health. This marked a shift in emphasis, which was characterized by assigning one administrative group the responsibility for several programs including social services, community health, rehabilitative services and mental health.

According to Splane,[26] however, advances in social welfare in general were somewhat limited during the Lougheed era. In part he attributes this to the poor relationship with the Federal-Provincial Social Security Review, which was a nation-wide endeavour beginning in 1974 and ending in 1983 to rationalize and improve Canada's social welfare system.[27]

This poor relationship between Alberta and the federal government, however, must be viewed in a much broader context. During this same period, Alberta, which had previously been a have-not province, very rapidly became one of Canada's wealthiest provinces. For example, the average annual increase in the gross domestic product (GDP) exceeded 20% and the per capita GDP rose from $7,648 in 1973 to $23,498 in 1983.[28]

Alberta's sudden wealth resulted in a reversal of the prior payment pattern to the federal government. In the four-year period from 1981 to 1984, for example, the federal government took $16.2 billion more in tax revenue out of Alberta than it spent in the province.[29] This imbalance in payments resulted in a declining interest in and conflict with federal initiatives. At the same time, the wealth of Alberta reduced its dependency on external funding for provincial endeavors. The development of a province-wide day care program which utilized for-profit agencies is a good example of Alberta's tendency to maintain its independence from the federal government. Because for-profit agencies were permitted to provide day care services, along with nonprofit agencies, Alberta excluded itself from cost-sharing the program with the federal government under the welfare services provisions of the Canada Assistance Plan (CAP).[30] The province, thus has lost millions of dollars per year by supporting a commercial day care system which does not qualify for federal cost sharing.

The socio-economic conditions of Alberta during the late 1970s and through to the early 1980s were critical in the development of social services. The province experienced a "boom-bust" cycle of rapid economic expansion and subsequent rapid decline. This phenomenon was a direct result of the high price of oil and very fast growth of the oil industry during the years of the rise of the Organization of Petroleum Exporting Countries (OPEC). Because of the "boom," the provincial population increased from approximately 1.5 million in the early 1970s to approximately 2.3 million in 1982, which was primarily due to the migration of people from other provinces in search of employment.

Economic growth, in conjunction with the associated increase in the population, resulted in a tremendous need for development of government programs. Public spending increased from $1.1 billion in 1971 to $10.8 billion in 1985, outstripping even the growth rate of the gross domestic product (GDP). The number of civil servants also grew by 200% even though the population it served only increased by 50%.[31] However, the boom did not last long and subsequent economic decline was accompanied by the current trend toward financial restraint. These changing conditions have demanded rapid responses and thus have made the task of providing appropriate welfare services very complex and controversial.

The Nature of Recent Developments in Social Services

The rapidly changing conditions of the early 1980s and the corresponding government attempt to restrain costs were the focus of much controversy. In May 1986, this controversy increased when Alberta Social Services publicly declared the intent to privatize. Even prior to this announcement, the Alberta Association of Social Workers had begun to develop arguments against the use of the private for-profit sector for the provision of direct social services. These arguments were formalized in a paper entitled "Alberta Association of Social Workers Position Paper on the Alberta Government Policy of Privatizing Public Social Services (The Commercialization of Caring)." This position paper, which was submitted to the Alberta government in June 1986, called for a moratorium on privatization of social services until after public hearings were conducted by a legislative task force throughout Alberta.[32] The Alberta government, however, did not act on the recommendations of the Alberta Association of Social Workers position paper. Instead, the Department of Social Services continued to transfer provision of services to both for-profit and voluntary agencies.

The key issue when examining recent developments in social services in Alberta is the extent to which the government has transferred the responsibility for provision of social services to the private sector: in other words, the extent of privatization. Thus the 1979-1987 period is examined below to determine both the extent to which government policy reflects the principles of privatization of social services and the impact of this policy on direct service provision.

The strategy for determining the nature and extent of privatization of the Department of Alberta Social Services involved three major components. First, Alberta's policy model for social services was examined. Its development was traced from the mid-1970s to the present to assess whether there are policies reflecting the principles of privatization which would involve the devolution of the government from direct services. The primary source of data for this specific question was government documents.

Second, estimates of expenditures 1979-1980 through 1986-87 and staff allocations were used to assess the extent to which policies to privatize have been implemented and have caused changes within the administration and direct service domain. The use of these figures should be considered within the context of their limitations. First, it should be pointed out that the figures represent estimates at the beginning of the year and not actual expenditures.[33] Second, because some reorganization of the department within subprograms has occurred, figures are sometimes not comparable between years. The specific areas of direct service to be examined are: (1) social allowance programs; (2) child welfare programs; (3) vocational rehabilitation services; and (4) services for the handicapped. In addition, centralized departmental support services is examined since change in this administrative branch of the department has been associated with changes in direct service areas.

The third component of this investigation involved examining the available data from the voluntary and nonprofit sector and the for-profit sector. Data relevant to the nature and proportion of the voluntary and for-profit sectors were very limited for several reasons. First, Alberta Social Services and other government departments do not tend to distinguish between for-profit and nonprofit or voluntary organizations in their accounting procedures. Expenditure records, for example, record the amounts allocated for grants, contracts, and direct purchase of services, however, the records do not indicate whether services were obtained from volunteer or for-profit organizations. Second, the lack of policy distinguishing between the volunteer and for-profit sectors seems to indicate a lack of concern for distinguishing between the sectors. External conditions, however, such as having to meet the nonprofit criteria of the Canada Assistance Plan (CAP) for cost sharing on welfare services, do affect certain areas such as the Family and Community Support Services Association of Alberta (FCSS) program. Third, the information available on the voluntary sector often does not distinguish between nonprofit voluntary organizations administered by a voluntary board with paid staff, and volunteers who provide direct service without pay. Finally, comparable data over time is not available.

Alberta's Policy Model for Privatization of Social Services

While rumors have been circulating for years about the privatization of the services delivered by the Department of Alberta Social Services, it was in May 1986 that the deputy minister, Michael Ozerkevich, publicly announced the intention of the Department of Alberta Social Services to privatize by "the contracting-out of programs, primarily to nonprofit, voluntary agencies . . . ."[34] The deputy minister stated that privatization was "not being done to cut costs." The intention, however, was "to reduce administration costs by contracting with private industry . . . ." For example, turning social allowance cheque processing over to the banks would reduce government administration costs.

Given these statements, it seems that the Department of Alberta Social Services has taken a firm policy position in favour of implementing privatization. The factors that moved the government to adopt this stance are further examined.

Causal Factors

Several factors set the stage for the onset of privatization in the 1980s. These factors can be categorized as "causal conditions" and "causal principles." The causal conditions are phenomena which have been external to the Department of Alberta Social Services and therefore out of government control. Causal principles, in contrast, consist of the policies and mechanisms employed by government to solve the problems created by external conditions.

In Alberta, the causal conditions have included historic, economic and demographic factors. First, the history of the development of Alberta Social Services indicates a tendency towards divestment or decentralization of responsibility for provision of social services to the municipal and community levels. Second, the Alberta economy over the last ten years can be most appropriately identified as a "boom-bust" economy. When OPEC oil prices soared in the mid-1970s, the Alberta economy boomed. It was not long, however, before oil prices dropped drastically, sending Alberta into a recession. Unemployment rates skyrocketed during the 1981/82 fiscal year. For example, the rate of unemployment for the overall working population (over 15 years of age) increased by over 300% to a high of almost 12% within the fiscal year.[35]

Demographic factors also set the stage for the change and development of new policies. Migration to Alberta from other provinces reached a high of 45,000 in 1980/81.[36] Migration contributed to a growth rate which peaked at 3.8% in 1981 and dropped to 1.6% in 1983/84. In addition, the structure of the family was changing, which was evident by the increasing number of single-parent families. By 1985/86, social allowance payments to single parents were projected to be almost 45% of the total budget for transfer payments to individuals.[37]

Revitalization of the causal principles for privatization was demonstrated in 1975, when a group of sixty Albertans travelled across Europe with Premier Peter Lougheed to collect information on innovations and products which Europe and Alberta could offer one another. One of the specific objectives of this endeavour included the observation and study of European innovations in the area of social services. The findings of the study pertinent to social services are summarized below:

> In Europe there seems to be an effort to decentralize public health and medical care, particularly noticeable in Britain and Sweden. While better management is seen to be one of the reasons for the reorganization, the main intention was to improve the quality of medical care, especially

in the neglected areas such as geriatrics, psychiatry and community services. Much can be learned from the successes and mistakes of reorganization in various European countries. Health and social service delivery is not well organized in Alberta and is unequally distributed through the province. If consolidation, reorganization and decentralization of planning and management of these services are to become government policy, there must be a developmental process with three major components clearly developed together:
1. Preparation of regional key executive personnel for the complex task of global management and priority setting at a regional level;
2. Central reorganization to produce back-up services which must be centralized. These would generally involve:
   a. planning and overall policy setting;
   b. program standard setting and monitoring of personal programs and services;
   c. service functions including budget allocation, management of capital expenditures and borrowing, including reviewing and authorizing hospital and health centre building, providing plans for facilities and providing data processing;
   d. information collection, collation, distribution and dissemination functions;
3. Enabling mechanisms for coordinated policy making and planning on a rational information base without the strangle hold of advisory committees currently impeding function in Britain.[38]

The findings and recommendations of this report set the framework in Alberta for a "staging" process of devolution of central government from direct service provision. The first stage of this process would be most appropriately referred to as the reorganization or decentralization stage. As indicated, the collection of information to develop reorganization and decentralization strategies began as early as 1975. The actual implementation of decentralization began in April 1981 with the regionalization of the department through decentralization of administration and provision of direct services.[39] Thus, the decentralization stage began in approximately 1975 and was implemented on a full scale in 1982.

Since 1983, with decentralization being relatively complete, the motivating principle has been productivity.[40] Thus, the second stage of the process may be called the efficiency stage. During this stage, increasing efficiency and responsiveness after decentralization became the goal and downsizing of the department continued to occur through attrition and contracting out for services.

Present Policy and Future Direction

The Department of Alberta Social Services recently released a report entitled, "Social Services Division Strategic Directions and Priorities for 1986-1989." This document outlines the mission of the department, as well as the principles and priorities related to the mission. These are outlined briefly below.

MISSION: The report states that:

> The mission of the Social Services Division is to ensure the development and delivery of services which protect and promote well-being, while *encouraging and supporting individual, family and community independence*, self-reliance and responsibility to the greatest degree possible.[41]

PRINCIPLES: In pursuit of the mission of the Department, the report indicates that the following principles are to be followed:[42]

1. *Basic Human Rights*
   The Department is committed to honouring and respecting human rights and fundamental freedoms and the dignity and worth of the person.
2. *Personal Responsibility and Independence*
   The Department believes that, while its services must be responsive to people's needs, services should not replace or interfere with the responsibility and initiative of individuals, families and communities to meet their own needs. To the greatest extent possible, services should develop and enhance independence; and should involve individuals, families and communities in the development and delivery of services which affect them. When services are provided, they should be delivered in a way which minimizes intrusion, disruption and restriction.
3. *Pre-eminence of the Family*
   The Department believes that services should help maintain and support the family as a healthy functioning unit, and that most people are best cared for within the context of their family unit.
4. *Prevention and Early Intervention*
   While recognizing the necessity of protection, crisis, treatment and rehabilitation services, the Department is also committed to providing a range of services which promote well being and prevent anticipated health and social problems.

5. *Quality Services*
    The Department is committed to provision of quality services, and to ensuring that services:
    — are available and accessible to all members of the service's target group within the scope of available resources;
    — are coordinated within the Department and with other government and community resources;
    — provide comprehensiveness and continuity of care;
    — are appropriate to people's needs;
    — encourage community resourcefulness, innovation and initiative;
    — are delivered by competent staff who are supported by effective administrative and supervisory practices and appropriate training and development opportunities.
6. *Accountability*
    The Department is committed to ensuring that services are delivered in accordance with its stated mission and philosophical principles, and that mechanisms are in place to ensure accountability for delivery of efficient, effective and economical services—including definition of program and practice standards, monitoring and evaluation.

PRIORITIES: In terms of priorities, the report stressed the following: (1) a shift toward more flexible and individualized services; (2) increased availability of services and community care alternatives; (3) increased delivery of services by nondepartmental personnel; and (4) effectiveness and productivity.

Overall, the mission, principles, and priorities of the report indicate that the department's policy is generally consistent with the concept of privatization. The first priority, "a shift toward more flexible and individualized services," introduces the concept of "empowerment of the individual." This concern about the empowerment of the individual is consistent with the recently adopted Federal Charter of Rights. While this priority is not clearly linked with the process of privatization, it does support the concept of diminished government intervention. The second priority, i.e., "availability of services" is a continuation of the decentralization process. Finally, the third priority, "delivery of service by nondepartmental personnel," is consistent with the devolution of responsibility for direct services by the department to the private sector.

Figure 3–1 ASSCH Total Budget Estimates—1979/80–1986/87

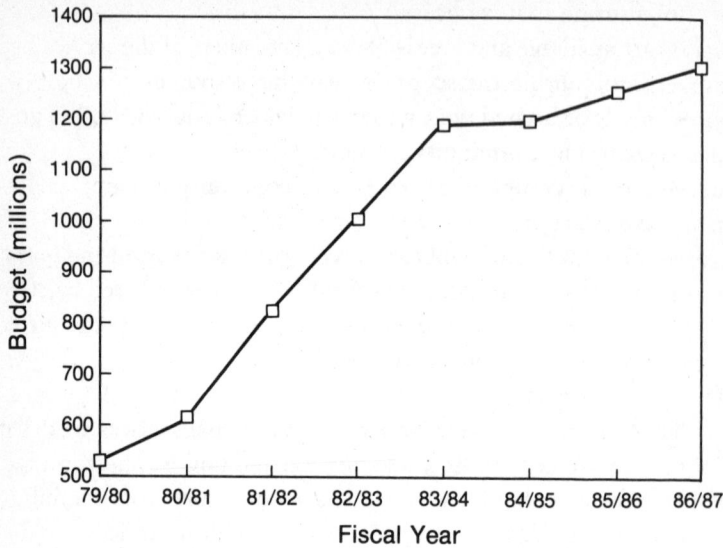

Figure 3–2 Permanent FT & Man-Yr Authorization—Total Dept. (Excluding AADAC), 1979–1987

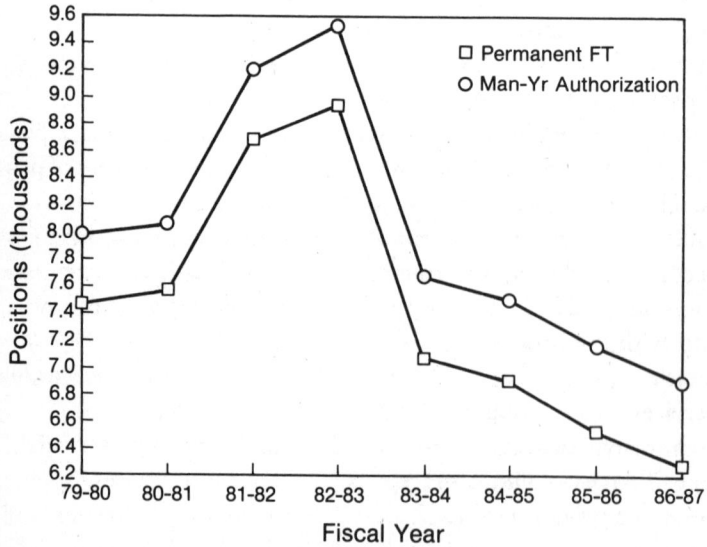

Social Service Administrative and Service Planning: Budget Estimates 1979-1986 and Man-Year Authorization

General Overview

The extent to which policies to privatize the Department of Alberta Social Services have been operationalized at the administrative and direct service level is examined by a review of the budget plans in four direct service program areas and the central support services. Two of the direct service programs, Social Allowance and Child Welfare, are statutory programs, while Vocational Rehabilitation Services and Services for the Handicapped are nonstatutory.

The 1986/1987 overall budget for the Department of Alberta Social Services is $1,306,267,706 (Figure 3-1). This represents an increase of 147% from the 1979/80 budget of $529,045,090. Figure 3-1 shows that the budget increased at a considerable rate between 1979/80 and 1983/84. The 1984/85 budget increased only marginally (i.e., 0.63%) over the previous year, but since the 1984/85 fiscal year, the budget has increased by 4% to 5% each year.

Figure 3-2 presents data pertaining to man-year authorization and full-time positions for the department from 1979/80 to 1986/87.[43] Note the substantial reduction of both man-year authorization (-19.39%) and full-time positions (-20.86%) from 1982/83 to 1983/84 and the continued downward trend to 1986/87. Expressed in actual numbers, man-year authorization decreased from 9525.1 in 1982/83 to 7677.4 in 1983/84. Furthermore, in the 1986/87 fiscal year, the department estimated man-year authorization at 6898.1, which was significantly lower than the 7979.1 man-year authorization of 1979/80. Overall, the decrease in man-year authorizations indicates staff downsizing, particularly after 1983/84. The very large decrease, however, from 1982/83 to 1983/84 was due to the transfer of responsibility for mental hospitals to the Department of Hospitals and Medical Care. This transfer included the loss of approximately 1700 man-year authorizations, which is demonstrated in Figure 3-2, and approximately $50 million from the budget, which did not substantially affect the overall budget (see Figure 3-1) since it was balanced by increases in other areas.

The main trends seem to be towards decentralization and increased efficiency. The speed with which these are being achieved could be described as pragmatic, since the overall budget has continued to increase (albeit at a slower rate since 1983/84).

Figure 3-3 Budget Estimates—Departmental Support Services, 1979–1987

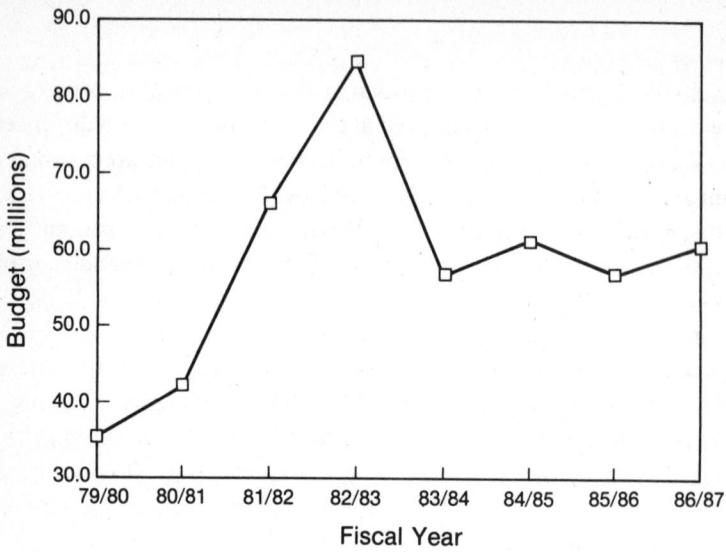

Figure 3-4 Permanent FT & Man-Yr Authorization—Departmental Support Services, 1979–1987

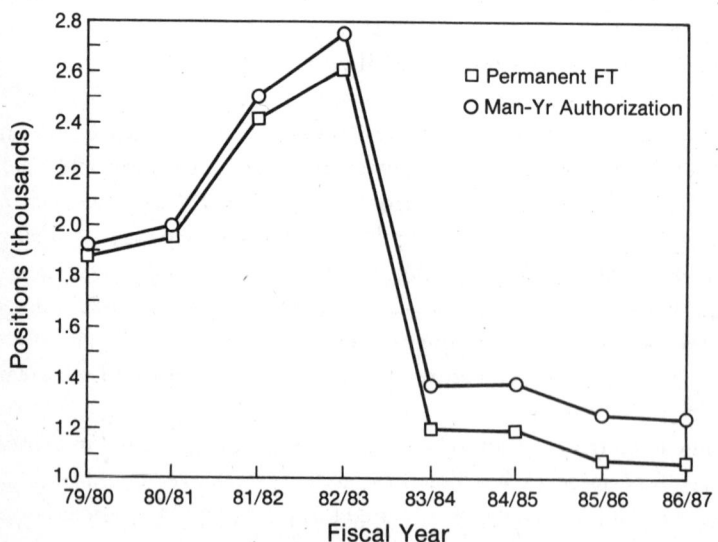

Departmental Support Services

Departmental Support Services consists mainly of senior management and central support services for the six regional areas located mainly at the head office in Edmonton, and thus does not include resources for the administration and provision of direct service. It is included in this analysis, however, because changes that have occurred with support services over the years provide strong evidence for decentralization, through transfer of responsibilities to regional offices responsible for service delivery, and for staff reduction where staff are not directly involved in delivery of services. Figure 3-3 reveals a substantial reduction (-32.7%) in the budget allocated to Departmental Support Services within a one-year period. The budget decreased from almost $85 million in 1982/83 to $57 million in 1983/84.

Figure 3-4 displays information regarding man-year authorization. It indicates that a logical corresponding drop in man-year authorization occurred in 1983/84. It is interesting to note that the drop in man-year authorization is more pronounced than the reduction of budgeted dollars. In part these reductions were due to the transfer of responsibilities for mental hospitals to the Department of Hospitals and Medical Care, and the transfer of administrative positions to the regions. This seems to indicate that dollars were being channelled away from centralized support staff to other areas such as computer hardware acquisition, technical support, and contracts since Information Systems' budget increased substantially beginning in 1983/84 and most contracts and grants budget lines increased.

Social Allowance

The objective of the Social Allowance Program is "to provide social aid to families and individuals in need."[44] The Social Allowance Program is organized into the following two administrative subprograms: (1) program development and support; and (2) several direct service subprograms. The direct services programs provide payments to the elderly, single parents, persons with physical and/or mental disabilities, employables, and special cases such as transients.

Figure 3-5 indicates a tremendous increase in the Social Allowance Program budget, which increased from $271 million in 1982/83 to $472 million in 1983/84. This represents an increase of 74.2% in one year. Obviously, this trend corresponds closely to the unemployment statistics during the "bust" period. Payments to employables increased from $44 million in 1982/83 to $120 million in 1983/84. It is interesting to note however, that in both of these fiscal years, payments to single-parent families

Figure 3-5 Budget Estimates—Social Allowance, 1979–1987

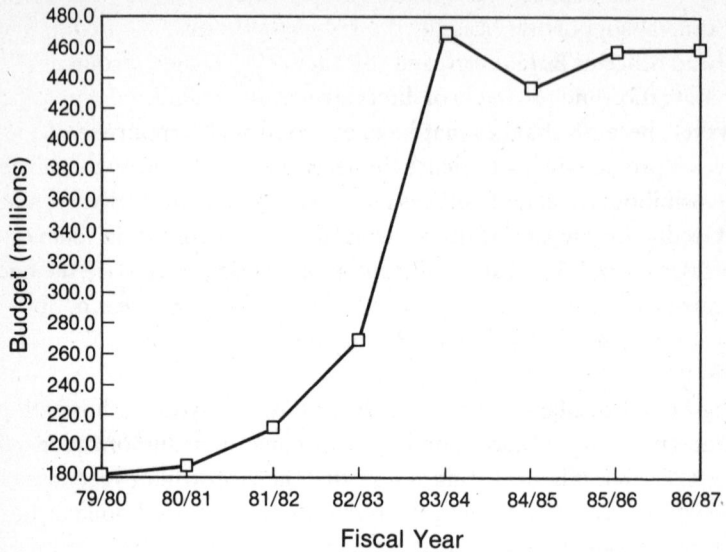

Figure 3-6 Permanent FT & Man-Yr Authorization—Social Allowance, 1979–1987

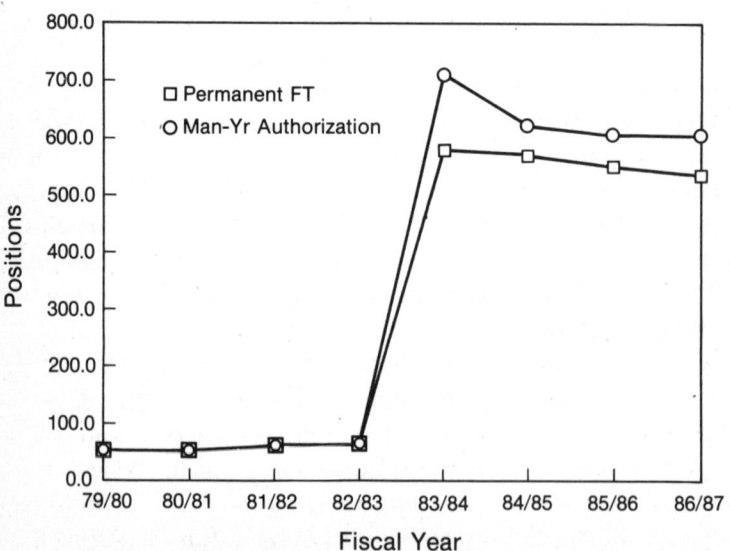

comprised almost half the total budget for this program. The decrease in budget from 1983/84 to 1984/85 is somewhat misleading, because actual expenditure data indicated that there was a $45 million dollar surplus in 1983/84, thus suggesting that the estimates for this fiscal year were very much higher than the need warranted.

Figure 3-6 indicates that the changes in man-year authorization are relatively consistent with the estimated expenditures. Thus, there is little indication of staff downsizing in this area. However, it should be noted that the ratio of staff to program dollars in this area is very low and therefore downsizing staff would have little effect on the department's overall staffing level.

Child Welfare
The objective of the Child Welfare Program is "to provide suitable environments for children committed to the crown either by the courts or by mutual agreement."[45] Child Welfare consists of the following subprograms: program development and support; guardianship of children; regional service delivery; family services; contracted residences; and residence and treatment in institutions. In the 1986/87 fiscal year, this program had a total budget of $127 million, which accounts for 9.7% of the total budget of the Department of Alberta Social Services.

Figure 3-7 indicates that the Child Welfare budget grew very rapidly between 1980/81 and 1982/83, increasing 55.5% in 1980/81, 26.3% in 1981/82 and 29.3% in 1982/83. In 1985/86, the budget decreased by 9.3%, most likely in anticipation of a decrease in the child welfare caseload resulting from the proclamation of the new Child Welfare Act (July 1985). This new Child Welfare Act emphasized the principle of "least intrusiveness," which reflected the government's belief in the autonomy of the family unit.

As Figure 3-8 illustrates, the man-year authorization also increased rapidly from 1979 to 1984, despite a decrease from 1981/82 to 1982/83. The largest increase occurred in 1983/84, when the man-year authorization jumped from 670 to 1352 positions, an increase of 101.7% within one year. However, the transfer of Regional Service Delivery as a new decentralized subprogram from Departmental Support Services during this time probably accounts for a substantial proportion of the increase in positions.

Vocational Rehabilitation Services
The objective of the Vocational Rehabilitation Services Program is "to develop and promote effective and efficient vocational rehabilitation

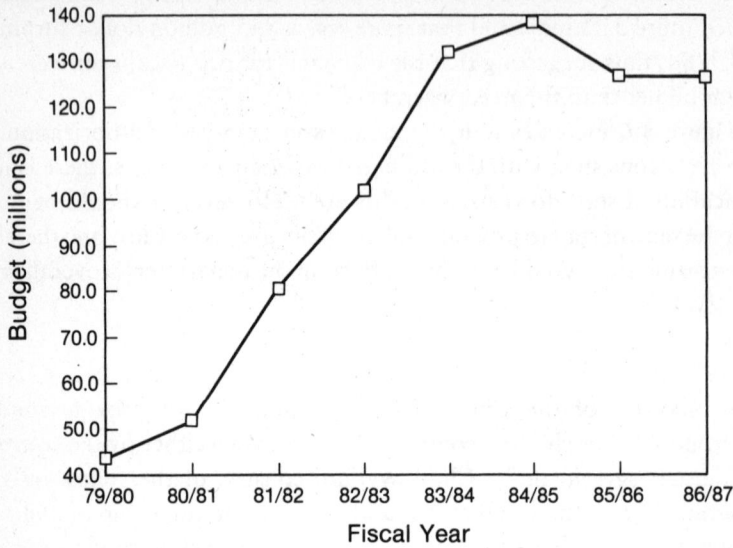

Figure 3-7 Budget Estimates—Child Welfare, 1979-1987

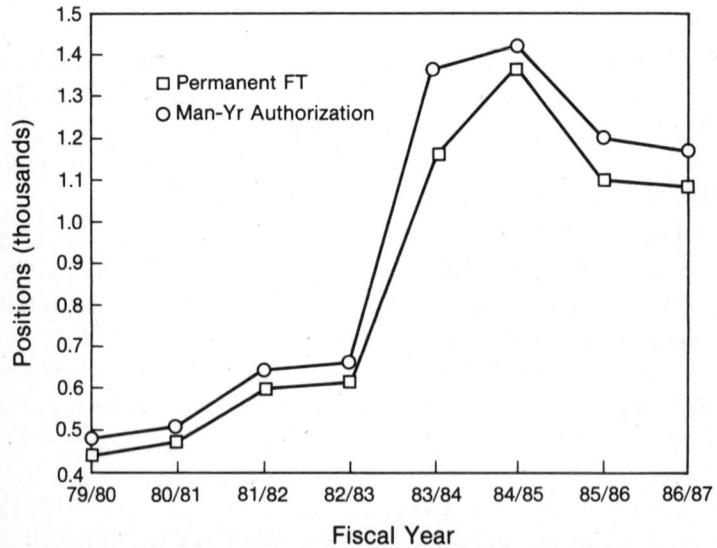

Figure 3-8 Permanent FT & Man-Yr Authorization—Child Welfare, 1979-1987

programs which assist disadvantaged and disabled individuals to become more self-reliant."[46] Vocational Rehabilitation services includes the following subprograms: program development and support; regional service delivery; and purchased services and agency grants. In 1986/87, the total budget for this program was $22 million, or 1.8% of the total budget.

Figure 3-9 indicates that the program budget increased significantly (88.9%) from 1980/81 to 1981/82 and then stabilized. The stabilized budget since 1981/82 seems to have been offset by a substantial decrease (-28.5%) in man-year authorization from 1981/82 to 1982/83 as is indicated by Figure 3-10.

Additional data on agency grants and purchased services indicate that as the man-year authorization decreased for the overall program, there was a substantial increase in grants and fee-for-service arrangements. In 1979/80, for example, grants and purchased services accounted for only 57.3% of the total budget for Vocational Rehabilitation Services. However, by 1982/83, this category accounted for 83.6% of the total budget. This trend continued to 1986/87; grants and purchased services still account for a projected 85.3% of the total budget, or approximately $19 million.

Services for the Handicapped

The objective of Services for the Handicapped is "to ensure the development and provision of care and rehabilitation services by community or the government, which enable handicapped persons to develop according to their potential, and where possible, to function in the community."[47] The subprograms include: program development and support; regional service delivery; purchased services and agency grants; and residential and treatment institutions.

The total budget estimate for this program in 1986/87 was $118 million, which accounts for 9.1% of the total departmental budget. As Figure 3-11 indicates, the budget estimates for this program have grown steadily since 1979/80 when it was allocated $49 million. In 1981/82 the budget increased substantially (50.5%). In contrast, Figure 3-12 indicates a steady decline in man-year authorization since 1982/83.

Examination of subprogram trends indicates a substantial increase in grants to agencies and purchased services, which would offset the decrease in the Department of Social Services staff. In 1986/87, for example, the proportion of the budget committed to grants and purchased services was 33.8%, which was an increase of approximately 14% since 1979/80. In contrast, residential treatment decreased from 76.1% of the budget in 1979/80 to 62.9% of the budget in 1986/87.

Figure 3-9 Budget Estimates—Vocational Rehabilitation, 1979–1987

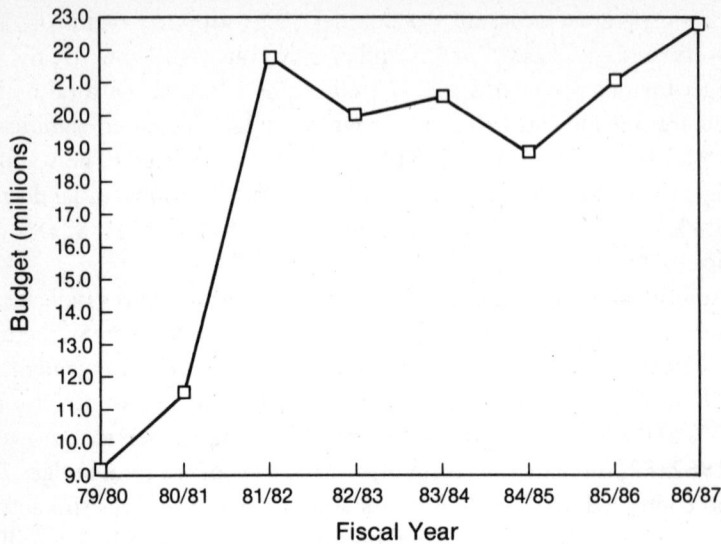

Figure 3-10 Permanent FT & Man-Yr Authorization—Vocational Rehabilitation, 1979–1987

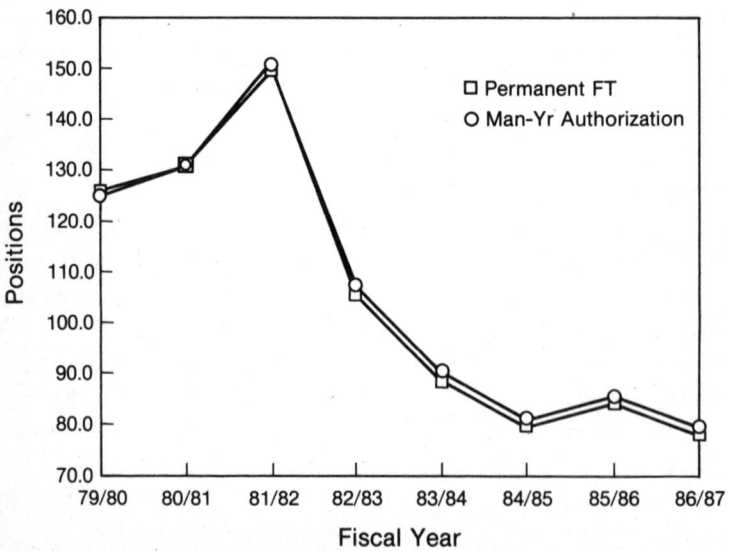

Figure 3–11 Budget Estimates—Services for the Handicapped, 1979–1987

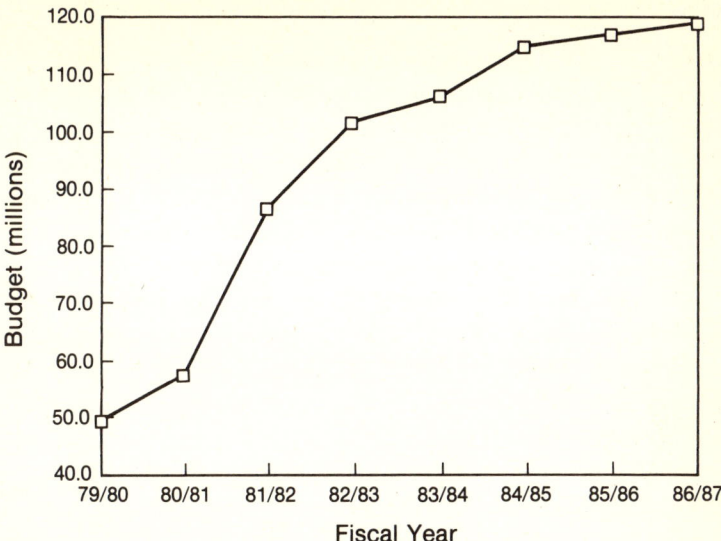

Figure 3–12 Permanent FT & Man-Yr Authorization—Services for the Handicapped, 1979–1987

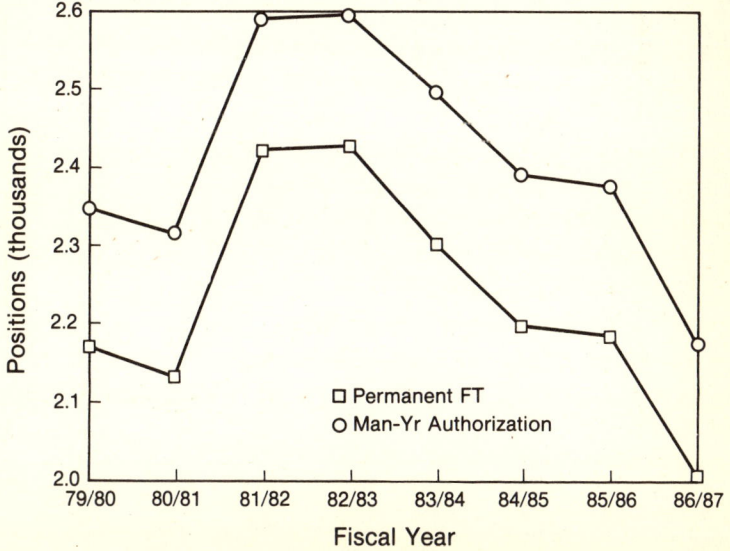

The Volunteer and For-Profit Sectors: Provision of Service

Voluntary Sector

The lack of available data on the voluntary sector is surprising, considering the importance attributed to such activities by governments and communities. Despite the lack of information, volunteerism seems rather pervasive in Alberta. A 1980 study by Statistics Canada indicated that 19.3% of Albertans worked as volunteers, compared to 15.2% of all Canadians generally. Of all volunteers in Alberta, 29.4% (compared with 31.5% for all Canadians) work for social service organizations. However, only 16.7% of Alberta volunteers (compared to 20.3% for Canada) provided direct social services to clients. Thus 42.4% of social welfare volunteers in Alberta (compared to 35.7% for all of Canada) did not provide direct services to clients. Rather, they performed other services such as board memberships, fund raising, and clerical support.[48]

A more recent survey of volunteers in Calgary indicated that over 50% did not provide direct services.[49] These findings suggest that approximately half of Alberta's social welfare volunteers could be involved in administrative or supportive roles for voluntary organizations, which probably have paid staff who provide direct services to clients.

The high proportion of administrative volunteers is in part due to the regulations of the Family and Community Support Services (FCSS) program mandated by the Family and Community Support Services Act (June 1981), which replaced the Preventive Social Services Act (1966). The intent of the new act was to involve citizens at the local level in services and activities that strengthen the family and community and to promote volunteerism.[50] Under this act, the provincial government provides funds for up to 80% of municipalities' expenditures for preventive social services, with the expectation that the municipality will provide the remaining 20% of the cost. The program requires that the services and activities be provided through the nonprofit or voluntary sector, that activities must be preventive in nature, and that services must be based on defined needs.[51] Most of these criteria are consistent with the "welfare services" criteria of the CAP. However, individual projects must be assessed in order to permit the province to recoup 50% of the 80% of funds flowed to municipal governments.

The budget figures available for the FCSS program in Alberta from 1979 to 1987 are contained in Table 3-1. It is interesting to note that substantial increases occurred in the budget every year except 1983/84. Overall the budget increased from $9.1 million in 1979/80 to $30.6 million in

Table 3–1 Total Amount of Budget for Community Resources from Family Community Support Services Program*

Fiscal Year (April 1 to March 31)	Total Amount of Budget	Percentage Change in Budget
Preventive Social Services		
1979/1980	9,196,092	—
1980/1981	11,865,570	29.0
1981/1982	17,118,750	44.3
Family and Community Support Services		
1982/1983	23,800,000	39.0
1983/1984	20,602,173	-13.4
1984/1985	21,222,158	3.0
1985/1986	25,300,000	19.2
1986/1987**	30,652,000	21.1

* The total amount of funding reflects the 80% of the projects' deficit costs which are funded by the province through FCSS. In some cases, however, the municipality may contribute more than the required 20%, or the projects may obtain additional funding elsewhere (e.g., through their own fund raising, United Way, Calgary Board of Health, etc.).

** Please note that at the beginning of the 1986/87 fiscal year, the Department of Community Health which administered the FCSS program was separated from Social Services and was placed with the Department of Community and Occupational Health.

SOURCE: Ron Gaunce, FCSS.

1986/87: an increase of 233%. In comparison, the overall budget for Alberta Social Services increased only 147% and the Child Welfare budget increased 190% within the same time period. These findings seem to indicate both a trend toward decentralization of responsibility for prevention services to the community level and the promotion of the growth of volunteer organizations.

For-Profit Sector
Very little is known about the role of the for-profit sector in the provision of social services in Alberta. As indicated above, FCSS funds are not accessible to this sector. There are no other statutes, however, which would exclude for-profit agencies. Day care is the most common service provided by for-profit agencies in Alberta. Seventy percent of day care agencies are for-profit [52] even though operating allowances provided to for-profit day care services are not cost shareable under CAP unless spaces are occupied by clients receiving a day care subsidy based on a needs test.

While the proportion of for-profit day care agencies is significant, the overall percent of for-profit agencies is thought to be considerably less. In a survey of 508 Calgary agencies, for example, only 19% were for-profit.[53]

Discussion and Conclusion

The objective of this chapter was to determine the extent to which privatization has been adopted by the Department of Alberta Social Services. This objective was facilitated by addressing the following research questions: (1) at the policy level, has Alberta Social Services adopted policies which reflect privatization or the devolution of the government from service provision; (2) at the administrative level, to what extent have the policies reflecting privatization been implemented; and (3) at the service level, how has privatization affected the balance of the voluntary and for-profit sectors? Below, the findings of this case study regarding these questions are summarized under the topic areas of policy and administration of service.

Policy of Efficiency
There is considerable evidence that since the late 1970s the Department of Alberta Social Services has attempted to adopt a policy to reorganize and increase efficiency. At least two stages of this policy can be clearly identified. First, in 1981 the "decentralization or reorganization stage" began and the department was regionalized into six administrative areas. Second, the "efficiency stage," which was characterized by downsizing through attrition and rotation, especially of central management, began after decentralization was widely implemented in 1983.

Given the relatively clear policy of efficiency over the last decade, it is interesting that there is little evidence in the budget estimates to indicate that the Department of Alberta Social Services has significantly reduced funding for direct service programs. Rather, since 1979, funding has increased substantially (i.e., 147%). These increases, for the most part, have been due to factors external to government policy; specifically, to the economic and demographic changes which are characteristic of a "boom-bust" economy.

While there were a few examples of specific program budgets decreasing from one year to the next, close examination of these situations usually indicated that the reduction followed a year in which a program was over-budgeted and had a large surplus at year-end. This situation is illustrated in the example of social allowance where a budget cut in 1984/85 was preceded by a large surplus in 1983/84.

Overall, the policy of efficiency indicates an attempt to control the government growth and increase the expenditures that can be cost-shared with the federal government such as in the area of day care. If restraint was the intent of the policy, it was aimed primarily at administrative resources.

Decentralization of Program Administration
The budget estimates from the five areas examined in this analysis indicate relative consistency with the stated policies of the department, depending on the program examined. The budget data of Departmental Support Services, which has been primarily a centralized administrative support unit, demonstrates a trend that is very consistent with a policy of downsizing administration and the devolution of government from service delivery. The overall budget for this area decreased substantially through the years examined. As well, the man-year allocations of this support program have decreased even more in proportion to the budget. These findings indicate a clear attempt to decrease administrative costs and, at the same time, to move decision-making closer to the provision of direct services.

The findings from the Vocational Rehabilitation Services and Services to the Handicapped program were also very consistent with a policy to privatize. Although the total budget of the programs increased over the years, the man-year authorization decreased. Further analysis indicated that the Department of Alberta Social Services shifted its involvement in these programs from direct service provision to allocating monies directly to those in need or through grants and contracts for provision of services by the private sector.

There were two programs which were less consistent with the policy trend toward privatization. First, the data from the Social Allowance program, which accounts for a larger proportion of the budget (i.e., 42% in 1986/87) than any other program, did not indicate that the program was being privatized. In contrast, the findings indicated that this program was very directly affected by the "boom-bust" economic situation, i.e., its costs increased directly with unemployment and the increase in single-parent families. The number of direct service staff allocated to this program is also low in proportion to the dollars that the program administers. Therefore staff downsizing would provide little gain and has not been implemented, however, there has been a move to make the program more efficient through automation.

The second program which has not been substantially affected by recent privatization is the Child Welfare program. The budget of this program grew rapidly in 1982/83 and has levelled off since then. The trend in man-year allocation corresponds closely to the budget, giving little indication that large scale change in service delivery has taken place. There are several reasons why this program has remained relatively stable. First, it is a statutory program and thus the department has both the legal mandate and direct responsibility for a child in need of protective services.[54] Second, the services that have been provided to children under the Child Welfare Act, such as group homes and foster care, have been in place for many years. Distinctions have not been made between services which have been traditionally provided by both for-profit and voluntary agencies. Finally, decreases in the child welfare caseload could be expected to occur as a result of the new Child Welfare Act proclaimed in July 1985.

The strong trend toward divestment, decentralization, and support of the voluntary sector is demonstrated by the very significant increases in funds provided for the FCSS program. The anticipated decrease in the caseload under the statutory mandate of the Child Welfare Act, because of the principle of least intrusiveness, may increase the caseload for the prevention and nonstatutory program.

Conclusion

Overall, the findings indicate that the Department of Alberta Social Services does have a clear policy to privatize service provision by contracting for services rather that providing them directly. This policy appears to be driven by a goal of efficiency but other factors also support this policy direction. First, there is a historical trend toward the devolution of responsibility to the municipal and community levels, including Indian bands, within the province's social services infrastructure. Second, there is currently a need to be flexible in service delivery because of an economic and demographic environment which has and may continue to change quickly. Third, this policy can be viewed as being consistent with the national trend toward empowerment of the individual as supported by the Charter of Rights.

These findings verify to some extent the statements of some of the department's senior managers who have indicated that the primary intent of decentralization and downsizing is not to cut dollars from the budget but to become more efficient by transferring monies previously used for internal government administration of programs to direct service.

The long-term effects of a policy of efficiency will be to change the implementation of social welfare services and related social work practice in the province. The primary role of Alberta Social Services will be to develop standards, monitor service delivery and tender service contracts to the nongovernment sector. Responsibility for maintaining the quality of service and motivating the client to identify problems and seek services will increasingly be transferred to the professionals and paraprofessionals providing these services through a variety of volunteer organizations and for-profit agencies.

Notes

1. Alberta, *Statutes*, 1907, ch. 10 and 1911-1912, ch. 2.
2. B.E. Krewski, *The Alberta Department of Social Services and Community Health: A History* (Edmonton: Alberta Social Services and Community Health Report, March 1979), pp. 3-13. The authors wish to acknowledge that much of the information used in the historical section covering 1905-1951 relies heavily on this work due to the lack of available information and the comprehensive and concise nature of Krewski's article.
3. Ibid.
4. Alberta, *Statutes*, 1907, ch. 4.
5. Alberta, *Statutes*, 1913, ch. 15.
6. Krewski, p. 13.
7. Statistics Canada, Census Canada, 1891-1971.
8. Alberta, *Statutes*, 1929, ch. 36.
9. Alberta, *Statutes*, 1919, ch. 21.
10. Alberta, *Statutes*, 1924, ch. 25.
11. Alberta, *Statutes*, 1920, ch. 31.
12. Krewski, p. 22.
13. Ibid., pp. 19-22.
14. Ibid., pp. 25-26.
15. Ibid., pp. 31-32.
16. Charlotte Whitton, *Welfare in Alberta, The Report of a Study* (Edmonton: Imperial Order, Daughters of the Empire, 1947).
17. Richard Splane, "Social Welfare Development in Alberta: The Federal-Provincial Interplay," in Jacqueline S. Ismael, ed., *Canadian Social Welfare Policy* (Montreal: McGill-Queen's University Press, 1985), p. 174.
18. Alberta, *Statutes*, 1949, ch. 86.
19. Krewski, p. 41.
20. Alberta, *Statutes*, 1967, ch. 27.
21. Alberta, *Statutes*, 1969, ch. 43.
22. Leslie Bella, "The Goal Effectiveness of Alberta's Preventive Social Service Program," *Canadian Public Policy* 8, no. 2 (1982), pp. 143-55.
23. Ibid., p. 143.

24. Statistics Canada, Census Canada.
25. Krewski, p. 43.
26. Richard B. Splane, "Alberta and the Federal-Provincial Social Services Initiative 1975-1985," in Jacqueline S. Ismael and Raymond J. Thomlison, eds., *Perspectives on Social Services and Social Issues* (Ottawa: Canadian Council on Social Development, 1987).
27. Ibid., p. 10.
28. Ibid.
29. Peter Cook, "Alberta Has Problems, But How Bad Are They?" *The Globe and Mail*, May 7, 1987, p. B3.
30. "Canada Assistance Plan." A Study Team Report to the Task Force on Program Review, June 10, 1985.
31. Cook, p. B3.
32. Alberta Association of Social Workers, *Alberta Association of Social Workers Position Paper on the Alberta Government Policy of Privatizing Public Social Services*, June 25, 1986.
33. Estimates were used instead of expenditures for the following reasons: (1) public account data are not available until almost two years after expenditures are actually made; and (2) a comparison of available expenditure data with estimate data indicate very little difference between the figures. (Note that large differences will be pointed out in the text when the data are available.)
34. "Social Services Privatization Beneficial—Deputy Minister," *Edmonton Journal*, May 6, 1986.
35. Statistics Canada Catalogue 71-001.
36. Alberta Social Services and Community Health, *Departmental Strategic Plan for the 1980s*.
37. Alberta Social Services and Community Health, *Estimates of Expenditures*, 1985-1986.
38. Department of Federal and Intergovernmental Affairs, *The Report of the Alberta Mission to Europe* (March 1976), p. 17.
39. Perry Kinkaide, "The Revitalization of Community Enterprise: The Alberta Case for 'Privatizing' Social Services," in Jacqueline S. Ismael and Raymond J. Thomlison, eds., *Perspectives on Social Services and Social Issues* (Ottawa: Canadian Council on Social Development, 1987), p. 23.
40. Ibid., p. 24.
41. Alberta Social Services and Community Health, Social Services Division, *Strategic Directions and Priorities 1986-1989* (February 1986).
42. Ibid.
43. Man-year authorization indicates the total number of manpower positions available to the department of program, including full-time positions, project positions, and wage salaries.
44. Alberta Social Services and Community Health, *Estimates of Expenditures*, 1986-1987.
45. Ibid.
46. Ibid.
47. Ibid.

48. Statistics Canada, *An Overview of Volunteer Workers in Canada—February 1980* (Ottawa: Minister of Supply and Services, 1981).
49. Janice Hillmo and Janet Harvie, "The Social Service Delivery Potential of Volunteers: A Privatization Issue." A paper presented at the 3rd National Conference on Provincial Social Welfare Policy, April 1987, Banff.
50. FCSS, *The Centre of Prevention*. A pamphlet publication of the FCSS Association of Alberta.
51. Ibid.
52. Carol Howes, "Experience Yields Warning," *The Calgary Herald*, July 23, 1987, p. A7.
53. Carol Howes, "Focus Turns to Funding," *The Calgary Herald*, July 23, 1987, p. A7.
54. Government of the Province of Alberta, *Child Welfare Act* (Edmonton, Alberta: Queen's Printer, July 1985).

4 Saskatchewan

MICHAEL O'SULLIVAN
SANDRA SORENSEN

Generalizations about the socio-economic and political reality of Canada are difficult to make given that the country is made up of (at least) eleven, rather than a single site of political and economic power. Even national social programs vary from province to province when they are cost shared and provincially administered. The battle to impose common ground rules for Medicare is a good example of how difficult uniformity can be to achieve.

An analysis of social policy in Saskatchewan is no exception. Saskatchewan, like all provinces, has a unique history which affects the specifics of how personal social services and income maintenance policies are formulated and delivered. One overwhelming fact of Saskatchewan life is the populist heritage of political struggle *against* the Eastern based interests that skimmed profits from the work of the province's settler-farmers, and *in favour* of a measure of security during those hard times associated with farm life in a harsh environment. This political struggle contributed to the 1944 election of the Co-operative Commonwealth Federation (CCF) government of T.C. Douglas. It also was a catalyst for many progressive social initiatives, some state administered and some community controlled. It is undoubtedly this political tradition that explains why Saskatchewan was often in the forefront of innovative social policy and more generous to its less advantaged citizens.

Much has been made of this latter point, to the extent of creating a myth about a socialist island in the Canadian capitalist sea. What has made Saskatchewan unique is more a question of degree than any substantial difference between it and the rest of the country. When the era of restraint was announced by Prime Minister Trudeau in 1975, Saskatchewan's New Democratic Party government joined in willingly, albeit not as gleefully as the Social Credit government in British Columbia, to name the most obvious contrasting example. Even the Conservative government of Grant Devine, while penurious in its approach to Social Services and especially to the income maintenance of single employables, was nonetheless constrained during its first administration by popular opinion from any further divestment of state responsibility in this regard.

The present era of restraint follows two expansionary periods with respect to the implementation of the welfare state. The first initiatives taken by the federal government during and following World War II, included programs for Unemployment Insurance, Old Age Security and Family Allowance. Although they frequently required provincial approval, these new programs were paid by federal revenues and delivered through the federal government.

The subsequent period of reform involved the provinces to a much greater extent. Many programs were cost-shared and delivered by the province. This period corresponded to the late 1960s Liberal government of L.B. Pearson which legislated Medicare and the *Canada Assistance Plan Act (1966)*.

The Canada Assistance Plan (CAP), was implemented at a time which in Saskatchewan, coincided with a particularly conservative administration, the Liberal government of Ross Thatcher (1964-71). It also coincided with an economic recession caused by depressed farm and potash prices. These two factors did not combine to create the conditions favourable to a creative policy of social assistance, although the Liberals did leave a positive legacy in the form of the *Saskatchewan Assistance Plan Act (1966)*. As a result of much improved economic factors, it would be the NDP administration of Allan Blakeney (1971-82) which would put in place a system of social service and assistance that truly reflected the objectives embodied in CAP.

This period of innovation under the NDP, despite the province's unprecedented prosperity, was to be short lived. By the beginning of its second term of office in 1975 the Blakeney administration's energies were increasingly being consumed with its economic policies. Notable was the fight to partially nationalize the potash industry, and the opening of the north to multinational uranium companies.

With the 1975 announcement of wage and price controls by Prime Minister Trudeau, the era of restraint was officially inaugurated. The Saskatchewan government fell into line with its 1976 budget of "responsible restraint." In fairness, it must be noted that despite its restraint program, Saskatchewan continued to be the most generous province in the country with respect to social assistance benefits. However, other innovative programs did not fare so well. The Family Income Plan (FIP) was reduced by inflation and became simply a welfare supplement, rather than an income supplement to the working poor modeled on the Guaranteed Annual Income proposal advocated at the time by Federal Health and Welfare Minister Marc Lalonde. Nor was FIP the only unfulfilled expectation. Although the economic boom continued well into the latter years of the NDP administration and vast amounts went to economic development, promises such as that made in 1973 to provide 13,500 day care spaces by 1979 fell 10,000 short when the target date arrived.[1]

We can not underestimate the hardships created by the federal and Saskatchewan governments' retreat from innovative social policies in the latter half of the 1970s. Wage controls and the abandonment of existing programs and policy reviews had serious consequences for social assistance recipients and the working poor. However, it is our view that the role played by the Trudeau, Blakeney and other governments was more that of preparing the climate of public opinion for more severe cuts in the future than they themselves actually undertook. For this reason, 1976, the year of the provincial budget of "responsible restraint," is a logical starting point for our consideration.

Continuities and Discontinuities

In studying Saskatchewan government social policies during the 1976-86 period, we examine the second and third Blakeney administrations and the first Devine administration. We note a major continuity and a major discontinuity in social services policies.

Continuity
Both the Blakeney and the present Devine governments can be seen as having a strong anti-state bias with respect to the delivery of personal social services. Like the CCF and Liberals before them, they looked to the nongovernmental sector to deliver these services. Their disinterest in fostering the delivery of personal social services through privately-owned,

profit-oriented businesses is evidenced by the refusal of both administrations, for example, to allow day care or home care services to be assumed by the profit sector. They preferred to provide these services through non-profit, nongovernment organizations.[2] The other side of this coin is that neither of these administrations undertook to deliver these services through state-run agencies.

A consensus exists which cuts across the provincial political spectrum and constitutes an anti-state bias which favours the community control of many social services. This consensus provides us with evidence that even in Saskatchewan, a province where politics is often stereotyped as the free enterprisers vs the socialists, this anti-state bias amounts to a popular ideology influencing all political parties. This has practical implications of considerable importance in the field of social service delivery.

Discontinuity

Discontinuity can be found in programs relating to income maintenance, job creation and the targeting of the "deserving poor," all of which are central to the Devine government's so-called "Welfare Reform." The income maintenance policy of the Devine government, introduced in 1984, the details of which are reported below, reduced Saskatchewan from first to sixth place with respect to the benefits provided single employables. It also disentitled 16 and 17 year-olds from eligibility and lengthened the waiting period for certain benefits for other categories of recipients. This amounts to a move away from the comprehensive programs of the past to a differentiation between various target groups, those who are considered less deserving and others who are referred to by officials as the "deserving poor." The ideological assumptions behind this term (and its unstated opposite) are obvious. For example, while welfare rates paid through the Saskatchewan Assistance Plan (SAP) were cut significantly in 1984, especially for single employables,[3] increases were directed to the electorally strategic, albeit deserving, senior citizens (in the form of home care, increased supplemental income through the Saskatchewan Income Plan for Senior Citizens and the construction of new residential and day activity spaces across the province). In 1984, the physically disabled community benefited as well.[4]

Integral to the welfare reform package is the Saskatchewan Employment Development Program (SEDP). This program identified and placed qualified workers on the welfare rolls in subsidized jobs. Employers in the private, municipal and nongovernmental sectors are eligible for this wage and benefits subsidy. However, the SEDP seems to be less a valid job creation program than it is a scheme to reduce the number of welfare recipients.[5] This "workfare" program also has the potential to significantly alter, through privatization, the policy, administration and delivery of social services in Saskatchewan.

NGO's as a Privileged Vehicle in the Delivery of Social Services.

Lord Keynes gave an economic justification for the liberal state to do what the social democrats had been urging since late in the nineteenth century: provide a social and economic safety net which would simultaneously reduce human suffering (the social democratic concern) while correcting deformations in the capitalist market (the liberal concern).[6] Under the impetus of World War II the state was thrown onto the center stage of socioeconomic intervention. However, no lasting consensus was ever reached about the balance between the state's responsibility and that of the community and the family. Government and nongovernment agencies, for-profit and nonprofit organizations, have played roles of varying importance in various fields of service delivery depending on the particular issue and on time and place.

Where state-delivered services are dominant, it is frequently justified by the *institutional redistributive model*, "which concerns itself with the development of universal policies providing services outside the market, based upon need." In this approach

> the government is accepted as having a key role to play in the development and maintenance of a social network of services designed to strengthen the individual and family in society; risks should be pooled and payment for services extended over time through the tax system or schemes of social insurance; policies, in practice, should be integrated and provided as of right.[7]

However, another approach, distrustful of direct state involvement in social services is the *residual welfare model* which is based on the premise that there are two "natural" (or socially given) channels through which an individual's needs are properly met: the private market and the family. "Only when these two institutions break down should social welfare institutions come into play—but only temporarily."[8]

There is invariably a lag between the time a problem becomes a socially recognized fact and the time the state accepts that they have a responsibility for that problem. For example, in the case of battered women, Transition Houses, established largely by women for women, are meeting this need as the state only slowly responds to this need.

Ironically, at least for those who view Saskatchewan politics as polarized between parties with across the board anti- and pro-state biases, the latter residual model has been embraced in some areas of social service delivery by the NDP, Tories and Liberals alike. Nor is this a recent development. The CCF, for example, promoted the creation of sheltered workshops for the mentally disabled that were state financed but run by the nonprofit Saskatchewan Council for Crippled Children and Adults. The Thatcher Liberals encouraged the development of special care homes for the aged through both profit (Extendicare) and nonprofit (church and municipal) auspices.

This preference of nongovernmental organizations (NGO's) came to be at the centre of the Blakeney government's strategy for the delivery of personal social services. The government also deinstitutionalized the care of mentally disabled. It was their policy that many services, from daycare to special homecare, were best provided by the nonprofit private sector with a level of provincial funding (which ranged from minimal, in the case of day care, to generous for services to the aged).

With respect to the reliance on the NGO's, Riches and Maslany note that of all the detailed changes in social service expenditures in the 1970s, ". . . . the most significant spending trend has been the major turn around in the allocation of funds as between government and non-government social services."[9] More specifically,

> Between 1972 and 1980 the share of government spending on such services provided directly under its own auspices dropped by nearly a half. Spending on NGO's rose from 40% to 67%. Between 1976 and 1980 the average annual rates of spending on government personal social services experienced a real decline of -(2.3)% down from real growth between 1972-1976 of 5.2%. Rates of growth for nongovernment services for the corresponding periods rose from 7.0% to 16.4%.[10]

Nor did this shift to NGO's, or more accurately quasi-NGO's, considering that many of them are "almost entirely dependent"[11] upon government funding, end when the Tories, led by Grant Devine, assumed office in 1982.

Making precise comparisons and drawing conclusions about the present government's policies is difficult because of recent changes in government accounting procedures. As well, programs have been shifted from

Table 4–1 Saskatchewan Subsidies to NGO's

Expenditures*	1971/72	1976/77	1981/82	1984/85
D.S.S. (Total)	33.20	155.20	319.00	328.40
Social Services Organizations	0.05	0.26	3.05	
Community Services	0.06	2.71	5.60	6.10
Service to the Handicapped	0.32	1.34	2.90	7.40
ESP**		1.48	2.18	2.25
SEDP***				9.10
Home Care				17.03
Total NGO's	0.43	5.80	13.70	41.49
Percentage	1.32%	3.70%	4.30%	12.6%

* In millions of current dollars
** Employment Support Program
*** Saskatchewan Employment Development Program

one department to another and others have been, for all intents and purposes, disguised under new budget headings.

Table 4-1 provides evidence of a measure of the support of both the NDP and Tory governments to NGO's. Our figures are incomplete and underestimate the point because they do not include items such as support for child care, the Senior Citizens Provincial Council or nonprofit nursing homes. Table 4-1 also indicates a shift away from comprehensiveness and towards the notion of targeting the "deserving poor," i.e., the aged, the house-bound, and the physically and mentally handicapped.[12]

Political consensus favouring the use of the NGO's as vehicles for the delivery of social services arises from the populist sentiment that the government should not usurp "the responsibility of the citizenry for assisting their fellow man."[13]

These ideas are reflected in the NDP's New Deal policies for social welfare in 1971. Included in the election manifesto of that year were major commitments to the decentralization of authority, the encouragement of community development, the promotion of community services for the mentally ill and decisions to be made with regard to making all homes for the aged either public or nonprofit organizations. While this last commitment suggests some ambivalence, nevertheless it is clear that the NDP on its election to office in 1971 was committed to following the community or nongovernment route.[14]

This consensus underscores Mishra's comment which, although made with respect to Ontario, is helpful in understanding Saskatchewan. He identifies "a populist strand . . . . which favours the development of modes of service provision that are nonbureaucratic, decentralized and community based" which tends "to overlap with those of the right for downsizing government with respect to service delivery."[15]

Whatever else may divide the policies and practices of the NDP and its political opponents, the anti-state bias with respect to the delivery of social services is not one of them. While the Blakeney administration may have departed from the Canadian norm in its use of state centred accumulation strategies in its potash and uranium sectors, NDP social initiatives, at least in respect to program delivery, represented far less a departure from that norm.

Welfare Reform: Cutbacks, Targeting and Job Creation

In early 1983, the new Conservative minister of Social Services commissioned a comprehensive review of the Saskatchewan Assistance Plan. This study, "A Productive Welfare System for the Eighties: A Review of the Saskatchewan Assistance Plan," provided the basis for far-reaching changes based on a philosophy that spoke of establishing "increased efficiency," and of providing "productive opportunities" to clients.[16] It would be characterized by (a) a worsening case-worker/client ratio;[17] (b) a significant decrease in individual benefits for single employables; and (c) a job creation program, the Saskatchewan Employment Development Program (SEDP), which would target about 4,000 of the 30,000 SAP case load for jobs subsidized under the Program.

Welfare Reform and the Attack on Universality

The Canada Assistance Plan (CAP), from which SAP received its matching federal dollars (and its policy framework), was one initiative in a network of national social security measures introduced by the Pearson government. The universalist nature of these programs was in sharp contrast with the partial, frequently "needs test" based programs that they replaced. Another important difference was that these programs, including CAP and its provincial counterparts, afforded a certain dignity to the recipient. CAP precludes, at least in theory, the payment of different benefits to different categories of persons in need. It also precludes schemes that involve "work for welfare" since assistance is considered a right as long as the recipient makes every reasonable effort at self support.[18] Despite these progressive assumptions, the provinces retained considerable discretion over local delivery and administration. Characteristically, most provincial programs failed to respect many of the more progressive CAP guidelines.[19] The major exception to this was Saskatchewan where the introduction of CAP coincided with a provincial welfare review by the Thatcher Administration. The resulting *Saskatchewan Assistance Plan Act* established a provincially administered program of social assistance with rates based on need, not on employability considerations. Employability categories were retained, but these were mainly for statistical purposes and for judging the level of work search expectations on clients.

Our generally favourable comments about CAP and SAP to this point should not be interpreted as meaning that we feel that when the provincial Tories came to office in 1982, they took over a nearly perfect system of social assistance. It was far from it. As early as 1973 even the federal government had recognized the system's shortcomings and had initiated a comprehensive review with a view to implementing further reforms in the direction of a Guaranteed Annual Income. This initiative was abandoned in 1976 in the face of the deepening economic crisis. This crisis also led to a chipping away of benefits by restraint-minded provincial governments, especially after the 1975 federal wage and price control initiatives gave legitimacy to such measures. Whatever CAP/SAP's shortcomings, its strengths cannot be denied, including the principle of universality and the view that assistance is a right of long-term clients and those only briefly requiring assistance.

Whatever continuity exists in Saskatchewan NDP and Tory thinking about the delivery of social services, it does not extend to their views on the universality of social programs. On the principle of universality, the Saskatchewan NDP is solidly within the reform liberal school of thought represented nationally by the social policies and reforms of the Pearson era. The Tories, however, are to the right of this position with elements in their party that are openly hostile to universalist notions. Unlike British Columbia where this rightist element captured the Social Credit Party and continues to dominate social policy decision making, in Saskatchewan this influence appeared to be more peripheral, at least during their first administration. (However, following their 1986 reelection this rightist influence would become dominant). The pre-1986 response took the form of cutbacks in benefits to the single unemployed and a targeting of the "deserving poor." This approach constituted a decisive break with the previously dominant ideology of universalism and was a throwback to the approach taken prior to the reform period of the mid 1960s. For this reason the provincial welfare reform can be seen as a reactionary program in the literal sense, that is, it rolled back social progress in Saskatchewan.

While the rest of Canada faced a severe recession in the mid 1970s, Saskatchewan and Alberta's economies were booming. Saskatchewan oil and potash sales provided unprecedented revenues to the province and the state-multi-national corporate joint ventures in uranium development created a major boom in the north. In Saskatchewan, unemployment rates were the lowest in Canada and so were the number of people on social assistance. However, when the Tories came to office in 1982 much of that had turned around. Potash and uranium prices fell dramatically as did oil prices subsequently. Investment dried up, government revenues decreased dramatically and unemployment went up with predictable results for social assistance. With unemployment reaching over ten percent in the early 1980s, up from four percent a few years before, the number of clients and their dependents on social assistance went from a decade low of 36,000 in 1976 to a 1985 high, slightly in excess of 61,000.[20]

Single employables saw their monthly benefits fall from $522 in 1983 to $345 in 1985. When lost purchasing power as a result of inflation is calculated this represents a real cut of 41.9%.[21] Saskatchewan fell from first to seventh place with respect to the level of payments to this category of welfare recipients.[22] Jeffery and Shadrack[23] argue that single employables now live at fifty percent below the poverty line.

Sixteen and seventeen year-old teenagers have been, for all intents and purposes entirely cut off welfare. It is safe to assume that the majority of such teenagers are pregnant girls whose disentitlement from benefits is of considerable concern, especially when we consider that Saskatchewan has the highest rate of teen pregnancy in Canada.

Nor does the list of cuts end here. The clothing allowance for welfare recipients is no longer available the first three months of entitlement and supplemental dental care is not available for the first six months because, as the minister said, "some people are going on welfare simply to get their teeth fixed."[24] In addition, a whole series of restrictions on such minutae as caps on lottery earnings, income tax regulations and personal assets have all been tightened up to the detriment of the recipient.

No category of recipient other than single employables has received long-term benefit cuts. However, because rates have been frozen since 1983, inflation has taken its toll. Client families have seen their benefits fall by nine percent because of inflation between 1982 and 1985.[25] Jeffery and Shadrack[26] have begun to document the human cost of this tightening of family budgets which, even while they remain the highest in Canada, are hardly generous to say the least. The fact that Saskatchewan is still, in virtually all categories except that of the single employables, the most generous province says less about this province's generosity than it does of the hardship faced by recipients elsewhere in Canada.

In addition to the cuts, the effort to reduce the cost of assistance was accompanied by an odious "blame the victim" campaign which included statements by the Social Services minister about the need to catch welfare cheaters and the establishment of a "fraud squad" that would monitor social assistance recipients. In response to criticism about the inadequacy of benefits then Social Services Minister Gordon Dirks arrived for a television interview carrying grocery bags and proceeded to lecture his listeners about how smart shopping could allow welfare recipients to live very nicely. Every prejudice the middle classes have towards the poor was appealed to in this campaign. Such a situation constitutes, in our opinion, a clear example of disentitlement,[27] one of the means by which government lessens its responsibility for the welfare of the country's disadvantaged sectors.

The net result of these policies is increased hardship. The fact that social assistance recipients and the working poor must increasingly rely on the food bank is symbolic of the depths to which the problem has reached. Food banks are more than an example of privatization. They represent an old-fashioned charity which has stepped in to fill the role that has been filled by the state in the post-war period. Graham Riches comments:

> . . . . private food is being substituted for public cash benefits . . . . the federal and provincial governments know that social assistance benefits are inadequate and are now depending on the voluntary sector to bail them out.[28]

Welfare Reform and Job Creation

Between 1980 and 1984 the jobless rate in Saskatchewan doubled with corresponding increases in the number of people seeking social assistance. Many were single employables. We have already outlined the government's response to the financial needs of these clients—they cut benefits. Convinced that many of these recipients were not actually seeking employment, the Devine Government also created the Saskatchewan Employment

Development Program (SEDP) and a parallel program, the Saskatchewan Skills Development Program (SSDP), raising the spectre of "workfare."

With respect to the SSDP, in order to be effective, a skills development program must create skills that are marketable. While no public evaluation of SSDP is available there is ample reason to question the effectiveness of a program whose first graduates, presented to the media by the minister of Social Services, were drywallers at a time when the unionized construction workforce was recording high rates of unemployment. Rather it would seem that the program's primary objective is simply to give the impression that action is being taken. With national and provincial unemployment rates in excess of ten percent, the problem is not so much the real or imagined inadequate skills of the labour force, as it is a structural problem that translates into lack of demand for labour. All the job training programs in the world will be of little effect until the demand for labour increases. The Saskatchewan Employment Development Program, also appears to be designed to reduce the number of people directly receiving social assistance rather than an effort to create meaningful and long term jobs.[29]

Under the NDP, job creation was addressed at a provincial level through the implementation of the Employment Support Program (ESP) in 1973. This program was designed as a means of providing employment opportunities for recipients of social assistance. As well as providing funds for job creation through project development (rather than subsidies to the private sector) for SAP recipients, ESP also catered to the special needs of clients for whom such things as age, family responsibilities, physical or mental disabilities, etc., acted as barriers to their attaining or maintaining work. ESP now primarily serves social assistance clients with physical and mental disabilities.

The effectiveness of job creation through employer subsidies has not been proven. American research found that up to eighty percent of the jobs created through such make-work programs resulted from the displacement of permanent positions.[30] There was a real increase in jobs created of only twenty percent of the program total. Even if this problem has somehow been avoided in Saskatchewan (department officials assure us it has, even though they can produce no documentation) one can question the programs' effectiveness getting people long-term productive employment. Social workers have reported confidentially that they have been told to target highly skilled workers for SEDP jobs. Frequently these jobs are well below the worker's competence or previous wage bracket. Even departmental officials will admit, off the record, that the jobs created are of the "paint the trim outside the factory" variety. With no available figures we wonder whether many SEDP "beneficiaries" would not have found more productive work faster had they been left free to look for it, rather than being tied up doing make-work well below their skill level.

The main beneficiaries of SEDP would appear to be those private sector companies which accounted for approximately one-half of the slightly over 2,000 placements in the first year of the program's operation. Furthermore the NGO's were, once again, recipients of the government's support as they employed about one-third of the workers placed. Local governments picked up the rest. All of these employers received a direct wage subsidy equal to the province's minimum wage plus a subsidy for benefits and overhead expenses for each SEDP client they employed.

Make-work painting the fences at a golf club is a long way from the innovation in job creation represented by ESP. Under the SEDP the worker is handed over to the employer whose needs are the first criteria for placement.

> While the rhetoric of job creation offers hope for many people the results appear to be mainly false promises. The strategy of providing incentives to the private sector in the belief that this will lead to the creation of jobs has not only failed but has also created additional hardship for the unemployed through, for example the reduction in benefits to single unemployed people on welfare.[31]

Do the SEDP/SSDP initiatives provide an, albeit initial, indication of privatization? We think so based on the potential inherent in the program design to significantly alter the policy, administration and service delivery in Saskatchewan.

The program policy clearly provides private sector incentives, through a $9.1 million wage and expense subsidy. The administration of the SEDP, the criteria for evaluating its effectiveness and efficiency; the uniformity of employment standards and training and the monitoring of the program with a view to client needs are not at all clear at the time of writing. However, there is a clear shift away from a program designed to meet clients' needs, such as the Employment Support Program, to a program designed to meet employers' needs. This constitutes a significant change in the power relations and accountability structures of a human service program. Various interests are served by this "innovative" program; but whose interest are primary? The government has reduced its long-term responsibility; clients are again employed for a period which may be long enough to qualify for federal Unemployment Insurance; and employers gain access to cheap labour.

The servicing of client needs by professional social workers is minimized in the program. That responsibility is shifted to the employer/employee relationship, especially when government and nongovernment agency staff are experiencing staff and program cutbacks and increasing case-load demands.

Conclusions

Research dealing with political events usually lags behind actual events; however, a survey of the available literature on public policy in Saskatchewan indicates that researchers continue to be much more interested in studying the NDP regime of Allan Blakeney, out of office since 1982, than in subjecting the Devine administration to scrutiny. This is not surprising given the inherent interest offered by studying a social democratic government in action although it has led to a situation where few detailed studies have been done on the current Saskatchewan situation. This means that rather than drawing definitive conclusions about the government, we are still at the stage of identifying themes for research.

With respect to the principle continuity that we have identified — the "anti-state bias" of all Saskatchewan governments in favour of community-based social service delivery, much more work needs to be done. We have presented this concept in the setting of ideological preference but such preferences arise from complex material realities. Often, of course, governments can turn mass ideological preference to their advantage. In this case it would seem that by encouraging NGO's and QUANGO's to deliver social services, the state can hand over responsibility while effectively maintaining control through the funding mechanism. The government can simply say to those who, for example, want more daycare: "take the initiative to establish new centres and we will be there with start-up grants and other subsidies." This keeps these critics somewhat at bay and puts the initiative for this essential service on users. At the same time, the state protects itself from critics who decry daycare as an abandonment of traditional values. The state can reply "we are only providing a minimal service to a small percentage of the parents of preschool children. No way are we undermining the essential role of the family." As Mishra suggests "community control" can become a cover for inaction. Much more research needs to be done and conclusions drawn about politicians' practice in this respect.

Data is required to examine the argument on whether private or community sector can deliver a cheaper service. Do nonunionized, invariably low paid employees in the community sector of social service delivery constitute a significant saving to the state? Some observers have argued that despite the low wages in this sector, there is no proof of substantial saving. We are skeptical. Low wages combined with low levels of service delivery add up to a budget cutting device, but clearly more work needs to be done on this. It will be useful to watch the effects of unionizing drives, conducted by public sector unions, among nongovernment workers. These unionizing efforts have provided legal protection and collective strength to previously isolated project workers, with inferior wages, benefits and job security compared to their counterparts in government service. Of interest to a future study would be the effect of community organizing and public awareness campaigns, conducted by coalitions of poor people, women, trade unions, churches and other community groups concerning social services programs.

Finally, we see a need for further work to identify the source for initiatives in social services delivery. Where is it coming from? When it is a private sector initiative, at what point is the state likely to accept responsibility? We noted previously that over the last several years in Saskatchewan (and across the country) women have come together in communities throughout the province to establish Transition Houses for battered women. Community and state support was sometimes forthcoming; however, more frequently these efforts were met with lack of support and indifference. In the past year, the Saskatchewan government through then minister of Justice, Gary Lane, announced its intention to prosecute batterers. However, to date the government has not improved funding or service to victims nor have they initiated rehabilitation or preventive education for perpetrators. Presumably the minister's statements constitute a testing of the waters on this issue. Is the public ready to accept greater state involvement in this "family matter?" What form would such involvement take? This, of course, raises the more general question of whether public opinion should be the principle factor in determining whether an essential service is offered.

On a more general point, we think that greater efforts can be made to put the provision of social service/assistance solidly into a basic human rights perspective, including one that situates this question in the sphere of the international socioeconomic obligations that Canada has undertaken. What constitutes an acceptable level of publicly financed social services is not an absolute. Fluctuations in the economy may affect society's ability to provide such services; however, there is a "bottom line" which is expressed in Article 22 of the Universal Declaration of Human Rights:

> Everyone, as a member of society, has the right to social security and is entitled to realization, through national effort and international cooperation and in accordance with the organization and resources of each state, of the economic, social and cultural rights indispensable for his dignity and the free development of his personality.

Can it be said that social assistance recipients in Saskatchewan are obtaining the "economic, social and cultural rights indispensable for his dignity . . ." in accordance with the resources of the country? We think not.

In the 1960s Canada set out on the new track with a social service network based on universality and comprehensiveness. The shelved federal social security review of Marc Lalonde was based on the premise that the process towards comprehensiveness should be deepened. In Saskatchewan, in the early years of its administration, the NDP responded to these progressive trends coming from Ottawa, although like the federal government, it largely withdrew from innovative programming by the mid-1970s.

Despite the popular belief that Canadians enjoy a cradle to grave welfare system, the reality is that in the 1980s Canada is farther from the goal articulated in the Universal Declaration than it was in the late 1960s. In saying this we are mindful of the economic difficulties facing Canada since the early 1970s. The question is less the amount of money spent than it is one of how creatively and with what priorities the available money is spent.

Future research will determine the effectiveness of Saskatchewan's "privatization" of job creation ventures for social assistance clients. How will the $9.1 million employer wage subsidy of the Employment Development program compare with the less expensive client interest centred program of the $2.5 million Employment Support Program? Will ideological preference triumph over a commitment to social service objectives?

Generally, we have favourably reviewed the NDP historical initiatives. In comparison with the Tory record, they do deserve favourable comment. However, once the NDP administration realized in the mid 1970s that the federal government had deserted the effort to develop comprehensive social programs, they too beat a hasty retreat and let their provincial programs languish. The fact that Saskatchewan remained number one in national social assistance provisions is less a favourable comment on the NDP than it is a devastating comment on the other provincial governments in this country.

It is difficult to know how much comfort to take in the observation that nowhere in Canada, with the important exception of British Columbia, have Reagan style neoconservative politics, been evident. Certainly such an ideology, if fully unleashed in Saskatchewan, could do tremendous damage.

The future in this respect is uncertain. In the 1930s, the influence of Keynes overcame the bankrupt monetarist theories that had failed to avert the Depression but which had been the prevailing orthodoxy in intellectually respectable and official circles. Those same theories are once again in vogue and Keynesianism has fallen into disrepute even, it would seem, in the NDP, once the most consistent carrier of modern reform liberalism.

The Saskatchewan NDP was, in 1986, attacking the provincial Tory government for its large deficits. Policy reversals frequently occur when a party moves from the opposition to the government side of the legislature. Nevertheless, such attacks legitimize the notion of balanced budgets and suggest that the NDP as government would strive to reduce the provincial deficit. Saskatchewan's current deficit results, in part, from the government's unwillingness to cut spending in the face of reduced revenues from lower uranium, potash, oil and agricultural prices. Any social-democratic government that is prepared to legitimize the mining of uranium by the great multinational energy corporations, as the NDP did during the Blakeney Administration, is equally capable of justifying spending cuts as a precondition to getting the province on its feet.

This temptation towards financial conservatism by any political party is tempered by the fact that the Canadian public is apparently not as tolerant of its Conservatives as the Americans appear to be of theirs. Prime Minister Mulroney was taught a lesson by the senior citizens of Canada when he attacked pension indexing. The people of Alberta certainly sent a signal to their government by electing seventeen NDP MLAs for the first time in the province's history in 1986. As Premier Grant Devine began his second term in office he was faced with a much stronger opposition and the electoral defeat of key cabinet ministers, including former social services minister, Gordon Dirks.

Changes of government, even from Tory to NDP, will not guarantee substantial improvements in social services as the latter years of the Blakeney government indicates. Social change will only come about as a result of a vigorous public alliance of trade unionists, women and native organizations, poor people's organizations and progressive social workers and other professionals who articulate and give political clout to a progressive, alternative vision of economic, social and cultural well-being.

Notes

1. Graham Riches and George Maslany, "Social Welfare and the New Democrats: Personal Social Service Spending in Saskatchewan 1971-81," *Canadian Social Work Review* (1983), p. 42.
2. It is noteworthy that, under pressure from its right wing, the Devine Government authorized public hearings into day care in 1984 under the chairmanship of MLA Joanne Zazelenchuk. Zazelenchuk recommended that profit day care be allowed in Saskatchewan but the government has made no moves to implement this recommendation.
3. Social Planning Council of Metropolitan Toronto, *Social Infopac* (March 1986), p. 4.
4. See the Budget Addresses by the minister of Finance, 1984 and 1985.
5. Little hard data is available on the Saskatchewan Employment Development Program as no publicly available evaluation has been done and civil servants associated with it refuse to be interviewed. Under such circumstances one must largely rely on hearsay evidence and off-the-record comments.
6. Christiane Buci-Glucksmann and Goran Therborn, *Le Defi social-democrate* (Paris: Maspero, 1981).
7. Graham Riches, "Who Cares? Politics and the Elderly in Saskatchewan," *Canadian Welfare* 52 no. 3 (1976), p. 5.
8. Ibid., p. 7.
9. Riches and Maslany, "Social Welfare and the New Democrats," p. 38.
10. Ibid., pp. 28-40.
11. Ibid., p. 44.
12. Table 4-1 is not as precise as one would like because of these difficulties but it serves as a useful guideline. Social Service Organizations, Community Services and Services to the Handicapped all represent financing of various NGO's delivering a range of personal social services. Social Service Organizations, which have recently been transferred to other budget headings, represented a general category covering a wide range of services, while Community Services are directed mainly to the aged. Services to the Handicapped refers to the physically disabled. As can be seen, all three of these categories enjoyed a rapid increase in the level of funding both under the NDP and the Conservatives.

   The Employment Support Program, the cooperative oriented, community-based job creation program mentioned above, continues to receive support but a listing of the major recipients of these funds indicate that it is now primarily directed towards "special needs" clients such as the physical and mentally handicapped.

   Expenditures on the Saskatchewan Employment Development Program, a make-work project that provides subsidies to employers to hire social assistance recipients, are referred to. While no public figures are available, departmental figures that the authors have seen show that one-half of the employers who have received subsidies are in the private sector and the majority of the remainder are NGO's. It is therefore not without significance that the second largest expenditure in Table 4-1 is the first year expenditure on a project that amounts to a direct subsidy to employers. The level of support for SEDP should also be compared with that given to the long-standing Employment Support Program.

Home Care refers to care for the house-bound, including (and one might assume, primarily) the aged. This is now administered by the Department of Health, a more politically palatable department in the minds of both the government and the elderly. Furthermore, housing this program in the Department of Health has had the effect of reducing the Department of Social Service budget by $17.03 million, all the while providing a major social service to an electorally important social group. The Home Care Program, though fully financed by the Department of Health, is solely administered through the nongovernmental Home Care Boards established in each city and region of the province.

13. Riches and Maslany, "Social Welfare and the New Democrats," p. 47.
14. Ibid., pp. 47-48.
15. Ramesh Mishra, "Public Policy and Social Welfare: The Ideology and Practice of Restraint in Ontario," presented at the Second Conference on Provincial Social Welfare Policy, Calgary (May 1985), p. 1. This paper also appears in Jacqueline Ismael, ed., *The Canadian Welfare State* (Edmonton: University of Alberta Press, 1987), pp. 327-46.
16. Bonnie Jeffery and Andy Shadrack, "Living Without Power," Social Administration Research Unit, University of Regina, Regina (1985), p. 3.
17. Saskatchewan Government Employees' Union, "Social Services: Are We All Being Short Sighted," Regina (1984), p. 4.
18. Graham Riches, "Speaker's Notes: Presentation to the Peoples' Budget Coalition," Regina (1984).
19. Ibid.
20. Saskatchewan Department of Social Services, "Monthly Statistical Bulletin" (March 1985).
21. Social Planning Council of Metropolitan Toronto, *Social Infopac*, p. 7.
22. Ibid., p. 4.
23. Jeffery and Shadrack, "Living Without Power," p. 6.
24. Handwritten notes from a press conference, March 28, 1984.
25. Social Planning Council of Metropolitan Toronto, *Social Infopac*, p. 8.
26. Jeffery and Shadrack, "Living Without Power," p. 8.
27. Mishra, "Public Policy and Social Welfare."
28. Graham Riches, "Food Banks and the Public Safety Net," *The Dome*, Regina (March 1986), p. 9.
29. Interviews with social workers.
30. R. Haveman, "Towards Efficiency and Equity Through Direct Job Creation," *Social Policy* 11, no. 1 (1981), p. 46.
31. Jeffery and Shadrack, "Living Without Power," pp. 40-41.

5 Manitoba

DENIS C. BRACKEN
PETER HUDSON

Introduction

The use of the term "privatization" as a rhetorical device to suggest a devolution of state responsibility for social services, the shrinking of the welfare state, and/or a method of reducing state expenditures during the ongoing "fiscal crisis," has tended to limit the examination of the relationship between the state and private social services as part of the welfare state. Generally, this relationship is considered within the context of attacks on the welfare state resulting in disentitlement, reductions in services, less universality and a range of other negative occurrences.

Manitoba has to a great extent been spared both this rhetoric and, more to the point, the largely negative policy developments which have accompanied such rhetoric in other provinces. This is not to imply that the province of Manitoba has been spared the adverse effects of the fiscal crisis of the West precipitated by the oil "crisis" of 1973 and apparent exhaustion of Keynesianism. Nor is it to suggest that there exists in Manitoba a firmly entrenched state-monopoly on social welfare provision. Rather it would appear that Manitoba is something of a unique case in the push for privatization that other Canadian jurisdictions have experienced during the 1980s. For example, there exists a relatively strong private, nonprofit voluntary (henceforth called simply "nonprofit") sector which has continued and in some cases even been strengthened in the past decade. Privatization, meaning the involvement of a private sector in service provision, has long been a fact of life for the welfare state in Manitoba. But privatization as a rhetorical term to describe attacks on the welfare state has not been, to date, a part of policy discussions.

The aim of this chapter will be to consider the issue of the privatization of social welfare services as it relates to the Manitoba context. In particular, it will demonstrate that, despite significant problems with the delivery of social services over approximately the past ten years, Manitoba has not experienced any significant reductions of social services provision to a "private" sector, particularly in the more pejorative sense of the term "privatization." First, there will be a consideration of the political and social service context of Manitoba with particular emphasis of the last ten years; secondly, there will be an examination of three specific service delivery areas which best highlight the state/nonprofit mix of Manitoba social welfare delivery; lastly there will be an attempt to provide some more general discussion on privatization and the welfare state in Manitoba.

For fourteen of the past eighteen years, the New Democratic Party (NDP) has formed the government in the province. This includes the past six years and, given the election of March 1986, indicates probably at least another three. In the period from 1977 to 1981, the Progressive Conservative party led by Sterling Lyon did form a government, but they were soundly defeated in the 1981 election. It would not be entirely accurate to suggest that the decision of the electorate in November 1981 was a wholesale embrace of social democracy. As one commentator has suggested: "The 1981 election was not so much a smashing popular triumph for the party (NDP) as it was a rejection of the Conservative government . . . [whose] promise of economic prosperity based on less government involvement in the economy did not bear fruit."[5] In terms of social welfare provision, there was a decrease or slowed level of growth in financial commitment during the years of the Lyon government. However, during a period of significant economic uncertainty (the 1981-1982 recession), the voters of Manitoba elected a political party with an obvious ideological commitment to the provision of social welfare. At a time when the most concerted attacks on the welfare state were being articulated by relatively powerful figures on the Right (e.g. Reagan and Thatcher), Manitobans elected (and subsequently re-elected) a government which would be opposed to a reduction in the welfare state.

Manitoba, however, has not been immune from the restraints imposed by high interest rates, reductions in federal funding, and an overall shortage of income experienced by governments across Canada. The record of the Schreyer NDP governments in Manitoba (1969-1977) might have led one to assume that a significant expansion of social service provision would have occurred following the 1981 election. And indeed, there have been some developments of a significant nature. However, one might be closer to the mark if one were to describe the role of government since 1981 as more in line with Mishra's concept of "maintaining." In this way, a "commitment to the principle of social protection based on universality and comprehensiveness" [2] combined with a desire to keep employment levels high through government action has resulted in no general loss of entitlements, services, or reduction in expenditures in social welfare. Some services, including those examined in this chapter, have in fact been expanded.

The question remains as to how this maintenance function was accomplished. A few political and economic initiatives have been attempted in response to the decline in government revenues. Manitoba has consistently argued for a number of years that declines in the growth of federal funding through the Established Programs Funding (EPF) formula and the 1982 changes in the equalization formulas have had a significant impact on the provision of health, education and social services. Federal transfers to Manitoba (in the form of shared cost programs, equalization and EPF) have gone from approximately 43% of total provincial revenues in 1980 to a projected 35% in 1985-86. Equalization payments alone have dropped from 18.3% of total provincial revenue in 1981-82, to a projected 15.1% in 1986-87. These changes in equalization have been interpreted by some as hitting Manitoba the hardest of any province.[3] Costs have not declined. Thus there have been consistent complaints from the provincial government that the inability to expand social services is a direct result of cutbacks by the federal government. (More accurately, perhaps, it has been a failure of federal grants to keep up with rising costs for these services.) The response of the federal government to these complaints to date has been a series of transitional supplementary payments related to equalization, designed to reduce the shock of reduction in federal funding.

A second approach has been to broaden the tax base within the province to make up for lost revenues from the federal treasury, and to push for federal tax reform. While actual tax reform at the federal level has not yet occurred, the province has moved to increase revenue through a series of tax changes, increases, and additions. The one most directly tied to the issue of social expenditures has been the Health and Education levy, which is in effect a payroll tax. Introduced in 1982 and increased in 1987, it places a percentage tax on business based on the size of their payroll, with payrolls under $100,000 exempt. As the federal government is a large employer in the province, it could be seen as a way of regaining some of the lost federal revenue.

Political events may also have played a part. The public decision by Henry Morgantaler to open a free-standing abortion clinic in Winnipeg in 1982 resulted in significant controversy in the province and no clear division of opinion along political lines. The French language controversy in Manitoba during 1984 virtually paralyzed the province, and with the exception of some Day Care legislation, virtually nothing of any legislative significance to specific social welfare programming occurred during this time period. The government avoided major controversial issues from then on, as the time approached for a general election. It should be pointed out however that a number of important developments which were begun prior to the language controversy, for example, restructuring child welfare delivery, were continued. As well, studies and recommendations have been received for major changes in certain social welfare areas. For instance, the report of the Manitoba Task Force on Social Assistance, which was submitted in August 1983 recommended that the province abandon the two-tier system of social assistance provision (municipal and provincial) and join with most other provinces in a one-tier, provincially operated system. The possibilities for the implementation of this recommendation have only recently been discussed. Although there are perhaps a number of reasons for this delay, the likelihood of increased cost to the province appears to be a significant one.

At the risk of oversimplification, one might be able to draw some conclusions as to the political and economic factors existent in the province, which resulted in the rejection of privatization and the development of a strategy to maintain existing services without significant cutbacks.

Manitoba has had a government for fourteen of the past eighteen years which purports to be ideologically supportive of expansion of social welfare services. In addition, in 1981 it received a clear message and mandate from the electorate that any significant government restraint in social welfare services (or in any other area, for that matter) would be unpopular.

But the government since 1981 has had energies diverted by two highly controversial issues, and has faced increasing limitations to its revenue base. These two opposing forces may explain why Manitoba has not clearly gone in the direction of great expansion in social services, or massive cutbacks in both expenditure and services. Rather, the focus has tended to be on protection of entitlements, limited expansion in certain areas and job creation, as these have been implied in the notion of "maintenance."

Despite this, the Manitoba experience can add to emerging theoretical discussions on the subject of privatization, particularly around the role of the private *nonprofit* sector in the provision of social welfare services.

A brief discussion of some demographic characteristics, particularly as they have changed in the past decade, might provide helpful information concerning the context within which Manitoba social services have developed to the present time.

Manitoba's population was approximately 1,082,500 as of February 1987 and has shown a steady increase since 1980, following a four year period of uneven decline. In the decade since 1977, the population has increased by 5.4%. An approximately 30% rural and 70% urban split has remained more or less constant in the past ten years. The age distribution of the population has shown some changes since 1977. The 0 to 17 age group has declined from 32% to 27% of the population, with the 18 to 64 group growing from 10% to 12%.

Of particular interest perhaps to a discussion on social services concerns the unemployment rate and changes in the labour market as it relates to women. Manitoba has consistently had a lower unemployment rate than the national average, as Table 5-1 indicates.

The various attempts to keep the economy moving in the direction of greater employment appear to have had at least some benefit, particularly when compared to the national unemployment figures for the same years.

Perhaps of even greater significance, however, is the change in the participation of women in the labour force in the ten years between 1975 and 1985. During that period, the number of women in the labour force increased by 43%, while the percentage increase of men in the labour force was only 7%. The strongest rate of growth for women was in the 25 to 44 age group. Clearly, women are not leaving the labour force in any permanent way during their childbearing years. There would therefore be some impact in the availability of women for more traditional child-rearing roles, and a concomitant increase in the demand for day care.

Some background on the history of the nonprofit sector in social services in the province provides additional information necessary for an understanding of the contemporary Manitoba situation. Since the last years of the previous century, social services in Manitoba (and especially in Winnipeg) have been characterized by nonprofit agencies providing statutory services as well as other services. As in other parts of Canada, religious institutions were the first established to provide for the needs of the European settlers and their descendants.[4] A Roman Catholic home for dependent children and the aged was founded in St. Boniface by the Sisters of

Table 5-1   Unemployment Rate %

Year	Manitoba	Canada
1978	6.5	8.3
1980	5.5	7.5
1982	8.5	11.0
1984	8.3	11.3
1986	7.7	9.6

Charity in 1884, and in 1885, the Christian Women's Union (a largely Protestant but nondenominational organization) established the Children's Home of Winnipeg. In 1898 the Children's Aid Society (CAS) of Winnipeg was established, having been modeled on the CAS of Toronto, as a private, urban and largely Protestant organization with prominent civic leaders forming its board. A large private sector, in some instances based not on religion, but on ethnic background (e.g. the Ukranian Mutual Benefit Association) or political belief (e.g. J.S. Woodworth's "All People's Mission" in the North End of Winnipeg) persisted into the post-war period. In one form or another, many of these in fact still exist.

Very little hard data is available to document in a comprehensive way the historic and current mix in the social welfare system between direct state delivery and that which is contracted or left to the private not-for-profit and the private for-profit agencies in terms of dollar allocations or number of clients. Data specific to the three major services examined in this paper, where it is available, is offered in the relevant section.

Neither can the authors document in a comprehensive way the impact or influence of the private, especially the not-for-profit sector, of special interest to this paper. Apart from the Social Planning Council, which is a membership organization of most of the nonprofit agencies in greater Winnipeg, and which acts occasionally in a research and advocacy role on general and particular social welfare issues, there is no organizational framework within which the private sector, be it not-for-profit or for-profit, acts in concert as a community of interest. Rather the private sector is organized within service areas and attempts to influence the public and government around matters particular to that service sphere. Some illustrations are provided later in this paper in discussing some of the implications (e.g. maintenance of advocacy services) of a strong private not-for-profit sector. One particularly interesting example from a service area not reviewed in this paper, is the work of the Society for Manitobans with Disabilities

(SMD). This is a large private nonprofit agency providing an array of rehabilitative, employment, group and individual counselling services to the handicapped (mostly the physically handicapped). In addition, it has made strong and sustained efforts to advocate on behalf of the general needs of the handicapped, particularly in terms of mainstreaming and access to those services available to the general community. It has been very successful in this effort—much more so than the previous nonprofit which the SMD took over and which had operated out of a charity philosophy, and much more so than any level of government. While not easily quantifiable, there has been an obvious and direct connection between the highly visible efforts of the SMD and substantial improvements in access, transportation, employment and, above all, a public image of the handicapped, transformed from that of recipient of charity, to that of provider of services and generally contributing members of the community.

Notwithstanding the absence of comprehensive, quantitative data to document the changing mix of delivery systems between public and private, it can be asserted that nonprofit sector participation has not only remained, but has grown in significance in Manitoba. This appears to be the case despite the great increases in state involvement during the expansion of the welfare state in the post-war era, and the more recent restraining of this expansion with, in some jurisdictions, a reversion to an increasing degree of reliance on the for-profit sector for social welfare provision. In addition, in some service areas, growth in the for-profit sector has been actively discouraged.

Child Welfare Services

The delivery system for child welfare services is our first illustration of the themes of this chapter. In terms of the traditional mix of direct state delivery and contracting out to the private, nonprofit sector, by 1980 the Children's Aid Society of Winnipeg alone accounted for more than 50% of the provincial appropriations for Child Welfare.[5] By the same date, there were in addition three other Children's Aid Societies serving the whole of the rural south, and a Jewish Child and Family Agency, with legal authority, located in Winnipeg. The northern areas were serviced directly by the responsible provincial department (currently named Community Services and Corrections—CSC), through six regional offices.

At the same time that the worst effects of the combination of recession and changing federal cost sharing arrangements were being felt or anticipated in the early 1980s, there were a series of crises in the system. The large Children's Aid Society of Winnipeg became the centre of controversy for its insensitivity to Native families, for its overly centralized organization, its almost exclusive focus on the protective function, its heavy reliance on institutional care, poor labour-management relations and alleged mismanagement of trust funds. In the rural areas Native organizations were demanding control over the delivery system, and the disastrous outcomes of several international adoptions of Native children were highly publicized.

The stage was set for change or reform which would be initiated by the province. There were two possible ways for the province to go at the time. It could have reasserted its need to control directly the service delivery system, in the name of restoring accountability. Legislative powers and administrative systems, including in the City of Winnipeg, were already in place to accomplish this. The opposite direction would be to devolve further the responsibility for the delivery to the private sector either for-profit or not-for-profit.

In fact the province chose the latter route of contracting out to the private sector, but more importantly, in terms of the focus of this chapter, specifically to the *nonprofit* sector. In the City of Winnipeg, the end point of an elaborate two year planning process saw the replacement of the CAS of Winnipeg with five regional agencies. A sixth assumed responsibility for an area of the city previously served directly by the province. The Jewish agency remained intact and in addition a Native agency, Mama-wi-chi-itita, was created and funded entirely by the province to provide a wide array of nonstatutory services on behalf of the Native population in Winnipeg. In short, provincial policy consciously established a delivery system for the City of Winnipeg which *extended* the tradition of delivery through the nonprofit community agency. It chose neither to assume direct control, nor to seek to contract out portions of the system to the private, for-profit sector.

Similar changes occurred in response to concerns expressed by Indian organizations regarding the quality of child and family services provided to members of the 55 bands in Manitoba. Between 1981 and 1983, a series of tripartite agreements were struck by which services delivered by the three southern rural CAS's and those delivered directly by the province in the north, passed to six newly established Indian agencies for all on-reserve families and children.[6] Here again the province might be said to be further contracting out services to the nonprofit private sector.

In attempting to quantify this trend, three base years were selected: 1976, 1980, and 1986. The resulting Table 5-2 illustrates the growth in the proportions of departmental allocations to the nonprofit agencies for Child and Family Services.

Table 5-2

Year	Total Allocations Child and Family Services	Operating Grants to Nonprofits (External Agencies)	% Allocations to Nonprofits
1976	18,494,145	3,486,376	18.8%
1980	25,899,247	5,621,212	21.7%
1986	48,275,750	18,518,368	38.4%

SOURCE: Public Accounts of Manitoba. Department of Health and Community Services, 1976 and 1980; and Department of Community Services and Corrections, 1986.

One of the obvious ways in which the proprietary or for-profit sector can play a role in the Child Welfare system is in the area of group home and institutional care. With regard to Group Homes, the for-profit sector's share of the market has remained fairly static, increasing only from 18.5% in 1982 to 19.9% in 1986. In institutional care, two of the major treatment centres have always been in the private nonprofit sector, funded on a per diem basis. Two others are operated directly by the province. One is primarily short-term custodial, while the other, a treatment centre opened in 1984, was established to avoid costly out of province placements, rather than as part of an anti-privatization ideology. In Group Home and institutional care, there have been no vigorous initiatives to discourage the for-profit sector, but assuming a basic level of adequacy provided by the nonprofit sector (Group Homes) and the mixed nonprofit and state provision (institutional care), there remains little incentive for the proprietary sector to increase its presence.

All of the above still begs the question of whether or not the province could have used or wished to use changes in the system as excuses or vehicles for fiscal restraint in Child Welfare Services. While contracting out to the private for-profit sector did not occur, the province could nevertheless have claimed cost efficiencies, budgetary restraint on the part of the provincial government and/or the agencies, instructed agencies to rely more heavily on unpaid volunteers in the guise of community involvement, initiated user fees for selected services and so forth. In fact none of this occurred. In the case of the northern and rural areas where some federal funds previously paid to the province were diverted to the Indian agencies, no diminishment of staff, or budgets of CAS's or regional offices occurred which can be directly attributed to the transfer. Within the City of Winnipeg, thirty-three new positions were created within the new community agencies. Between the fiscal years ending March 1985 and March 1986, there was a 10% growth on the departmental budget. Of the $15 million in increased expenditures, $6 million, or 40%, was for child and family services.[7] Over a longer period, between the years 1976/77 to 1986/87, Child and Family Service expenditures rose from $21.2 million to $52.7 million—an increase of 148%. The authors used the Consumer Price Index for Manitoba in order to place these figures in constant dollars. Needless to say, these adjusted figures are much less dramatic, but still show an increase from $32.6 million in 1977 to $39.8 million in 1987 (22%). This was true over a period when the child-in-care population actually declined. As of December 31, 1976, there were 4,025 children in care in the Province of Manitoba, compared to 3,656 at the same time in 1986.

With regard to user fees, one of the obvious places to implement is in adoption services. Here new legislation expressly prohibits the receipt of fees for such services and provides heavy fines for violators. While this legislation was designed specifically to prevent intrusions by the for-profit agency into adoption services, it also effectively inhibits the possibility of user fees being implemented by the present delivery system.[8] Going even further, the same legislation provided for a limited subsidy to adoptive parents in cases involving a special needs child.

All this is not to say that the provincial government was unconcerned about expenditures. From the outset of planning for decentralization in Winnipeg, the minister had consistently and publicly stated that no new monies would or could be allocated to the system. It was asserted that this was to be a new and improved system, but not a more expensive one. It appeared as though the province only allocated more funds to the system when it was clear that it could not function without them. Considerable controversy had surrounded these major changes and the provincial government had placed a portion of its political fortunes in their success. It could not afford to allow the new agencies to founder for lack of adequate financial support.

In short, recent changes in the Child Welfare delivery system gives evidence of a form of privatization not often considered in many theories on that subject: namely, heavy and sometimes growing reliance on the *non-profit* private sector. Moreover, it is not inevitably accompanied by financial cutbacks or renunciations of state responsibility.

Homemaker and Home Care Services

Services provided to people not in need of acute or constant personal care, such as the elderly or those recovering from illness or hospitalization have traditionally been provided by family or private medical services. However, little emphasis was placed on such "community care," until the mid-1970s, when concern over rising costs for institutionalization resulted in consideration of less or even de-institutionalization as a lower cost alternative.[9] As well, the concept of remaining in the community gathered support particularly in the case of the elderly. In Manitoba, the Home Care program was started in 1974 by government as a way of providing support for community living for people where institutionalization was the less attractive alternative. There was no substantial "private sector" with which government had to compete, due to the high cost of private home care which existed on a very limited basis at the time.

Homemaker and Home Care services are provided by a combination of government, voluntary, and for-profit agencies, with the government by far the largest employer and funder. Funding for the services is divided between the Department of Health and the Department of Community Services and Corrections. These services present an example of the mix of public, voluntary and to lesser extent, for-profit sectors all involved in service provision. While not strictly kept out by policy or regulation, the for-profit sector clearly has limited involvement. This is done by keeping the direct costs to the consumer at a minimum for government and voluntary sector services while providing a reasonably high level of service. The for-profit sector to compete must therefore put their level of service even higher, with high direct costs to the consumer as the result.

Home care services are provided by the Department of Health through the Office of Continuing Care. The program is designed to "provide an alternative to institutional care by assisting individuals who require support services in order to remain at home."[10] A majority of those receiving care are the elderly, although it also includes some measure of support for the physically handicapped.

Services offered through the Office of Continuing Care include a variety of home care services such as health supervision and education, and social service counselling. The staff is made up of nurses, social workers, homemakers, and orderlies. Other services include nursing services, certain auxiliary health services through LPNs, aids and orderlies, therapy from occupational and physiotherapists, and what is described as "home help" which includes performance of household duties and/or personal care.

Eligibility for the services offered by the Office of Continuing Care is based on an assessment of health-related need, and income is not a consideration, nor are fees charged to the individual. When home care services for the elderly and infirm were established in 1974, it was government that accepted responsibility for funding and administering the program. This has not changed. Some nursing services are in fact contracted out on an overload basis to certain private, for-profit health care corporations when the need arises. However, this does not have an impact on the direct cost borne by the consumer (which remains at zero).

The Home Care program has shown a pattern of growth similar to Child and Family Services. In the decade 1976 to 1986, the numbers of persons receiving services rose steadily from a monthly average of 3,290 in 1976 to 9,945 in 1986—an increase in excess of 200%. In the same decade, actual expenditures rose from $4.7 million in 1976 to $24.5 million in 1986. Even adjusting for inflation, the constant dollar increase was 151%, by far the sharpest increase being from 1980/81 to 1985/86 (95%).

During this period of growth, the provincial Department of Health established a Home Care Orderly Service in 1984 "to meet the needs of the physically disabled and other Home Care clients" who required assistance with personal care. Of special interest in the context of this paper is that previously this service had been contracted out to the private, for-profit sector. However, government thought that it could be provided in a more cost-effective manner through a publicly operated service.

Homemaker services are provided within the Home Care program as one of a possible range of services provided to clients. There is also a very much smaller service specifically called "Homemaker Services" provided to assist families for social reasons as opposed to health reasons. These services are provided by the voluntary sector, specifically child and family service agencies as well as other voluntary agencies working with families (e.g. the Family Service Association). This may be done under the authority of the Child and Family Services Act when, in the opinion of a child and family service agency, a need exists on the part of a family for assistance in homemaking and/or child care. Such services are subsidized by the provincial government through the Department of Community Services. The Child and Family Services Act does provide for the charging of means-tested fees to families for homemaker services, although this provision does not appear to be uniformly applied. The agencies providing this type of homemaker service have exercised considerable discretion, based on consideration of the family situation, in determining whether or not the fees scheduled should be applied.

The for-profit homemaker and home care services are used by the aged, infirm or by families on a direct cost basis to the consumer. While their range of services is wider than the publicly provided ones, the costs make them prohibitive for the average person in need. Thus, their impact on social services delivery is negligible.

Manitoba's experience with Home Care Services has thus been somewhat different than with Child Welfare Services. In the latter case the state has discharged its responsibilities in large measure through contracting out to the private nonprofit sector. In the former case, the state has developed and maintained a universal service, primarily without user fees, under direct state control. While there is a small role to play for the nonprofit sector, the role of the proprietary, for-profit sector is miniscule.

Day Care Services

In recent history, the mix of delivery of day care services in Manitoba has involved exclusively the private sector. The role of the public sector has been to subsidize in order to limit user fees (and therefore maximize accessibility—a very important objective), set standards, licence and inspect. Until the 1970s, the for-profit sector was limited mainly to individuals caring for children of others in their own home, unlicenced and regulated only by consumer satisfaction. During the 1970s, the corporate sector began to establish licenced centres especially for the full time preschool age child, concentrated exclusively in the larger urban centres (primarily Winnipeg). Even so, in that portion of the day care delivery system which is subject to provincial legislation and regulation (i.e. licenced), the private nonprofit agencies have dominated.

Perhaps the most direct government position with respect to the involvement of a for-profit sector of social services is in the day care sector. Recent legislation in the form of a Day Care Standards Act and Regulations indicates that in this area at least, the for-profit sector is actively discouraged while a not-for-profit sector is clearly enhanced.[11]

The Day Care Standards Act and Regulations provide for three sorts of provision for public funding of Day Care Centres. A start-up grant is provided for new centres based on the estimated number of spaces to be created. In 1985, this was set at between $238 and $292 (depending on the age range of the children) per space. Secondly, an operating or maintenance grant is provided based in the number of children registered in and in attendance at the centre. For preschool centres, for example, this sum was set at $940 per child per year for 1985. Finally, a subsidy is provided on application from the parent(s), but paid directly to the centre on behalf of the family. This subsidy is a net income tested payment, the ceilings for which vary with family size. For example, in 1985, two parents with two children in day care would receive a full subsidy of $11.25 per day if the net family income was approximately $16,000 or less. The same family would receive no subsidy if its net income is in excess of $30,000.

Several provisions of the Day Care Standards Act and Regulations actively and deliberately promote the development of a nonprofit delivery system over the for-profit delivery system. First, none of the above funding provisions are available to the for-profit sector. The sole exception is a grandfather clause involving some 200 for-profit spaces which permits the subsidy to be paid on behalf of families, but *not* start-up grants or operating grants. Even this limited subsidy to the for-profit sector has a double edge in that these spaces are subject to statutory limits placed on the daily fee permitted to be charged for each child. No centres receiving any kind of assistance on behalf of a child can charge more than one dollar per day over the maximum fee subsidy. (In 1986 this was $11.25, meaning that the fee cannot be more than $12.25 in such cases.)

Second, the licencing provisions of the Day Care Standards Act and Regulations are quite stringent. Apart from the usual physical standards, a 1:8 ratio of staff to children is required at all times through the day. All centre directors are required to be qualified graduates from an approved community college program or its equivalent by 1988. In addition, a proportion (two-thirds in the case of preschool care) of child care staff will be required to possess this training by the same date. Certain types of equipment, space and levels of play activity are also required. Finally, a maximum of 70 spaces only is permitted for any one centre.

Except for what is termed private home day care, always less than four children, all day care centres and family day care homes (4-8 children) are *required* to seek a licence. Thus the for-profit centres cannot (or will not be able to after 1988) be assured that profit margins are obtainable by way of less qualified and lower paid staff, or any other kind of diminishment of standards. The for-profit sector can charge whatever the market will bear, but presumedly there are some limits to this. While a subsidised nonprofit has statutory ceilings placed on its maximum daily fee, this is compensated by the three sorts of subsidies available to it, which are not available to the for-profit centres.

It is clear that these policies embodied in law and regulation are designed to firstly maintain the private sector as the sole delivery agent for day care services, but more specifically to enhance the role of the nonprofit sector. Whether or not the current mix of nonprofit and for-profit delivery of day care services will change as a result of the new Day Care Standards Act and Regulations is too early to say. Unfortunately provincial statistics distinguish between centres which are unfunded and those which are funded. This is not necessarily the same as for-profit and not-for-profit. All for-profit centres are unfunded (except for the "grandfather" spaces previously mentioned), but so are a good number of nonprofits either because they are happily self-sufficient or because they are awaiting the allocation of sufficient funds to the Day Care Program. A data base is in preparation which will distinguish the for-profit and the nonprofit sectors in the near future. In the meantime it can only be said that as of March 1986 an estimated 91% of all licenced day care spaces were provided by the nonprofit sector, most of which were governed by consumer (parent) boards.[12] Staff of the Day Care Directorate believe that this figure represents as increased share of the market by the nonprofit sector, but cannot verify it. They also believe that this share will further increase.

What can be documented, important to one of the themes of this paper, is growth in state provision for the system. Total expenditures on Day Care Services (including salaries of departmental staff as well as grants and subsidies), rose from $1.36 million in 1976 to $20.9 million in 1986. Adjusted for constant dollars, the increase was 635%—by far the service with the strongest rate of growth.[13]

One final comment is pertinent to the theme of this paper. The simultaneous objectives of maximizing access through subsidy programs, continuing growth in spaces, upholding standards and discouraging the for-profit sector, is limited by the ability of the state to make the necessary funds available. In this regard there are some indications that despite the enormous growth in state expenditures the demand for day care services continues to far outstrip the supply of spaces, especially subsidized spaces. For example in December 1984, seventy percent of all day care centre spaces (excluding Family Day Care) were receiving provincial funding. A year later this figure had dropped to 66%. In the same period 355 new funded spaces were created (a 4.4% increase), but nonfunded spaces increased by 22.4% from 3,458 to 4,232.[14] The critical distinction here is not between for-profit and nonprofit, but between funded and unfunded. The growth in unfunded spaces would indicate that many families may be using unsubsidized services which they can ill afford, even if they are offered on a nonprofit basis, simply because provincial funding cannot match the growing need.

In addition, and despite the growth in licenced spaces commensurate with increased state expenditures (from 4,795 in 1976 to 14,775 in 1986), waiting lists appear to persist. In this situation, the current residual role of the for-profit sector could potentially be expanded in ways that only it knows best. This comment specifically refers to day care offered by subsidiaries of some large corporations, such as Crown Life (Playschools) and Great West Life (Mini-Skools). Furthermore there remain a multitude of private home day care arrangements which, if involving less than four children, do not require licencing. No controls or data exist regarding affordability or quality of care in these arrangements, or the extent to which parents are using this type of care as a less satisfactory alternative to licenced day care. Advocates for expanded state provision for day care appearing before the Federal Special Committee on Child Care, claimed that such care was still the single largest type of arrangement. There is no reason to believe that this situation is markedly different in Manitoba.

General Issues

This discussion of these service areas would suggest that the traditional mix of direct state delivery and contracting out to the private nonprofit sector has been maintained in Manitoba. The proprietary sector has not been encouraged, and in one instance has been actively discouraged (although without results to date). The nonprofit sector has assumed a somewhat greater role over the past five years, but this has not been accompanied by disentitlements or overall reductions in expenditures. For example, funding levels for the voluntary agencies provided by Manitoba Community Services (including the new child and family service agencies) have increased by approximately 25% over the past five years (fiscal year 1982-1983 through 1986-1987). The same data suggest that just over 50% of the total departmental budget increase over the same period is accounted for by an increase in funding to the voluntary social service sector. At the same time the *overall* level of state commitment to the three services examined has increased in the past decade, despite the slowed and, in some instances, decreased expenditures during the Lyon administration. In short, the continuation and expansion of a voluntary sector in Manitoba has been accomplished by a somewhat increased commitment to services rather than the reverse.

There are more general issues, other than fiscal, which concern the consequences of the large and increased role assigned to the private nonprofit sector in service delivery: deprofessionalization, diminishment of advocacy services, issues of quality, and lack of accountability.[15] There has been no appreciable trend towards the deprofessionalization of services accompanying recent changes. In child welfare the combination of the shortage of professionally trained Native workers and the desire of the agencies to employ Native workers has resulted in very high percentages of untrained or in-service trained workers staffing these agencies, but most of these positions are new. They do not represent the replacement of professional with nonprofessional staff. The Manitoba Association of Social Workers (MASW) attempted to monitor this question in the period 1984-86 and found no evidence that deprofessionalization was occurring in Winnipeg's newly regionalized system.[16] The Day Care Program has recently embarked on an ambitious program to upgrade the qualifications of staff, and the nonprofit sector was fully supportive of these changes.

Contracting out services to the proprietary sector and assigning of statutory services to the nonprofit sector has been observed as sometimes leading to diminished willingness on the part of the agency to advocate on behalf of the client group and for the service in general.[17] This does not appear to have been the case in contracting out child welfare services to the nonprofit sector. The Indian child welfare agencies in particular, but joined by other agencies, lobbied vigorously and partially successfully for the new legislation to reflect what was perceived to be their interests and needs. The regional agencies within the City of Winnipeg lobbied equally vigorously, publicly, and again partially successfully, for the allocation of new monies for the system, particularly for expanded substitute care facilities, prevention programming and child abuse services. A very effective advocate for day care services has been a province-wide organization formed mainly from a membership of all the nonprofit centres. This Manitoba Day Care Association heavily influenced the new legislation and has been instrumental in keeping day care needs and shortfalls high on the government's agenda.

Issues of quality of services are far too subjective to treat seriously in the limited space available in this paper. The decentralized child welfare system has been under attack. There have been serious concerns about the quality of service provided. There have been a couple of tragic deaths of children in the care of the new Winnipeg agencies and other seemingly ill-advised repatriations carried out by the Indian agencies without proper planning or follow-up. None of the critics, however, are suggesting "nationalization" of the system, or for-profit privatization remedies.

In the day care system, some comparisons have been made between the quality of service in the for-profit systems and the nonprofit systems in which the latter features more favorably. The study, carried out by the Day Care Directorate using a random sample, showed that 47% of the nonprofit directors had recognised qualifications compared to 14% of the for-profit centres. Staff/child ratios were 1:4.7 compared to 1:6. Only 5% of the nonprofits exceeded 70 spaces compared to 23% of the for-profit centres. With regard to a minimum level of program and play activity only 2.4% of the nonprofits, while 18.0% of the for-profits were shown to be below the minimum. Less than 11% of the nonprofits did not conform to minimum standards regarding space and equipment compared to nearly 32% of the for-profit centres.[18]

Finally the province continues to wrestle with mechanisms which would satisfactorily resolve the contradiction which is inherent in contracting out statutory services; namely, that it is legally responsible for services, but risks losing some of the ability to control those same services. Basically, it is an issue of accountability, which becomes particularly acute when the legislative, judicial and executive functions are discharged by three entirely different systems, as in Child and Family Services. Recent changes involving even further devolution of executive functions to the nonprofit agencies has served only to subject the issue to renewed scrutiny.

Some attempt has been made to resolve this issue through amendments to the 1974 Child Welfare Act, their incorporation into the new Child and Family Services Act (1985), along with other new provisions in the latter act. There is now a strengthened statement declaring the Province of Manitoba's authority in giving or withholding an agency charter, or in intervening in any other way it sees fit. These powers have indeed been exercised including the highly controversial dissolution of the former CAS of Winnipeg in 1983 and, more recently, the suspension of a director of one of the newly created agencies by the minister. Section 4 of the new act gives the director of Child Welfare more active responsibility for monitoring the agencies, and to receive and hear complaints from anyone affected by administrative actions of the agency. Section 7 obliges agencies to make permanency plans for children in their care, and the director of Child Welfare is obliged to review the status and treatment of all children in care at least once a year.

Difficulties remain in that while provincial authority is asserted, there is still a lack of specificity in the relationship. Tensions between the provincial authority and the autonomy of the agencies continue to surface periodically. In addition, budgets are struck on the basis of a historical baseline, rather than on service plans and objectives, which would serve as tools for evaluation and accountability. Statistical reporting is required of the agencies but this yields little data on quality of service. A licencing function for group homes and other substitute care is carried by the province, but there is no effective way for the province to monitor quality of foster care.

In Day Care, the Community Child Day Care Standards Act was proclaimed in October, 1983. This legislation classified day care settings by age and numbers of children cared for, and set standards for each type. These standards are specific as to the physical and staffing requirements for each category of centre or home. Most significantly it required minimum educational and training requirements for staff, provided funds for upgrading of existing staff and set out a specific time frame for implementation.

A Day Care Directorate assumes responsibility for the investigatory and licencing function, but also co-ordinated monitoring by other officials such as fire inspectors and public health nurses. A review of activities and programs is an integral part of the licencing process. In no small part because the small nonprofit agencies were involved in, and indeed initiated, these changes, there appears to be strong and effective accountability mechanisms to ensure minimum standards in licenced care services.

A heavy reliance on the private nonprofit sector for the delivery of Child Welfare and Day Care services does not appear to have led to deprofessionalization, weakening of advocacy services or lack of accountability. Advocacy efforts, on the contrary, appear to have been strengthened. Attempts have also been made to strengthen accountability to the government for minimum standards and quality of service. These attempts are so far only partially successful in the case of Child and Family services, but have been successful in the case of Day Care.

Concluding Comments

The preceding discussion should give some indication that Manitoba has not faced the pressures for privatization that have been evident elsewhere. It should also be apparent that the reasons for this are not related simply to ideological commitment (although that clearly is a factor), but involves more complex processes at work, including a specific historical set of circumstances. As well, the fact that Manitoba has not followed the actions of other jurisdictions in reducing expenditures through disentitlements and cutbacks in services does not mean necessarily that the province has continued to develop and maintain social services as if the fiscal crisis never existed.

As mentioned at the beginning of this chapter, it would appear that whether by default or by design or by some combination of both, Manitoba has developed an approach to social welfare in the 1980s akin to the notion of "maintenance." In this case, commitments to full employment and to universality of social welfare programs continue. "State action continues to be viewed as positive and attempts are made to harmonize economic and social objectives . . . ."[19] This maintenance function has relied on the historical combination of government and nonprofit service delivery, to the point of enhancing the nonprofit sector in some areas like child welfare. In other areas, there has been an apparent, conscious de-emphasis on aspects of for-profit service delivery, as in day care.

Government has not moved rapidly in the direction of expanded direct government provision. Despite the opportunity to abandon the voluntary child welfare service model in 1983, the government chose to maintain the voluntary sector in this area. Similarly, a strong voluntary sector is actively supported by government in day care. Clearly there exists in Manitoba the commitment to the voluntary sector (backed by government funding, regulation and in some cases ultimate statutory responsibility) in areas of social service provision.

An issue to be addressed then is the rationale for a voluntary sector in Manitoba. Fiscal savings and, it would seem, deprofessionalization, do not appear to be factors, as neither is occurring. History is no doubt important; the nonprofit sector has been active for all of this century and part of the last. More significantly perhaps is the emphasis currently given to decentralization and community involvement without any concomitant reduction in either commitment to social welfare or provision of services. There does not exist either a strong residual concept of charitable institutions or a free market ideology of the for-profit sector in social services. Rather, there is an apparent belief in the role of the state as a guarantor of equality of access to services and maintenance of standards, while placing less emphasis on the actual provision of the service by the state. Historical precedent and some measure of practicality no doubt help to determine whether service is provided by the state or voluntary sector. While there are dangers to over-romanticizing the powers of the "community" as well as in trying to identify an ideological commitment clearly at work in Manitoba, the voluntary sector continues to be a force in social service delivery.[20]

Two critical points need to be made, however, with respect to the

Manitoba approach to social welfare in the 1980s. One is that the de-emphasis on for-profit services provision is not uniform. For example, there are grants and subsidies available only to nonprofit day care centres. The presumed impact of this will be a decrease in the for-profit sector, as it would be difficult to recover costs and make a profit. Similarly, there is no subsidy to for-profit adult-care homes (formerly known as guest homes and designed mostly for short stays), while there is a per diem subsidy to nonprofit adult-care homes.[21] However, the level of subsidy to nonprofit and for-profit nursing homes (also referred to as personal care homes) on a per person per day basis is the same. It appears that there is no conscious effort being made to phase out for-profit service delivery in all areas, and that there is inconsistency between and within government departments.

Perhaps more importantly, government has not explicitly excluded the for-profit sector. Instead, it has tended to rely on market forces, specifically the profit motive and supply and demand, to keep the for-profit sector at bay. In those areas where the for-profit sector competes with the nonprofit public sectors, government is directly or indirectly (through enhancement of the nonprofit sector) providing as equal or better service at a lower direct cost. But reliance on market forces means being subject to them if they change. For example, speculation on the (at least short term) increase in for-profit day care, despite specific attempts through regulation to make it unprofitable, must include the notion of a demand far exceeding supply, and a willingness on the part of the consumer to pay the potentially higher costs of the for-profit sector.

As well, the existence of a for-profit sector, however small, could have an influence on debates surrounding future developments in social welfare. A change in ideological commitment on the part of government, particularly on the grounds of cost and private sector efficiency, could result in the enhancement of the for-profit sector. Such apparently was the outcome of the Thatcher government in Britain and the relationship between the National Health Service and private health care.[22]

A wider question to be addressed, but perhaps too great to be dealt with properly in this context, concerns the ability of any Canadian province to maintain both sufficient economic activity and a reasonably comprehensive welfare state, within the Canadian federation and the increasingly integrated, U.S. dominated North American economy. It would appear that Manitoba has attempted to do both through its various employment schemes (termed the "Jobs Fund") and the commitment to its social welfare and health care systems. How successful this has been and how long it can continue are unclear. What is clear is that the concept of privatization in the negative sense implied in other Canadian jurisdictions is not an issue nor does it appear to be high on anyone's social policy agenda in Manitoba.

Acknowledgements

The authors wish to acknowledge the kind assistance of Alfred Black, Sid Frankel, Kathy Kristianson and Kathy Reid of the Manitoba Department of Community Services and Corrections, and Sherry Mooney of the Manitoba Department of Health for providing some of the information used in this chapter. All errors and opinions are the responsibility of the authors.

Notes

1. N. Wiseman, *Social Democracy in Manitoba: A History of the CCF-NDP* (Winnipeg: The University of Manitoba Press, 1983), p. 151.
2. R. Mishra, "Public Policy and Social Welfare: The Ideology of Restraint in Ontario," in J.S. Ismael, ed., *The Canadian Welfare State: Evolution and Transition* (Edmonton: The University of Alberta Press, 1987), p. 333.
3. M. Decter, "Taxation—A Review and Recommendation for Reform," Final Report to the Government of Manitoba (Winnipeg: The October Partnership, November 1986).
4. The following brief historical comments of the nineteenth century period are based on a discussion in D. Fuchs, "Child Welfare in Manitoba 1898-1928," unpublished paper, Department of History, University of Manitoba (n.d.).
5. This data is taken from an examination of Child Welfare budgets undertaken by Professor Brad McKenzie, School of Social Work, University of Manitoba, in 1983. It is an unpublished brief used primarily as teaching material.
6. P. Hudson, "Manitoba Indian Child Welfare System: In the Balance," in J.S. Ismael and R. Thomlison, eds., *Perspective on Social Services and Social Issues* (Ottawa: Canadian Council of Social Development, 1986).
7. Manitoba, *The Child Care Challenge for Canadians: A Brief Submitted to the Special Committee on Child Care by the Government of Manitoba* (Winnipeg: Department of Community Services and Corrections, June 1986).
8. This is set out in Section 65 of the Child and Family Services Act, S.M. 1986 Chapter 80.
9. Cf. A. Scull, *Decarceration Community Treatment and the Deviant: A Radical View,* second edition (New Brunswick, N.J.: Rutgers University Press, 1984).
10. Manitoba, Department of Health, *Annual Report, 1985-1986* (Winnipeg: Department of Health, 1986).
11. Manitoba, *The Child Care Challenge for Canadians.*

12. Ibid.
13. Manitoba, *Public accounts for the Province of Manitoba, 1986* (Winnipeg: The Queen's Printer for Manitoba, 1987).
14. Manitoba, Department of Community Services and Corrections, *Annual Report, 1984* (Winnipeg: Department of Community Services and Corrections, 1985); Manitoba, Department of Community Services and Corrections, *Annual Report, 1985-1986* (Winnipeg: Department of Community Services and Corrections, 1986).
15. These issues cover a number of service delivery areas including those discussed in this chapter, except Home Care services as these are delivered almost exclusively by the state.
16. Manitoba Association of Social Workers, *Report of the Committee on Regionalization* (Winnipeg: MASW, 1986).
17. D. Bracken, "The Voluntary Correctional Agency in the Welfare State: The John Howard Society of Canada," paper presented to the annual meeting of the Society for the Study of Social Problems, Washington, D.C., August 1985.
18. Manitoba, *The Child Care Challenge for Canadians*.
19. Mishra, "Public Policy and Social Welfare," p. 333.
20. Beyond the scope of this chapter, yet still important, is the nature of the voluntary sector in Manitoba. The extent of its ability to innovate, to respond more directly to local issues, to provide the same standards of service across the province, its dependence on government funding, etc., are issues yet to be addressed.
21. A. Santin, "Seniors' Home Operators Seek Provincial Funds," *Winnipeg Free Press,* March 2, 1987, p. 3.
22. A.J. Willcocks, "In Defense of the National Health Service," in P. Bean, J. Ferris and D. Whynes, eds., *In Defense of Welfare* (London: Tavistock Publications, 1985).

6 Ontario

RAMESH MISHRA
GLENDA LAWS
PRISCILLA HARDING

Major developments in public policy and the controversy surrounding them are often encapsulated in a single keyword. Privatization seems to have emerged as such a keyword for social policy development in the eighties. But as an authority warns us the very nature of such keywords makes their meaning "uncertain and often tendentious."[1] Since the first chapter of this volume provides a working definition of the concept, this chapter will not be concerned with definitional problems as such.

Although privatization derives its rationale largely from the difficulties of welfare capitalism, especially financial constraints on the government since the mid-seventies, it has several other bases of support which must not be overlooked. One of these lies in the populist and left-wing critique of the social services. Put simply, it is the criticism that the social welfare state has become inordinately large, bureaucratic and centralized, and remote from the people whose needs it is meant to serve. Here the anti-state sentiments of grass-roots activists and others, who favour citizen participation and self-management, come into play. As a result, these progressive objectives of debureaucratization and decentralization of services begin to overlap with neoconservative aims of downsizing government. Novick, for example, outlines the development of community-based or alternative services in Ontario in recent years. He describes them as small-scale responses "to the rigidities of the social service professions and the institutional service sectors."[2] Recently, a report of the Social Planning Council of Metropolitan Toronto identified more than two hundred struggling community-based programs in Toronto without consistent core funding.[3] Subsequently the Ministry of Community and Social Services approved a neighbourhood support grants program to be cost-shared with the United Way and the City of Toronto, legitimizing the role of grassroots community-based operations.[4]

At the national level, the argument for replacing state-delivered services with nonprofit self-managed services has been made very clearly by the Canadian Association of Social Workers in its brief to the Macdonald Commission. The brief states that "our quarrel is not with *what* we have but *how* it is administered. We think that the democratization and decentralization of administrative structures of the Welfare State" will make social programs more popular.[5] It goes on to urge the Commission to "consider voluntary organizations and associations of employers and employees as vehicles for the administration of social benefits. Community-based voluntary associations are a long-established tradition in Canada. They are nonprofit in nature (and)...deliver a broad range of human services. They are capable of doing more."[6] Indeed the idea of empowering the community and allowing groups and communities to define their own needs and manage their own services goes back to the sixties. It is a continuing refrain in the field of social welfare. It is important to acknowledge its relevance for voluntarism and privatization not only because it is based on principles and objectives which differ substantially from the neoconservative version of privatization but also because it provides, unwittingly, a convenient legitimization for government withdrawal from service delivery.

Furthermore, at a pragmatic or empirical level, certain other policies and perspectives in social welfare have tended to merge with privatization. Deinstitutionalization as a service ideology and policy predates the rise of fiscal conservatism in Ontario. Its influence can be seen not only in the fields of mental illness and the handicapped but also in many areas of service provision including corrections. It too has provided a rationale for small-scale and decentralized facilities based in the community. The ideology and objectives of deinstitutionalization have lent a good deal of support to the privatization of service delivery. Government policy statements have seized upon the idea of a shift from the institution to the community as a ready-made justification for privatization. It is important, therefore, to bear in mind that privatization is a multi-faceted phenomenon. Somewhat disparate objectives, concerns and values—associated with the right as well as with other ideological positions and also with certain pragmatic developments—have tended to coalesce in the move towards privatization. In looking at the changes that have taken place in Ontario's social services over the last ten years or so the influence of these various social and ideological currents is apparent but also hard to distinguish. A further problem is that of distinguishing between the rhetoric and ideology of governments and their practice with regard to social welfare. It would be a mistake to infer practice from ideological pronouncements. Taking these points into consideration, this paper will seek to examine the sources, the nature and the scope of privatization in Ontario. It will focus on service delivery but within the context of privatization policies understood in the broader sense.

The Social Services in Ontario: A Historical Overview

It is useful to begin with a brief outline of the development of social welfare in Ontario. Legislation of 1791 created two provinces of Upper and Lower Canada. Upper Canada (Ontario), while retaining the general application of English common law, explicitly rejected the poor law.[7] Assistance to the needy was, in effect, seen largely as a private concern. From the early decades of the nineteenth century, however, the government began to assist philanthropic effort. The Charity Aid Act of 1874 regularized the system of grant-in-aid by providing for grants to private charities, conditional upon their meeting state-imposed regulations.

By the closing decades of the nineteenth century, industrialization and urbanization had progressed a good deal in Ontario and reformers, lay as well as religious, were increasingly concerned over a number of problems. These included child neglect and child welfare. Such voluntary effort led to the successful lobbying of the Ontario legislature to pass the Children's Protection Act of 1893. It initiated what is now a century-old partnership in which publicly-mandated child welfare services are delivered by the Children's Aid Society, a nongovernment organization funded by the government. During the latter half of the nineteenth century, the provincial and municipal governments also began providing some institutional facilities, such as asylums for the insane, institutions for the mentally retarded, schools for the deaf and blind, and homes for the aged. Thus began what has been described as a "dual system of social services in Ontario—one set of institutions operated by local or provincial government authorities, and another by church or secular auspices usually with a subsidy from the public purse."[8] There is little doubt however that at the beginning of this century the initiative still lay with voluntary effort and philanthropy.

Spurred on by the Great Depression, the 1930s saw the beginning of a more substantial government involvement—both federal and provincial—primarily in the area of income support for the needy but also in social welfare more generally. Concern with the largely uncoordinated service system in the province led to the establishment of a Department of Public Welfare, the predecessor of today's Ministry of Community and Social Services. The war years saw greater involvement of both levels of government in the control and regulation of the economic and social conditions of life. It was, however, during the post-war decades, especially in the sixties, that major advances were made in providing for the basic needs of all citizens through public services.

Lang and others have documented the rise of the social service state in Ontario after World War II.[9] Ontario's population grew from nearly 4 million at the end of the war to over 6 million in 1960 and 7.5 million in 1970. These were the years of baby boom as well as substantial immigration, and also of heady economic growth which Canada shared with other Western nations. Ontario's expenditure on health, education and welfare rose from a modest 3.8% of the Gross Provincial Product in 1946 to 13.1% in 1971.[10] In 1966 the Canada Assistance Plan (CAP) provided for a 50% cost sharing with the federal government for a wide range of social programs for the needy. CAP undoubtedly spurred the growth of the social services. In constant dollars, Ontario's expenditure on social services rose from $12.13 per person in 1963-4 to $83.91 in 1981-2, close to a sevenfold rise.[11]

It is important to bear in mind, however, that this spectacular growth in state welfare, far from superseding the nongovernmental organizations in fact helped in their proliferation. The secret of this relationship is that the government funded a variety of voluntary organizations, old and new, and entrusted many of them with the delivery of services. The growth of government did not mean a decline of the nongovernmental sector, indeed quite the opposite. Moreover, this post-war expansion of social welfare activities also helped the development of a commercial sector—profit-making organizations involved in the delivery of social welfare.[12] Such, in brief, is the context of the more deliberate policy of privatization pursued by Ontario from about the mid-seventies.

Ontario: Between Retrenchment and Restraint
(A) THE COMMITTEE ON GOVERNMENT PRODUCTIVITY AND THE SPECIAL PROGRAM REVIEW

Western governments—national and provincial—have responded to the economic crisis of the seventies and beyond in a variety of ways. Elsewhere, Mishra has suggested that their approach to social welfare can be grouped under five different headings: Dismantling, Retrenching, Restraining, Maintaining and Transforming.[13] Ontario's Conservatives seemed to have adopted an approach that falls somewhere between retrenchment and restraint. If they have endorsed the ideology of retrenchment, their practice has been far more pragmatic, leaning towards restraint. Privatization in Ontario, until the fall of the Progressive Conservatives from power in 1985, must be seen in the context of such an ideology of retrenchment.

Long before Reaganomics and Thatcherism came to symbolize a new departure in the social policy of Western countries and long before the Bennett government in British Columbia seemingly decided to move in that direction, the Province of Ontario had embarked on a program of downsizing government which, in retrospect, appears impressive in its candour and pioneering role. The reports of the committee on Government Productivity (COGP) (1969/73) issued in the early seventies mark the beginning of the process. The reports warned that in opposition to the trend of the 1960s, the 1970s would see a sluggish growth in government revenue and a strong pressure (fuelled by existing program commitments and emerging demands) towards higher levels of public spending. It was therefore imperative for the government to be as cost-effective as possible. The committee was primarily concerned with improvements in the structure and functioning of the government from the viewpoint of increasing efficiency and cutting costs. It saw the privatization of service delivery as a potential instrument for realizing these objectives. Drawing a distinction between policy-making and program delivery the committee argued that whereas the former must remain a function and a direct responsibility of the government, i.e., the relevant department or ministry, the latter could be delegated. It should therefore be possible "for a ministry to contract for programme delivery, with agencies both inside and outside the government."[14] The committee was in favour of "selective reprivatization of programme delivery" which it believed could "tap community skills and resources." Such skills might be found "in nonprofit organizations, in private, profit-oriented corporations, or in community corporations organized by special interest groups."[15] More generally, the committee emphasized the need for organizational diversity and flexibility to face the challenge of varied and changing demands on government services; from this viewpoint too privatization of service delivery seemed a good idea. Moreover, it could act as a brake on government growth, provide more cost-effective service delivery (especially in the form of a contract of service based on competitive tender) and help develop a closer relationship between the government and the community.[16]

Partly in response to the committee's report, the Budget of 1972 proposed to slash growth in provincial spending and reorder priorities so that new needs might be met without additional outlay.[17] But it was not until after 1975, following the report of the Special Programme Review Committee (SPRC), that Ontario's policy of retrenchment of social expenditures and programs really got under way. The SPRC was set up by the government to "inquire into ways and means of restraining the costs of government through examining issues such as the continued usefulness of programmes, alternative lower cost means of accomplishing objectives, and the problem of increased public demand for services in an inflationary period."[18] The SPRC looked at social and economic issues through the lens of neoconservatism. It saw growing public expenditure as a threat to the economic future of Ontario. It believed that the provincial budget deficit was fueling inflation, pushing interest rates up and crowding out private investment. It firmly rejected the option of reducing the deficit by raising taxes as that would discourage enterprise, investment and productivity. The urgent problem, according to the SPRC, was not simply to contain government spending but to "face up to the difficult job of cutting it back."[19] And this was precisely the agenda it set out for the provincial government.

The SPRC made detailed recommendations (some 184 of them) and set specific targets for downsizing government and reducing social expenditures. It advocated user charges for services such as health care and more stringent means tests and selectively for income maintenance services. It laid special stress on cutting back public sector employment. The SPRC noted that the biggest element in government spending was the cost of labour. Moreover, since the public services were labour intensive the clamour for improved services nearly always meant more public employees.[20] It expressed serious concern over a growing trend towards large wage settlements in the public sector and was anxious to put a brake on this development. While noting with satisfaction that the government had taken steps to reduce growth in the provincial public service and had proposed further reductions, the SPRC cautioned the government against complacency. It stressed that every effort must be made to control the growth of employment in the public sector and to increase productivity, and recommended further reductions in the provincial public service complement.[21] Although the SPRC did not connect this policy explicitly with its suggestions for the privatization of service delivery, there is little doubt that containment of public employment (with all its cost implications) has formed an important context in which the argument for the greater use of nongovernmental organizations (NGO's) for service delivery has taken shape in Ontario. It urged the government to "explore the possibility of transferring back to the private sector some of the activity that it currently undertakes."[22] The SPRC also touched on deinstitutionalization and the prospects of developing community-based services. Seeing the latter clearly as a low-cost alternative, it encouraged the development of these services under the auspices of private organizations and individuals.[23]

The reports of the COGP and the SPRC, taken together, may be seen as providing, *inter alia*, the rationale and policy orientation for privatization in the province. In particular, the philosophy of social welfare articulated by the SPRC, which was directly concerned with public expenditure and its control, and the general tone of its detailed recommendations have informed much of social policy development in the province since 1975. That year the budget included a 2.5% cut in the civil service complement. It required that all ministries absorb in their estimates for the year inflation-related cost increases, postpone building projects wherever feasible, and make a thorough assessment of the efficiency, effectiveness, and relevance of major spending programs.[24] The period of retrenchment and restraint had officially begun. From Table 6-1 we can see that public expenditure as a percentage of Gross Provincial Product (GPP) fell from 17.5 to 15.5 between 1975/76 and 1980/81. During the same period, the provincial budget deficit as a percentage of the GPP fell from 2.8 to 0.7. Indeed the province seemed to be within reach of its target of a balanced budget based on reduced *public* expenditure rather than higher taxes. The next two years were, however, years of high inflation and a sharp economic recession. The level of expenditure rose sharply but resumed its decline again in 1983-84; the budget deficit shows a similar pattern. The dramatic decline in the growth rate of *social* expenditure can be seen from Table 6-2. From a three-yearly (1973-75) average of 56.3% it plummeted to 10.7% in 1976-78 and fell to 5.9% in 1979-81. Table 6-3 tells a similar story in terms of social expenditure as a percentage of the GPP. In short, whatever indices or measures we choose to employ the result is the same: the level of public, including social, expenditure declined appreciably from about the mid-seventies as a result of the policy of retrenchment and restraint.

In general, provincial policy has favoured underfunding rather than the elimination of mainstream services and programs or the tightening up of eligibility as the strategy of restraint. The fiscal squeeze, together with inflation restraint programs such as the "6 and 5,"[25] have meant reduced public sector employment, lower wages and salaries in the public services,[26] postponement of capital expenditure in human services and in the case of provincial income maintenance programs a reduction in benefit rates.[27] The policy of fiscal restraint followed by the province has created the conditions in which privatization of service delivery has been occurring both by design and default. But to what extent has service delivery been privatized and what form has privatization taken? These questions are difficult to answer as there are no clear benchmarks and the necessary data are hard to come by. As pointed out already, in the personal social services sector the NGO's—both nonprofit and for-profit—have been a part and parcel of Ontario's system of social welfare. However, the period under review also shows some new departures, notably the growth of fee-for-service contracts. Taking the personal services sector as a whole, available evidence suggests that changes have been piecemeal and marginal so far. They have also been uneven—varying from one ministry to another. Moreover, despite the general endorsement of privatization by the two reports mentioned above, the government's action and policy statements have been cautious. In this respect the Ontario Conservatives, as might be expected, have charted a pragmatic and incremental rather than an ideological and radical course. We shall briefly review the policy and practice of privatization with reference to three government departments: the Ministry of Community and Social Services—the social service department of the province—and the Ministry of Health and Ministry of Correctional Services. Our focus will be on the personal social services rather than on such general services as medicare, education, housing or income maintenance. It should also be pointed out that our concern will be with the provincial rather than, say, the municipal level of policy.

(B) THE MINISTRY OF COMMUNITY AND SOCIAL SERVICES

Community and Social Services (COMSOC) provides most of what are traditionally understood as personal social services. It is also in the delivery of these, e.g., child welfare, that NGO's have been especially prominent. COMSOC's heavy reliance on NGO's predates the policy of privatization initiated in the province in the seventies. However, the recent policy stance has provided a rationale for the long-standing "partnership" between the government and the NGO's and for a further impetus towards the use of the NGO's.

Table 6-1 Public Expenditure and Budget Deficit as a Percentage of the Gross Provincial Product in Ontario

Year	Expenditure	Deficit
1975/76	17.5	2.8
1976/77	16.7	1.8
1977/78	16.5	2.1
1978/79	16.1	1.3
1979/80	15.7	0.6
1980/81	15.5	0.7
1981/82	16.0	1.2
1982/83	17.2	1.9
1983/84	16.8	1.5
1984/85	16.6	1.0

SOURCE: *Ontario Budget*, 1984 and 1985.

Table 6-2 Growth-rate of Expenditures (constant dollars) of the Provincial Social Service Department Over 3-Year Periods

	Ontario	All Provinces
1966/67 – 1969/70	124.2	61.6
1969/70 – 1972/73	46.4	49.9
1972/73 – 1975/76	56.3	46.1
1975/76 – 1978/79	10.7	12.4
1978/79 – 1981/82	5.9	12.6

SOURCE: H. Philip Hepworth, "Trends in Provincial Social Services Department Expenditures 1963–1982," in J.S. Ismael, ed., *Canadian Social Welfare Policy* (Kingston and Montreal: McGill-Queen's University Press, 1985).

Table 6-3 Social Expenditure* As a Percentage of Gross Provincial Product in Ontario

1972/73	10.19
1975/76	10.45
1978/79	9.07
1981/82	9.83
1984/85	10.05

* Budgetary Expenditure on Social Development Policy Field (comprising the Ministries of Citizenship and Culture, Colleges and Universities, Community and Social Services, Education, and Health). Calculated from *Ontario Statistics 1984* and *Ontario Budget, 1985*.

As noted earlier, the sixties saw a large expansion in the social services. In 1972 the Ministry of Community and Social Services was constituted with enlarged functions and responsibilities. In the same year a task force was appointed to review the government's role in the provision of social services. Reporting in 1973 the Hanson Task Force advised rather bluntly that COMSOC "should operate programmes only when no other organization is willing or able to do the job satisfactorily."[28] It advocated program diversity and flexibility which would offer competing alternative services. These recommendations of the Hanson Task Force were in line with those of the COGP and together they "stimulated the already large and influential proprietary or profit-making social service sector to consolidate and extend its partnership with the traditional government and voluntary social services."[29] Indeed, the work of the task force was "a watershed in the provision of social services in Ontario in the next decade."[30] Ten years later, consistent with the Ontario tradition and the rationale for privatization articulated in the province in the mid-seventies, the ministry outlined its service delivery objectives in the following terms. It was to *"strengthen the capacity of the community* [emphasis added], in partnership with the ministry, to deliver a range of services responsive to the needs of individuals and families, in a way which supports their self-reliance within the community."[31] In short, nongovernmental organizations and groups were seen as forming a necessary part of Ontario's social welfare mosaic.

The services funded by COMSOC are largely delivered by nonprofit organizations. For example, the core of children's services are delivered by Children's Aid Societies. These nonprofit organizations are legally mandated to provide services and are almost entirely funded by the government. Other nonprofit organizations are involved in operating group homes and other forms of children's residences, day care centres, home support services and a variety of "prevention" programs. The for-profit sector is thus far involved mainly in the provision of children's residences and day care facilities. In 1983 some 34% of all beds in children's residences were accounted for by the for-profit sector.[32] In day care, the commercial sector accounted for 47% of the places compared with 39% nonprofit and 14% municipal places.[33] In recent years growth has been mainly in the nonprofit sector with both commercial and municipal day care places posting a slight decline in their share.

Services for the physically and mentally handicapped—both children and adults—are also largely in the hands of nonprofit organizations. For example, in 1984 there were 140 approved workshops serving over 7,000 developmentally handicapped adults in Ontario[34] which organized and ran assessment services, life skills and vocational training, job placement programs and sheltered employment. These workshops and related services were offered by voluntary agencies with the ministry providing grants for the construction, acquisition or renovation of workshops and the purchase of basic furnishings and equipment.

Homes for the Aged, which cater for the elderly who do not need nursing care, show that a higher proportion of beds (2/3) are in the municipal than in the voluntary nonprofit sector (1/3). (There are no commercially run old age homes which receive government funding.) But in recent years the balance has been shifting towards the voluntary sector. The moratorium on capital expenditure (a part of fiscal restraint) is undoubtedly responsible for the relative decline of the public sector. Since 1973 the number of beds in the public sector had risen by a mere 3.8% compared with a 14.7% rise in the nonprofit sector.[35] The emphasis on the home care of the elderly has resulted in the growth of homemaker and nursing services. These services are provided by nonprofit as well as proprietary agencies.

The policy of deinstitutionalization has had a considerable impact in corrections. COMSOC's involvement in the justice and corrections field is through juvenile offenders. Here again with the emphasis on community-based services the private sector has come to play an important part. Services contracted with nongovernmental groups and agencies include Victim-Offender Reconciliation projects, Community Service Orders/Attendance Centres, One-to-One Workers, Employment Counselling, Drug Counselling, Observation/Detention Homes. Probation supervision of juveniles is also contracted out in a limited number of cases.[36] In a consultation paper the ministry stated that purchase of services, e.g., for observation and detention, "represents a substantial cost-saving compared with the establishment of new direct government-run facilities."[37] Further, it allows the ministry to provide more flexible, alternative forms of detention care suited to the needs of particular communities.

Many of COMSOC's services are cost-shared with the federal government under the Canada Assistance Plan. CAP funding regulations favour the use of nonproprietary organizations.[38] Moreover, COMSOC itself does not provide funds directly to commercial organizations. It is the municipalities or nonprofit agencies such as Children's Aid Societies that purchase services from proprietary agencies with funds provided by COMSOC. Thus although proprietary organizations are well-represented in some areas of the ministry's services, overall the voluntary sector remains the chief service provider. Privatization has not, at least thus far, meant simply commercialization.

(C) THE MINISTRY OF CORRECTIONAL SERVICES

Unlike COMSOC, the Ministry of Correctional Services (MCS) has not traditionally employed NGO's in the delivery of its services. The ministry's "services" such as prisons, mean to punish and detain the wrongdoer, have been state operations. The involvement of NGO's in corrections has been in connection with the welfare of the discharged prisoner. In Ontario this involvement dates back to 1929 when the Citizen's Service Association, the forerunner of the John Howard and Elizabeth Fry Societies, began to provide needed and useful services to discharged prisoners. In recognition of their general good work, including aftercare, the ministry began to provide such organizations with annual grants. However, these grants remained small and the role of the agencies remained somewhat limited until the advent of the policy of deinstitutionalization. In the late 1960s and early 1970s the ministry was influenced by the shift in penal philosophy away from the traditional institutionally-based incarceration towards community-based forms of correction. At the same time the province was embarking on a policy of restraint and retrenchment of public expenditure. The result of these twin influences was the development of community-based alternatives to incarceration and a significant increase in the use of NGOs.

Thus the Temporary Absence Program, introduced in 1969, grew rapidly in the 1970s. In 1972 the Volunteers Programs Branch was set up. Three years later the ministry launched the Community Resource Centres—halfway houses, located in the community and operated by private agencies under contract for inmates actually serving a sentence.[39] In 1978 when the MCS was reorganized, a separate Community Programs Branch was established with a focus on probation and parole services. In the late 1970s, with the switch from imprisonment to community-based alternatives, probation and parole grew rapidly as methods of dealing with offenders.[40]

These developments were paralleled by the increasing use and funding of NGO's by the ministry. To meet increasing demands for community services, the MCS developed a Grants Program which involved the policy of promoting the development and involvement of private agencies in corrections by making available unconditional grants.[41] This can be seen as the first stage of privatization in corrections, i.e., increasing the capability of the private sector through the award of general grants. The second stage, more crucial for the development of privatization, began in 1975 with the move towards contracting for services with private agencies. The following figures show the dramatic rise of contracts eclipsing the paltry growth in unconditional grants. In 1975/76 the ministry disbursed $116,416.00 in grants but over $1 million in contracts; in 1981/82 the corresponding figures were $346,488.00 and $10 million. In short, grants rose three-fold but contracts rose ten-fold. In 1975 the MCS had entered into only 15 contracts; by 1981 the number of contracts had risen to 224.[42] Increasingly the ministry has been purchasing services under contract from NGO's in such areas as the Community Resource Centres, Community Service Orders, Employment Life Skills Programs, Alcohol/Drug Abuse Programs, Victim Services and the like. The NGO's involved are nonprofit in nature and are led by such names as John Howard Society, Elizabeth Fry Society and the Salvation Army.

It is important to note however, that the MCS seems to have adopted privatization as a carefully planned and a somewhat delimited approach to service delivery.[43] In this the MCS differs from the other two ministries reviewed in this paper both of whom have followed an ad hoc and piecemeal approach without articulating a clear and specific role for private service delivery. It is likely that since the use of NGO's for service delivery is a somewhat recent development in the field of corrections, dating from about the early 1970s, the MCS has been able to fashion a more coherent policy orientation. It could also be that the very nature of the field of corrections has encouraged a more cautious stance. The report of the Workload Management Committee (1978), concerned with the probation and parole service, provides a good example of this approach. This committee saw probation and parole as a key human service but thought that "it cannot and should not undertake the burden of providing all services to offenders." Rather the service should "establish better links and more effective cooperation and use of community agencies and resources."[44] The report made a distinction between certain "core responsibilities" which would remain with the service and other ancillary services which would be supplied by community agencies. The committee went on to identify certain areas of core responsibility in probation and parole.[45] In practice, the distinction between core and noncore areas is not easy to maintain but there is at least an attempt here to formulate a clear rationale for privatized service delivery within corrections. The Community Programs Branch, a separate section established by the ministry in 1978 to promote the funding of community agencies and to keep track of the funds going to these agencies, provides another indication of the planned and controlled approach of the MCS.

The systematic use of volunteers is another aspect of privatization much in evidence in the field of corrections. In 1978 volunteers in probation and parole services were said to be increasingly augmenting the work of paid staff. Apparently they had contributed time equal to 100 full-time staff members, a saving estimated at $1 million.[46] In 1980 the ministry reported that a sum of $260,000.00 had been devoted to programs for the initiation, development and support of voluntarism. In 1985 the ministry estimated that the 5,000 or so volunteers in corrections represented half of all volunteers working within the human services in Ontario.[47]

Lastly, it should be noted that the MCS does not appear to employ proprietary organizations in service delivery with the exception of some operations connected with prisons e.g., prison industry.[48]

(D) THE MINISTRY OF HEALTH

The Ministry of Health (MOH) differs from the other two ministries in that unlike COMSOC it does not have a general commitment to nonprofit forms of service delivery; and unlike the MCS it does not appear to have followed a carefully considered and delimited policy of privatization. The MOH has been more pragmatic and open-ended in its approach to these issues. Thus the last Conservative minister of Health is on record as saying that there was "no overall policy with respect to which services may be provided by for-profit operators but rather each situation must be considered on an individual basis."[49] The same minister also affirmed the government's belief that "private enterprise has a place in the provision of health care services in the province."[50]

In the area of personal social services with the ministry, the nursing homes are perhaps the best known example of privatized service delivery. They are predominantly commercial ventures engaged in providing nursing care for the elderly and also for the mentally handicapped and ex-psychiatric patients. Of the 332 licensed nursing homes in the province in 1983/84, only 24 were run by municipal or nonprofit organizations. The rest were for-profit homes.[51] Moreover, in recent years the commercial sector has expanded rapidly. Between 1979 and 1983 the number of beds in proprietary homes increased by 38.9% compared with an increase of only 8.8% in the voluntary sector and 5.5% in the government sector.[52] Commercial organizations now provide over one-half of Ontario's nonhospital residential services for the elderly.

The last ten years have seen a growth in the domiciliary services provided under the ministry's Home Care Program. These include nursing, homemaking, physiotherapy, occupational therapy and the like. Traditionally these services have been provided by the voluntary sector represented by such organizations as the Victoria Order of Nurses and the Red Cross. While the ministry has been contracting for services with these organizations there has been a noticeable increase in the number of commercial agencies operating in this field. Apparently in Metropolitan Toronto their number has tripled since 1974.[53] In 1983/84 one-half of the MOH's contracts under the Home Care Program, on which some $18 million was being spent, were with commercial agencies.[54]

Deinstitutionalization, insofar as it affects the MOH, has centred largely on the closure of psychiatric hospitals and the discharge of mental patients in the community. From about the early 1960s there has been a steady decline in the number of beds in public mental hospitals.[55] While to some extent this has been counter-balanced by an increase in beds in psychiatric units of general hospitals, the turnover of psychiatric patients has increased significantly. More particularly, the move away from large psychiatric hospitals and towards a variety of community-based alternatives has meant an increasing use of nongovernmental facilities. In 1964 the Homes for Special Care Program was started to encourage the supply of small residential facilities for ex-psychiatric patients. Twenty years later over 6,000 people, discharged from provincial mental retardation or psychiatric institutions, were under the jurisdiction of this program. The residential facilities involved—nursing homes and residential homes for special care—are private, for-profit operations.[56] It is estimated, however, that the majority of ex-psychiatric patients live in commercial rooming or boarding homes with scarcely any support services.[57]

It is no secret that deinstitutionalization of the mentally ill and retarded has often meant discharging them into the "community" with totally inadequate facilities and arrangements. In response to this situation the ministry established the Adult Community Mental Health Program in 1976. Under this scheme, community-based services and programs have been funded. To take rehabilitation as an example, by the end of the 1970s some 42 programs had been funded. These were delivered by a wide variety of agencies, both governmental and nongovernmental, such as the local general hospital and the Canadian Mental Health Association.[58] In 1983/84 the ministry's grants to community mental health programs (excluding alcohol and drug programs) came to over $30 million.[59] A wide variety of sponsors were involved such as local general hospitals, the Canadian Mental Health Association, regional health units, and the Ontario March of Dimes. It appears that in the delivery of community mental health services, at any rate, the ministry is in favour of using nonprofit organizations.

In sum, although the MOH has been following a pragmatic line on privatization there is little doubt that under the general policy of fiscal restraint in the province and as a result of deinstitutionalization and the trend towards community-based services, the role of the private sector in the delivery of personal health care services has been growing. Furthermore, unlike COMSOC, whose services are cost-shared with the Canada Assistance Plan which favours nonprofit forms of delivery, the MOH is not restricted by any regulations inhibiting the use of proprietary services. Not surprisingly, the MOH seems to have few qualms about using the commercial sector. Indeed, this is also evident from the ministry's initiatives in the field of hospital administration and management, a topic that is not pursued here.[60] It is likely that the personal social services for which the MOH is responsible will be privatized further and that the profit sector will play a prominent part in some of the service areas.

Summary and Conclusions

This paper has explored the nature, sources and extent of privatization of social services in Ontario. Progressive Conservatives who ruled the province until mid-1985, have had a clear ideological commitment to the privatization of social welfare—in the broader sense as well as in relation to service delivery. In any event Ontario's personal social services, residential and domiciliary, have historically been delivered by private agencies funded by the government. In this sense, service delivery was largely in private hands already when the government made an explicit commitment to the use of NGO's. Thus to a large extent privatization in Ontario has meant a renewed commitment to the use of NGO's in service delivery and to moving further in that direction. Overall the nonprofit sector remains pre-eminent but it is likely that in at least some of the service areas the for-profit sector will grow. In part because the NGO's have been a part and parcel of Ontario's social welfare for a long time and the greater use of NGO's did not seem a new departure, the government departments concerned have not collected—and in any case not published—systematic data which would make a quantitative evaluation of the recent changes feasible.

Undoubtedly, a new and significant development is the growth of fee-for-service contracts between the government and the nonprofit sector. The potential of contracts in changing the relationship between the government and the voluntary sector, in particular the latter's role in social welfare, is very considerable. Traditionally, voluntary agencies have had the role of reformers, advocates and innovators rather than routine service providers. With the replacement of general unconditional grants with fee-for-service contracts they are in danger of becoming mere service providers, sometimes little more than contractors serving a particular department or ministry. The rapid growth of contracting in the field of corrections, for example, has led to some soul-searching among nonprofit organizations. A draft paper by the John Howard Society of Hamilton, for instance, calls for a clear articulation of the Society's mission and a reassessment of its position on contracting for services. The paper also recognizes the implications of relying heavily on government funding and looks for a diversified funding base.[61] There is little doubt that contracting, in an environment of cost-reduction and fiscal squeeze and the encouragement of competition between agencies, is likely to "commercialize" the nature of voluntary agencies and also their relationship with the government. The consequences of such a development are not easy to foresee.

The privatization of service delivery raises many important issues only some of which can be mentioned here. The role of the voluntary nonprofit sector within the welfare state is one of several unexamined questions that has been pushed to the fore in recent years as a result of privatization. It is a question that needs to be answered by all the main parties concerned. A related question is the role of the commercial sector within social welfare. As we have seen, both the attitude towards, and the scope of commercialization differs among the three human services departments reviewed in this paper. While some of the differences are historical in nature others may have to do with the characteristics of the services themselves. Nonetheless there is a need to clarify the legitimate sphere of activity for the commercial sector in social welfare. A further question is whether there is an optimal mix of government and nongovernment, nonprofit and for-profit, agencies within the broad field of service provision and delivery. And if there is, then the relevant criteria for such a division need to be spelled out clearly and the outcome of such a policy approach evaluated carefully. The consequences of a drift into privatization, based on unexamined assumptions about its supposed advantages, are likely to be harmful to most of the parties involved, notably clients, service workers and voluntary agencies.

The issue of the commercialization of the social service system in Ontario has been examined thoroughly in a recent study of the Social Planning Council of Metropolitan Toronto (SPCMT).[62] The study found a good deal of ambivalence in government statements at the ministerial level regarding the use of proprietary agencies in human service delivery. Yet the study also found a clear trend towards the growth of commercial programs. In light of this situation the SPCMT has called for a moratorium on the commercialization of human services until the provincial legislature can undertake a thorough review of the nature, extent and implications of commercialization.[63] We might add that a similar inquiry into the changing relationship between the government and the nonprofit sector, in light of recent policy developments, would be highly desirable.

Following the elections in May 1985, a minority Liberal government, dependent on the support of the New Democratic Party, took office ending over forty years of Progressive Conservative rule in Ontario. Two years later the Liberals won a landslide victory and formed a majority government. This government does not subscribe to the ideology of Retrenchment of social welfare and from this viewpoint privatization, in the wider sense at least, has likely slowed down if not halted. Despite fierce opposition from the medical profession, the Peterson government has passed a law banning extra-billing by physicians. But if recent changes in the province point one way, developments at the federal level since 1984 point the other way. With the advent of a Conservative government in Ottawa the ideology of Retrenchment rather than Restraint holds sway. Substantial federal cutbacks on social spending are on the agenda and could have a considerable impact on provincial social welfare policy.[64]

The three main sources of privatization in social welfare seem to be neoconservatism, deinstitutionalization, and the movement for debureaucratization and community control. They are not of equal strength nor are they identical in their policy implications. Yet all three seem to be important elements of contemporary social reality. And in this sense privatization may be here to stay. This chapter has examined government policy towards privatization rather than the dynamics of the privatization process itself. The latter concerns larger issues which need to be explored within the framework of the political economy of privatization. In any case, the ideologies and interests involved in the process, and the intended and unintended outcomes in the different service sectors, and for the different parties concerned, are among the issues raised by this overview of privatization that would repay careful study.

Notes

1. David Donnison, "The Progressive Potential of Privatization," in Julian Le Grand and Ray Robinson, eds., *Privatization and the Welfare State* (London: Allen and Unwin, 1984), p. 45.
2. Marvyn Novick, "Social Policy: The Search for a New Consensus," in Donald C. MacDonald, ed., *The Government and Politics of Ontario* (Scarborough: Nelson, 1985), p. 335.

3. Social Planning Council of Metropolitan Toronto (SPCMT), *Neighbourhoods Under Stress* (Toronto: SPCMT), p. 11.
4. SPCMT, *SCPC News* (February, 1986), p. 11.
5. Glenn Drover, "Beyond the Welfare State: Brief to the Royal Commission on the Economic Union and Development Prospects for Canada," *The Social Worker* 51, no. 1 (1983), p. 141.
6. Ibid., p. 143.
7. Allan Moscovitch and Glenn Drover, "Social Expenditures and the Welfare State: The Canadian Experience in Historical Perspective," in Allan Moscovitch and Jim Albert, eds., *The Benevolent State: The Growth of Welfare in Canada* (Toronto: Garamond Press, 1987), p. 15.
8. Donald Bellamy, "Social Policy in Ontario," in Ontario Social Development Council, *The Province of Ontario: Its Social Services* (Toronto: Ontario Social Development Council, 1983), p. 31.
9. Vernon Lang, *The Service State Emerges in Ontario 1945-1973* (Toronto: Ontario Economic Council, 1974).
10. Ibid., p. 52.
11. H. Philip Hepworth, "Trends in Provincial Social Service Department Expenditures 1963-1982," in Jacqueline S. Ismael, ed., *Canadian Social Welfare Policy* (Kingston and Montreal: McGill-Queen's University Press, 1985), p. 144.
12. Bellamy, "Social Policy in Ontario," pp. 39-40.
13. Ramesh Mishra, "Public Policy and Social Welfare: The Ideology and Practice of Restraint in Ontario," in J.S. Ismael, ed., *Canadian Welfare State: Evolution and Transition* (Edmonton: University of Alberta Press, 1987).
14. Committee on Government Productivity, Interim Report No. 3 (1971), p. 50.
15. Ibid.
16. Ibid., pp. 50-51.
17. *Ontario Budget 1972* (Toronto: Ministry of Treasury, Economics, and Intergovernmental Affairs, 1972), p. 5.
18. *The Report of the Special Program Review*, 1975, Preamble.
19. Ibid., p. 1.
20. Ibid., pp. 95-97.
21. Ibid., p. 316.
22. Ibid., p. 37.
23. Ibid., pp. 44-45.
24. *Ontario Budget 1975* (Toronto: Ministry of Treasury and Economics, 1975), p. 17.
25. Refers to federal legislation of 1982 which, *inter alia*, restricted federal public service wages to 6% in 1983 and 5% in 1984. The provinces were expected to and generally followed the federal government in placing similar restrictions on provincial public service wages. See e.g., *Ontario Budget 1983* (Toronto: Ministry of Treasury and Economics, 1983), p. 44.
26. Wages, salaries and benefits together as a percentage of total budgetary expenditures fell from 12.57% in 1972/73 to 10.55% in 1982/83. Calculated from *Ontario Statistics 1984*, Table 27.9, p. 592.
27. Between 1975 and 1982 general welfare rates in Ontario were eroded by over 30% and family benefits by about 25% in purchasing power. See Social

Planning Council of Metropolitan Toronto (SPCMT), *Social Infopac* 1, no. 3 (1982). Increases in welfare benefits up to 1984 had done little to restore the substantial erosion of purchasing power earlier. Since 1985 the situation has improved however. See SPCMT, *Social Infopac* 3, no. 4 (1984) p. 1; SPCMT, *SPC News* (November-December, 1985), p. 1.

28. Task Force on Community and Social Services, *Report on Ministry Role and Capabilities* (Toronto: Ontario Ministry of Community and Social Services, 1974), pp. 3-4.
29. Bellamy, "Social Policy in Ontario," p. 44.
30. Ibid., p. 43.
31. *52nd Report for the Fiscal Years 1982-83 and 1983-84* (Toronto: Ministry of Community and Social Services), p. 71.
32. Social Planning Council for Metropolitan Toronto (SPCMT), *Caring for Profit: The Commercialization of Human Services in Ontario* (Toronto: SPCMT, 1984), p. 50.
33. Ibid., p. 43.
34. *52nd Report*, p. 33.
35. SPCMT, *Caring for Profit*, p. 110.
36. Probation Officers' Association of Ontario (POAO), *Privatization of Community Corrections in Ontario*, p. 3.
37. *Consultation Paper on Short Term Legislative Amendments* (Toronto: Ministry of Community and Social Services, Children's Services Division, 1977), p. 85.
38. SPCMT, *Caring for Profit*, p. 26.
39. POAO, *Privatization of Community Corrections*, p. 3.
40. See S.L. Davis, "Seduction of the Private Sector — Privatization in Ontario Corrections," MSW Thesis, Carleton University, Ottawa (1980), pp. 35-36.
41. Ibid., p. 21.
42. POAO, *Privatization of Community Corrections*, p. 12.
43. Ibid., p. 4.
44. Ibid.
45. Quoted in ibid., p. 9.
46. *Report of the Minister of Correctional Services 1978*, p. 15.
47. *Report of the Minister of Correctional Services 1985*, p. 46.
48. John Howard Society of Ontario, "Privatization and Commercialization of Correctional Services," mimeo (1986), pp. 18-19.
49. Keith Norton, Minister of Health, quoted in SPCMT, *Caring for Profit*, p. 28.
50. Ibid., p. 27.
51. Ibid., p. 30.
52. Lorna Hurl and Christa Freiler, "Privatized Social Services: The Ontario Experience," a paper presented at the 2nd Conference on Provincial Social Welfare Policy, at the University of Calgary, May 1-3, 1985, p. 6.
53. Estimate. See SPCMT, *Caring for Profit*, p. 39.
54. Ibid.
55. G.F. Heseltine, *Towards a Blueprint for Change: A Mental Health Policy and Programme Perspective* (University of Western Ontario, 1984), pp. 21-22.
56. SPCMT, *Caring for Profit*, p. 34.
57. Heseltine, *Towards a Blueprint for Change*, p. 145.

58. Ibid., p. 123.
59. *Regional Allocation of Estimated Expenditures on Mental Health Services* (Toronto: Ontario Ministry of Health, 1985), p. 22.
60. See SPCMT, *Caring for Profit*, p. 38; Ontario Ministry of Health, *Annual Report 1981/82*, p. 10; Ontario Ministry of Health, *Annual Report 1982/83*, p. 7.
61. John Howard Society of Ontario, "Privatization and Commercialization," pp. 31-34.
62. SPCMT, *Caring for Profit*.
63. Ibid., pp. 106-8.
64. Over the next five years (1986-91) Ontario is expected to lose $2 billion in federal support as a result of cutbacks in transfer payments to provinces. See *Ontario Budget 1985* (Toronto: Ministry of Treasury and Economics, 1985), p. 2.

7 Quebec

YVES VAILLANCOURT

Introduction

At first glance, privatization of social services does not appear to be high on the Quebec agenda of issues for public debate and government action. A closer inspection nonetheless reveals that social services in Quebec are presently undergoing important transformations, and that within this shifting context, the stakes involved in the privatization of social services make it a subject of growing concern.

Over the past few years, and especially since the election of a new Liberal government under Robert Bourassa in December, 1985, the question of privatization has acquired increasing status on the government agenda. This official interest in privatization would appear to focus less on social services than on health services and is mostly clearly concentrated on Crown corporations.

Public debate on privatization of health services was launched shortly after the re-election of the P.Q. government in April 1981, when Jacques Parizeau (then Finance minister) made a highly publicized speech extolling the virtues of user fees.

It was also during the P.Q.'s second term of office (1981-1985) that privatization of Crown corporations was debated with the idea of placing

Crown corporations such as the Sidérurgie du Quebec (SIDBEC), the St. Hilaire sugar refinery, and the Quebec Liquor Board outlets, back in the hands of private business. However, it was with the Liberals' return to office that the question of privatization of Crown corporations really began to occupy centre stage. Indeed, immediately on forming a new Cabinet on December 13, 1985, Premier Robert Bourassa took a significant first step in this direction by creating a new cabinet position of minister for privatization. Pierre Fortier was the first incumbent appointed to this post. The following elements were included in his mandate, as stipulated by decree:

> That [. . .] the minister for privatization, under the authority of the finance minister, be responsible for reviewing and analyzing the role of the state enterprises in a socio-political context which is marked by reduced state intervention in the economy and heightened confidence in the values of enterprise, individual initiative, and market forces to ensure the economic growth of Quebec . . .[1]

As a minister not lacking influence in Cabinet, Fortier hastened to have a government policy drawn up on the issue of privatization. Decisions on certain specific cases of privatization soon appeared before the public. The initial work undertaken by the minister dealt more specifically with privatization of Crown corporations. This was indeed the kind of privatization referred to by Mr. Fortier in public statements made since his nomination, and in the two successive reports published by him personally under the auspices of the "Comité des sages"[2] over which he presided. These publications, along with Mr. Fortier's frequent public statements throughout 1986, were quick to target a dozen Crown corporations as likely contenders for partial or total privatization in the short term. Among such corporations were the Raffinerie de sucre du Québec, Québecair, SOQUEM (the Québec society for mining exploration), DOFOR (a lucrative subsidiary of the Société générale de financement), Société nationale de l'amiante (a Quebec asbestos corporation), SOQUIA (Société Québécoise d'initiatives agro-alimentaires), REXFOR, SOQUIP, and Madelipêche.[3]

Without blurring the distinction between privatization cases involving Crown corporations or health services and those dealing specifically with social services, over the past few years the debates on privatization of Crown corporations have fostered the emergence of a general ideological climate, one which is not without impact on declarations and actions pertaining to privatization of public services, and of social services in particular.

It should not be inferred from the relative lack of media coverage on this subject that Quebec currently faces no problem of privatization of social services. To the contrary, significant processes have been set in motion over the past few years in Quebec, ones which are in keeping with a vision of privatized social services. The most striking manifestation of these processes would appear to be in the area of social services for elderly people, young people, and women. But before turning to the concrete changes in thought and practice on the subject of privatization of social services, let us briefly examine the theoretical and historical parameters which, in our view, can scarcely be overlooked if we wish to proceed with a rigorous description and analysis of what is happening at present. Given that there has been little research on the subject in Quebec, we have to be content with rather modest objectives for the present chapter. Our specific aim here is to do some initial spadework on the privatization of social services, concentrating on a description (rather than an evaluation) of what is taking place.[4]

Privatization goes hand in hand with a process of state withdrawal. It represents the reverse side of nationalization, and is measured accordingly against a backdrop of state involvement. For this reason, our analysis of the current processes of privatization must take into account how social services were organized in the past, and the legacy inherited by the present organization of social services, giving particular attention to the place held by public social services within this system. In a given society (or province), the degree to which social services have historically come under public control would to some extent condition what is possible in terms of privatization. Clear processes of privatization would not readily be encountered in a province whose system of social services had been traditionally organized under the private sphere. In fact, the state can only withdraw from delivery of certain services to the extent that it was formerly involved in such services. But, if we take the example of a province whose system of social services had already been brought under state or public control to a significant extent—as we think would apply in the case of Quebec—it would then theoretically be possible to witness certain processes of state withdrawal, and of privatization.

The Historical Legacy

It is clear that the historical evolution of a system of social services must be taken into account in examining the processes of privatization within a current context. Indeed, it would be risky, if not impossible, to examine these processes in Quebec or other parts of Canada, without considering the organization of social services inherited from the past. If we want to be able to discern and assess whether (or to what extent) there are processes of privatization at work in any given sector, we have to make the necessary detour of reconstructing the historical background.

Our hypothesis is as follows: in Quebec, the historical relationship between private and public sectors in the area of social services resembles a complex amalgam formed from the sedimentation of two highly distinct—or rather, mutually exclusive—strata. The first stratum, inherited from the period before 1970, is marked by an omnipresent private sector within the system of social services. The second stratum, inherited from the first phase of the reform which took place during the 1970s, is characterized by omnipresent state involvement in the system of social services. Paradoxically, in almost all of Canada, Quebec might well be the province with the most privatized social services (before 1970) and also the most public ones (after 1970). Moreover, given that our past informs and shapes our present, we might suggest the idea that opposites co-habit the Québécois subconscious: some distant memories foster mistrust of the private sector, and other more recent ones nurture a fear of the public sector.

The Legacy of the Distant Past: Extensive Private Involvement
According to the Castonguay-Nepveu Report, the Government of Quebec contributed $150 million towards the funding of social services designed for children, young people, elderly people, and families, during the 1970-1971 fiscal year.[5] Although public funds provided by the Quebec government represented more than 85% of costs defrayed by the institutions and agencies which delivered these services,[6] these institutions were all private at the time, whether nonprofit or commercial.

This assertion may come as a surprise, as some interpretations of Quebec history suggest that the modernization of Quebec society—understood to mean a movement towards deprivatization, extension of public control, and secularization—arose during the feverish years of the Quiet Revolution (1960-1966), and in all sectors of collective life at once. This is not an accurate reading. Although the years between 1960 and 1966 constitute a particularly intense period of social ferment and transformation, the Quiet Revolution as a period of modernization lasted up until the beginning of the 1970s. To be sure, in some areas such as primary and high school education, the modernization movement had begun in a clear and decisive fashion in the first half of the 1960s. But in other areas such as social services, it was not until 1971 that an indepth reform got underway after a gestation period of several years.

At the dawn of the 1970s in Quebec an entirely private system of social services remained intact, although it was full of cracks and under fire since the 1950s from increasingly broad sectors of the population. Far from being homogenous, this private system resembled a shattered mosaic whose private components were no less diversified than its whole. In order to reconstruct this mosaic, which provided the backdrop for the system of social services in Quebec in 1970, it would be useful to identify its various components.

1) There were social services delivered by volunteer and community organizations which were the legacy of previous decades, forming a more traditional network of charities and social welfare groups financed by various annual fund-raising drives. These fund-raisers were organized by the "Fédération des oeuvres de charité canadiennes-françaises" for the French Catholic sector, and by other similar federations for the Jewish, English Catholic, and English Protestant communities. The types of groups which immediately come to mind are the St. Vincent de Paul Society, mission homes for itinerants, and the YMCA. These services were part of the nonprofit private sector.[7]

2) There were social services delivered by new types of volunteer and community organizations which were established in low income neighbourhoods in the big cities and in depressed rural zones to confront the acute social problems left untouched by the more traditional organizations working in social services. For example, protest groups and "citizen's committees"—specifically, the "maisons de quartier," welfare rights groups, and community youth groups (such as the Bureau de consultation jeunesse)—arose in the second half of the 1960s.[8]

3) A broad range of social services designed for families, children, women, and elderly people, were also offered under the Quebec law on public assistance (Loi d'assistance publique du Québec). Passed in 1921, this law was still in force in 1970, although its obsolescence had been common knowledge since the end of World War II. Despite its misleading name, the law on public assistance provided a general legislative framework under which private nonprofit social service institutions were recognized as "public assistance" institutions. Through its provisions, the Quebec state had, since 1921, been partially subsidizing health and social services delivered by "public assistance" institutions operating services within the doors of the institution and outside the doors of the institution. The public assistance scheme which stemmed from this legislation was at first characterized by

a rigorous system of tripartite funding in which the institutions themselves, the municipalities, and the province each contributed one-third of the funds. In the 1950s, however, the provinces' share began to increase as the diminishing payment capacities of municipalities and institutions forced the latter to reduce their share. By the early 1960s the municipalities had practically dropped out of the picture; and with escalating costs outstripping the private institutions' capacity to pay, the lion's share of funding fell on the province. By the end of the 1960s, the following types of institutions were still involved in social service distribution under the Quebec public assistance legislation:

a) social service agencies offering general or specialized services (about 40);
b) nursing residences (about 160 in all) for elderly people and other adults, representing a total capacity of 13,700 beds (or 67.6% of the residence facilities for the adult and elderly population);[9]
c) institutions for children who had been abandoned or were otherwise in difficulty (80), representing a total capacity of 9,150 beds (or 65% of the residence facilities for children);[10]
d) other institutions for "unwed mothers," handicapped persons, etcetera. It should be specified that these social services covered by the public assistance plan were of a private, nonprofit nature; in addition, they were for the most part denominational (notably in the French-speaking community), coming under the administration of either male or female religious orders.[11]

4) Outside the scope of the law on public assistance, curiously enough, were social services for the young and the elderly provided by for private commercial institutions incorporated under the law on private hospitals. In the area of nursing residences for the adult and elderly population, there were 243 such commercial institutions, representing 5,614 beds (or 27.7% of the residence facilities available for this category of clientele).[12] Concerning social services for young people, there were 36 commercial institutions incorporated under the law on private hospitals, representing 2,892 beds (or 20.5% of the total residence facilities for young people in difficulty).[13]

5) Social services for young people were also delivered by nonprofit institutions which were incorporated under the old youth protection act, rather than the law on public assistance. According to the Report of the Castonguay-Nepveu Commission, this type of arrangement involved 18 institutions with an overall bed-capacity of 2,042 representing 14.5% of the facilities in this sector.[14]

6) There were also private commercial social services, often dispensed

clandestinely or without authorization.[15] We are referring here to home care services and to social services provided for elderly or disabled persons in unauthorized nursing residences.

The Legacy of the More Recent Past: Extensive State Involvement
The private distribution of social services still prevalent in the early 1970s, ten years after the start of the Quiet Revolution, represented a peculiar anachronism. The days of this private model were numbered, however. Since the 1950s, with the rise of anti-Duplessis feeling, it had come under attack from the working-class and more popular movement, and from reformist circles of the new petty bourgeoisie which had strong aspirations for the democratization of Quebec society. It is important to understand as well that such aspirations for greater democracy converged at that time with a demand for heightened intervention in social development and social services on the part of the Quebec state. During the 1960s, as the Quiet Revolution developed in sectors such as health and education, it became increasingly evident that the private system of social services had outlived its purpose. The *Boucher Report* published in 1963 had vigorously exposed the inadequacies of private nonprofit agencies operating in the social sphere, and of theories portraying the state as a complementary or residual supplier, and had emphasized the need for reorganization of the social services through state planning and guidance.[16] The *Boucher Report*'s recommendations on public assistance and social services were not immediately put into practice. However, the thrust of the report left its imprint on ideas, evaluations, and plans emanating from government departments involved in the social sphere. This was especially true in 1965 and 1966, while René Levesque headed the Ministry of Family Affairs and Social Welfare.[17] Rising trade union struggles in the hospital sector and unionization in social service agencies throughout the second half of the 1960s gave added impetus to plans for government reform in social services.

When the Castonguay Commission began its work at the end of 1966, it was clearly challenged and influenced by the general ideological and political climate of the time. Such was the vigorous onslaught against the obsolete private system of social services that the commission found itself compelled to join in the attack.

In order for us to reconstruct the Castonguay-Nepveu Commission's assessment and recommendations on social services, we need to refer to Part II of Volume VII, published in 1970, for the section on commercial (profit-making) social services; and, for the section on voluntary (nonprofit) social services, to Parts I and II of Volume VI, published only in 1972, more than a year after Claude Castonguay left the chairmanship of the commission to head what would later become the Ministry of Social Affairs (Ministère des affaires sociales (MAS)).[18]

A clear and concise analysis of the private commercial sector was produced by the commission on social services. In hindsight, it is striking to note the harshness of its assessment:

> While recognizing the services it has rendered and still renders, we are forced to observe that the profit-making sector acts on the basis of motives and pursues objectives which are incompatible with the fundamental principles on which the health plan and the social services plan we have proposed must be built . . . .
>
> We do not claim that persons who engage in the profit-making sector of bed or residential care have all, without exception, sought only to gain financial advantage. What we do believe is that bed and residential care services, which are the product of an activity whose essential goal is to satisfy human needs, must be remunerated of their just value but without opening the door to exploitation of man by man. It is not the persons but the system we disapprove of because of the abuses it gives rise to and because of the obstacles it places in the way of integrating methods of care distribution and social services, planning such systems and the participation of citizens. Furthermore, we have observed how impossible it is for the state to subject the profit-making sector to stringent standards, and its powerlessness, when these standards exist, to control their application.[19]

The commission was not content to just brandish this rather brutal judgment. Based on a well-supported line of argument, it set itself the task of explaining how the profit motive constituted a source of abuse and represented an obstacle to planning, participation and quality of services.[20] It then went on to draw the conclusion which stemmed logically from this assessment: " . . . we have come to the conclusion that commercial enterprise has no place in the operation of health care or social welfare institutions through direct or indirect state subsidies."[21] From then on, private profit-making institutions could continue to operate, but under two specific conditions: they were required to have a permit, and could no longer count on "direct or indirect state subsidies."[22]

On the other hand, the commission's analysis in Volume VI concerning the voluntary private sector, though somewhat marred by long and tortuous passages, arrives at an equally harsh assessment. Private, nonprofit social services were judged to be inadequate in terms of efficiency, easy access, and accountability of services.[23] Paradoxically, this private form of organization even came under criticism for being too bureaucratic: "The social services system was of an authoritarian type, administratively in a vertical line and bureaucratic."[24] The contradiction between the private nature of institutions' legal structure and the extensively public nature of their sources of funding, was forcefully exposed.[25] In terms of recommendations, Volume VI advocated a bold reform which, without suggesting that the private nonprofit sector should disappear altogether, nonetheless called for its sharp reduction in favour of public system institutions. Such institutions were to be the backbone of the system. Recommendations 1, 20, 21, and 22 of Volume VI well illustrate the commission's views on this subject:

> The commission recommends:
> 1. THAT a system of public social services be instituted, with a view to assisting persons, natural groups and communities, and to promoting their development.
> 20. THAT the government recognize the need for a private social services sector.
> 21. THAT such private social services sector be completely independent of the state in its financing and in the implementation of its objectives.
> 22. THAT the private social services sector concern itself principally with the particular needs arising from the subjective attitudes and values to which public services cannot respond satisfactorily, the new needs which constantly emerge in a changing society, the unforseen needs brought about by emergency situations and, finally, the socio-cultural aspirations which by definition cannot be incorporated within a system.[26]

These four proposals summarize several dozen pages of convoluted and sometimes ambiguous text. One of the sources of ambiguity stems from the fact that the private sector referred to in the text is never clearly identified. However, considering both the context and the development accorded specifically to the private profit-making sector in Part II of Volume VII, it seems clear that the passages devoted to the private sector in Volume VI can be interpreted as referring to the private nonprofit sector. Ambiguity also arises from the murky distinction—more showy than useful—between social services designed to meet "special needs" (which would be allowed to exist provided that they did not come under the public sector or resort to public financing), and those intended for more universal needs (which would come under the public sector).

We offer the following interpretation of the Castonguay-Nepveu Commission's position on voluntary private social services. In our view, the commission wanted to recommend that the voluntary private sector be brought under state control. It did not, however, want to legitimize and support the transfer of all private nonprofit services, programs and organizations from the private sector to the public sector, because it considered some components of the private sector to be less relevant than others.[27] The commission therefore armed itself in advance so that the government then in power would not be forced into a position of having to absorb the entire private nonprofit sector. To do so, the commission thought it necessary to assert clearly that the contribution of the private nonprofit sector was legitimate and relevant, while at the same time proposing "essentially the institution of a coherent system of public social services which could be adapted to the most general situations and needs of present society."[28] In this way, without clearly saying so, the commission advocated an indepth reorganization of social services in which the public sector would be the main component, while the voluntary private sector acted "as a complement or extension of the public system."[29]

The reform in social and health services which was set in motion in the 1970s, after passage of the law on health services and social services (Loi sur les services the santé et les services sociaux)[30] in December 1971, although not adhering exactly to the model advocated by the Castonguay-Nepveu Commission, was nonetheless inspired by it, at least in terms of the issues which interest us in this chapter. This legislation constituted the blueprint for a reorganization of health and social services, which called for a bold process of deprivatization and increased state control. It called on five types of institutions to form the main components of the new system, all of which were public; regional councils on health services and social services (CRSSS—Conseils régionaux de services de santé et de services sociaux), health care centres (CH—Centres hospitaliers), centres offering social services (CSS—Centres de services sociaux), reception centres, which included nursing residences and rehabilitative centres (CA—Centres d'accueil), and local centres for community services (CLSC—Centres locaux de services communautaires). Among the five types of institutions, two were new inventions (CRSSS and CLSC), and three were the outgrowth of changes in previous institutions (CH, CSS, and CA). In basing itself on these five types of public institutions, the reform represented a strong move towards increased state involvement. This did not mean, however, that everything would become public. The December 1971 legislation was more moderate than what had been recommended by the Castonguay-Nepveu Report, especially the status of commercial private-sector services. On this matter, the legislation provided for two types of private, profit-making institutions. Specific provision was made within the public system for a type of "private state-subsidized institution" (Art. 1, c. 176, 177, 177.1), which could receive public subsidies; and implicit allowance was made, through licensing provisions (cf. Art. 136-148), for another type of private institution thereafter categorized as "private self-financing." Unlike private state-subsidized institutions, those in the private self-financing category had to be financially self-sufficient, relying on patients' contributions, and could in no way depend on state subsidies. At the same time, these institutions were to give precedence to "light cases" involving a more autonomous clientele, as the "heavy cases" requiring more care implied higher costs than the majority of patients—mostly elderly people—could afford.

Thus the health and social services reform in Quebec which was mainly carried out in the 1970s inevitably brought with it a considerable expansion in the role of the state. In the 1970s, the social service system which had so recently depended to a great extent on the commercial or nonprofit private sector, very quickly became one in which the public sector clearly formed the main component, thus relegating the various private agencies and services to a complementary—indeed, residual—role. In the sphere of homes for the elderly, for instance (to take a sector fiercely coveted by private entrepreneurs in some provinces, such as Ontario), in 1976-1977, public nursing residences had 13,392 beds at their disposal, representing 79.5% of the total facilities.[31] Granted, if the private self-financed nursing home facilities were added to those of the private state-subsidized sector, and if foster homes were included in the commercial private sector, this would raise the figures for bed and residence capacities in the private commercial sector. But even with such calculations, public sector facilities would still be found to exceed those of the private sector.

In summary, moves to open up the state's role in social services continued to be made until the late 1970s and early 1980s. For its entire first term of office following the November 1976 elections, the P.Q. government determinedly pursued the reform which had been launched under the previous Liberal government. With Denis Lazure heading the Ministry of Social Affairs, the P.Q. government imposed a kind of moratorium on the commercial private sector covering nursing residences and rehabilitative centres (CA). On this subject, it is interesting to recall that when the P.Q. came to power in the fall of 1976, a growing sense of foreboding pervaded the private network of rehabilitative centres (for mentally handicapped young people) which were controlled by the ANBAR Institute.[32] Moreover, this concern was not entirely unfounded: in 1977, institutions from the ANBAR network which were operating on Montreal's South Shore and in the St. Jerome region were bought out by the Quebec government, and became public sector institutions.[33]

The advance of state involvement in social services continued at an astonishing pace until the beginning of the 1980s. A few figures showing changes (between 1978-1979 and 1982-1983) in the number of unionizable staff members employed by various institutions under the social affairs sector, are highly significant. Such changes are significant in that the five-year period referred to was marked by sweeping budget cuts in Quebec (as in most parts of Canada), in which public social services were especially hard hit.

Still, in Quebec, the effects of budget restraints were experienced later in the social services than in the health services. In the hospitals, budget restraints and job cutbacks began in the 1977-1978 fiscal year. In social service institutions, it was not until the 1979-1980 fiscal year (or even the 1981-1982 year marked by drastic cutbacks), that brutal restraints were introduced. During the five year period in question, from 1978 to 1982, the size of unionizable staff:

a) dropped by 6,516 (6.5%), in public health care centres on the whole (i.e., hospitals offering extended care, short-term care, and psychiatric care);[34]

b) dropped by 204 (6.8%), in private state-subsidized health care centres;[35]

c) rose by 2,374 (105.5%), in the local centres for community service centres (CLSC's);[36]

d) dropped by 199 (4.5%), in social service centres (CSS);[37]

e) rose by 1,409 (6.5%), in public nursing residences and rehabilitation centres (CA);[38]

f) dropped by 1,026 (33.9%), in private state-subsidized nursing residences and rehabilitation centres (CA).[39]

These statistics call attention to a significant phenomenon: even at the beginning of the 1980s, public nursing residences and rehabilitative centres (CA) were still growing in relation to their private counterparts. This observation is confirmed by other figures on the number of public and private state-subsidized CA's in the same period. In fact, the number of public and private nursing residences and rehabilitative centres rose by 10.4% in that period, from 413 to 456 institutions. By comparing developments in the public sector with those in the private sector, we observe that the number of public CA's rose by 21%, from 319 to 386, whereas the number of private state-subsidized CA's dropped by 25.5%, from 94 to 70.[40]

Thus, throughout the 1970s and early 1980s, the commercial private social service sector was held in poor esteem, and found itself on the defensive. A vigilant and mistrustful attitude toward the commercial private sector was shown by the Quebec Ministry of Social Affairs, especially during the period in which it was headed by Denis Lazure. Institutions from this sector were tolerated rather than supported. The owners of nursing homes and private rehabilitation centres (CA's) seem to have been traumatized by these years, and events from this period have left rather painful memories. At the time, they felt threatened and were under the impression that development of the public sector was a direct move against them. This is what comes through in rereading the history of the 1970s found in some of the briefs to the Rochon Commission, presented in the spring of 1986 by employer associations from private commercial institutions such as ACHAP (the association of private hospitals and CA's) and ACAPA (the association of private self-financed CA's). The latter, in its brief, maintains the belief that private commercial establishments were simply boycotted during the 1970s.[41]

On the other hand, private nonprofit organizations, although undergoing a period of relative disgrace, still remained numerically important at that time. The more traditional network of self-help groups and community agencies, which had been carried over from the previous decades, went through an unspectacular and little esteemed period in their history but did not disappear. Moreover, a host of new volunteer groups and community organizations, which had sprung up with the citizens' committees of the 1960s, continued to develop around issues pertaining to the rights of elderly people, welfare recipients, the unemployed, minimum wage earners, and tenants. These organizations, often called popular groups, form part of a progressive "sphere of influence." Unlike their more traditional competitors, these groups often had to squabble with the state in order to obtain and conserve a funding base, however tenuous, and a bit of room for manoeuver.

Nonetheless, although private voluntary organizations were both numerous and active in the area of social services throughout the 1970s, they had trouble gaining recognition and surviving financially, in a historical context in which the network of public organizations received most of the limelight. It is important to recall that during the years of growing state involvement in social services, charitable organizations like the Fédération des oeuvres charité canadienne-française (which became Centraide-Montreal in 1974), went through an identity crisis and had problems raising funds from the general public to finance private-sector voluntary groups.[42]

Government Declarations on Privatization

Theoretically, government declarations and actions are two distinct components of government policy, and this calls attention to the frequent appearance of contradictions between the two. But for contemporary Quebec, a rather significant convergence between rhetoric and practice deserves note. It is interesting to try to retrace the evolution of government policies, paying particular attention to official declarations and practices in turn.

The Quebec government's use of the concept of privatization is a relatively recent phenomenon. This does not mean, however, that declarations pertaining to the privatization of social services have only surfaced since 1985 or 1986. On the contrary, a more precise analytical framework which is attuned to both commercial and voluntary types of privatization allows us to pick up indications of pro-privatization arguments in government circles as early as 1979 or thereabouts. We assert, in short, that government statements and actions pertaining to the privatization of social services in Quebec have developed in two successive waves.

The pronouncements which accompanied and legitimized the first wave of privatization began to appear in 1979, towards the end of the P.Q.'s first term of office. Such declarations began to take on more sophistication and daring in 1981, during the P.Q.'s second term, in a context marked by intensified budget restraints and new awareness of the limitations of the welfare state. This approach, which we would term "communitarist," never refers explicitly to the concept of privatization. It prefers to fall back on more positive concepts which would have individuals, their surrounding friends and families, and local communities "taking charge" of their own problems. Against the limits of the welfare state—the weight of bureaucracy, the confines of paternalism and its ensuing dependence—it proposes boundless possibilities of aid and solidarity rooted in natural and primary support systems. The state's limited capacity for paying thus calls on society to bank more boldly on the contributions of "natural helpers" and volunteer organizations of all kinds. This approach also maintains a highly critical view of professionals, particularly singling out unionized professionals in pubic agencies delivering social services. While portraying such professionals as self-interested and self-serving, it celebrates the more generous and selfless intentions of nonprofessionals or semi-professionals working in volunteer and community organizations on the outskirts of the government sector. As an aside, it is worth noting that this approach embodies the most excessive elements of the critique of state control found in the 1971 reform, and uses the reform to legitimize and carry out a reduction in state involvement.

We first find this type of communitarist rhetoric in the late 1970s, in official documents of the Ministry of Social Affairs which deal with government policy on home care services for persons with restricted autonomy, such as elderly people or those with handicaps.[43] In the documents pertaining to elderly people, particularly from 1979 on, various issues are at stake: a strategy for providing nursing homes is seen as having limitations, and conversely, a strategy for maintaining such people in their own homes is seen as having advantages. This would of course imply noninstitutionalization or deinstitutionalization. On the other hand, public home care services are perceived as having limitations: " . . . one can only be impressed by the vast quantity of human and material resources which the state would have to devote to home services if we were to depend on the state solution alone."[44] As a logical consequence, less should be required of the state and public services, as the state approach is too costly; and there should be more direct individual participation ("finding one's own solutions") and "involvement by the family and the community, voluntary (or volunteer) acts by its members, self-help and other forms of activities which combine resources from the community."[45] Taking its argument even further, the Ministry of Social Affairs adopts a more formal stance in favour of community types of privatization: it asserts that the state should provide material support for volunteer organizations offering home care services. In other words, the very state which, in the late 1970s, was putting the brakes on a policy of nursing residences and rehabilitative centres and was instead emphasizing home care services (while being very careful not to commit itself to public responsibility for such services), was now in favour of having these services taken on by the private nonprofit sector: "In order to help groups representing the elderly and handicapped, the state must ensure the security and survival of volunteer organizations, rather than looking to replace them."[46]

This new communitarist line was refined over the years, and during the P.Q.'s second term of office from 1981 to 1985, was handled skillfully by the Ministry of Social Affairs. We find a good illustration of this in an official MAS document from April 1981, in which the ministry formally announced the completion of the CLSC network,[47] presenting CLSC's as a vehicle "to help the population take its problems in hand and solve them."[48] This line permeates the arguments put forward by ministry spokespersons in 1982, 1983, and 1984, in preparing and implementing the transfer of "front-line" resources from the community health departments (DSC) and social service centres (CSS) in turn, to the local centres for community services (CLSC).[49] In light of this reasoning, CLSC's may paradoxically be seen as public institutions which have the capacity to act as a lever for privatization of the voluntary kind. This is no doubt one of the factors explaining the ease and readiness with which organizations such as the Quebec Federation of CLSC's adopted (and elaborated on) this line of argument.[50] This may also help us understand the popularity of the British *Barclay Report* (and of a few local efforts) among those heading the Ministry of Social Affairs and the Quebec Federation of CLSC's, during the same years.[51]

The communitarist line was even more strikingly pervasive in a series of official documents published by the Ministry of Social Affairs in 1985. We are referring in particular to texts tracing department intervention and policies on issues pertaining to mental health, old age, and violence against women.[52]

Following the elections in December 1985, the P.Q. continued to polish up this line of argument from the opposition bench.[53] The Liberal Party, however, from the time it came to power, proved itself to be more ambivalent and less confident in its capacity to adopt the communitarist line as its own. For example, communitarist arguments were singularly absent from the three reports of the "sages" (headed by Messieurs Scowen, Gobeil and Fortier) published early in the summer of 1986.

Nonetheless, the new Liberal government seems more comfortable with the privatization line favouring the commercial sector. It is here that the second wave we mentioned earlier makes its appearance. To be sure, as we indicated in our introduction, government declarations since 1985 have contained more ample references to the privatization of Crown corporations than to that of state-run services. But it is our hypothesis that the line promoting privatization in its most global sense winds up fostering an ideological penchant for privatization with regards to public services in general, and to social services in particular. It can hardly be thought that the line of argument on privatization of social services is on its way to becoming the official government line. Nevertheless, it still remains an argument which stems from the thought and writings of a few influential ministers (such as Paul Gobeil) and a handful of well-known business personalities of liberal persuasion (such as Claude Castonguay).

We will be content here to point out that, in the *Gobeil Report* published in July 1986, the section on social and health services was fraught with a strong bias in favour of commercial types of privatization.[54] This report recommended, among other things, "the possibility of conferring complete hospital management onto outside firms," "the privatization of small or medium-sized health centres," and "more vigorous application of the policy of contracting-out to private firms for the management of support services." Up until that point, the recommendations referred more specifically to the hospital sector. But such recommendations are of no less importance for the social service sector. Moreover, when it came time for the report to refer more explicitly to social services, no attempt was made to disguise sympathy for the profit-making private sector: the report emphasizes the legitimacy of the 60 private nursing homes and rehabilitation centres then in operation (out of a total of 236), and specifies that "this mix of private and public should be maintained in any future development of services."[55] In the same vein, the Gobeil Report, in noting competition between urban CLSC's and private general clinics, proposes that the conflict be managed by simply eliminating the urban CLSC's, thus giving the commercial private sector precedence over the public sector.[56] As for the regional health and social service councils (CRSSS), the same report, after reiterating a few of the criticisms aimed at the councils, hastens to recommend their total elimination.[57] And, finally, the specter of commercial privatization also haunts the Occupational Health and Safety Board (CSST) insofar as the Gobeil Report advocates a reform which would allow insured employers to apply to private insurance companies rather than to the public insurance company which comes under the board itself.[58]

During the same period, similar arguments in favour of commercialized social services are also found among business personalities associated with the Quebec Liberal Party, such as Claude Castonguay, president of the Laurentian Insurance Company. In April 1985, in a two-article series published in *Le Devoir*, Mr. Castonguay proposed the idea of reinstating the principle of contracting-out within the hospital sector, and spoke highly of the possibilities offered by private nursing homes and rehabilitation centres:

> Development of the necessary resources and equipment might be improved by allowing and encouraging the private sector to set up and administer certain types of institutions.

> [. . .]
> It has been clearly demonstrated in the United States and in other provinces in Canada that the private sector could very well develop more than sufficient resources to meet a good portion of the need for nursing homes and rehabilitative centres for elderly people and the chronically ill. To achieve this objective, it would require only that the legislation and existing regulations be revised and that certain fiscal incentives be introduced to promote the development of the necessary resources.[59]

It is rather astonishing to hear these statements coming from a man who, fifteen years earlier, had been associated with Part II, Volume VII, of the report of the Castonguay-Nepveu Commission, with its harsh and devastating critique of the commercial private sector in the sphere of health and social welfare.[60] How times have changed between 1970 and 1985! The commercial private sector (which only yesterday had been on the defensive), now seems to be enjoying a more favourable image and is back in style once more, after fifteen years' disgrace.

Privatization Practices

It now remains to be seen whether privatization practices involving social services have followed the government line over the past few years. At this stage in our research, the ensuing text will necessarily take on a rather exploratory and superficial tone. We can now suggest a certain number of hypotheses which subsequent research will enable us to verify.[61] We will examine what is taking place in the private nonprofit sector, before turning to its commercial counterpart.

Voluntary-type Privatization[62]
It is our hypothesis that from the end of the 1970s onwards, the Ministry of Social Affairs, while working on a new line of argument, also endeavoured to develop new practices under a strategy of voluntary privatization. This new policy found specific expression in a certain number of consistent moves undertaken every year since that time in the areas of home care, services for battered women, and youth services. In this period marked by severe budget restraints (and implicitly, state withdrawal from delivery of services), the Quebec state seems to have taken care in developing and implementing a policy of material support for certain volunteer and community organizations, particularly those responsible for nongovernmental

social services involving elderly and handicapped people, women, and young people.

Since the late 1970s, the Quebec government has equipped itself with a global policy on home care which contains a more specific policy of support for volunteer organizations providing home care services. In an interview conducted in February 1979, one year after entering office, Deputy Minister Jean-Claude Deschênes was forthright in acknowledging that the state should support volunteer organizations "which are in need of some financial support," specifying that "the state will no longer be able to assume all the roles played by these organizations," and that there was room for "collaboration." He then referred to pressure being put on the Treasury Board (by those in charge of the Ministry of Social Affairs) to convince it to release new support funds, despite the context of restraints, for certain nongovernmental agencies in the nonprofit sector:

> We are still in the process of making strong present actions on behalf of volunteer organizations. We are aware that many groups may merit the department's assistance, and receive partial aid from the institutions. We would like to define our policy more clearly with regard to such organizations, and intensify our efforts in trying to convince the bodies concerned.[63]

A new program of support for volunteer organizations offering home care services was indeed set up during this period by the Ministry of Social Affairs. By the 1979-1980 fiscal year, it was already providing financial support for a number of "meals on wheels" services for elderly people, but the funds thus authorized were minute, representing from about $100,000 to $150,000 per year. However, starting in 1979-80, the prescribed budget, along with the number of volunteer organizations receiving support, began to increase significantly from year to year: in 1979-80, there were 216 organizations which received assistance, with a total budget of $1.5 million; in 1980-81, 325 organizations, with a total budget of $2.3 million; in 1981-82, 381 organizations, with a total budget of $3.3 million; in 1982-83, 410 organizations, with a total budget of $3.7 million; in 1983-84, 458 organizations, with a total budget of $4.0 million; in 1984-85, 480 organizations, with a total budget of $4.5 million.[64] It might be observed, as an aside, that from 1980-81 to 1981-82—the year in which budget restraints for social services were the most severe—the Social Affairs' budget for assisting volunteer home care service organizations saw a 43.5% increase. These are new indications of voluntary privatization.

As of 1978-79, the Ministry of Social Affairs began to define a policy of support concerning shelters for battered women and other categories of women in difficulty. In 1978-79, the Ministry of Social Affairs set aside $250,000 in credits to subsidize two shelters; in 1979-80, it granted $645,000 for 11 homes; in 1980-81, $1,310,000 for 18 homes; in 1981-82, $1,370,000 for 21 homes; and in 1983-84, it granted subsidies to assist close to fifty homes for battered women.[65]

The Ministry of Social Affairs similarly got involved in financing youth centres ("Maisons de jeunes"), in the second half of the 1970s. Starting off rather slowly, between 1976-77 and 1979-80, the ministry granted subsidies to only two youth centres. But beginning in 1979-80, it began to intervene more boldly, subsidizing 10 or so of these centres. In 1980-81, 15 youth centres were subsidized, with a total budget of $593,000; in 1981-82, 18 centres, with a total budget of $654,000; and in 1983-84, 41 youth centres were subsidized.[66]

In the P.Q.'s final two years in power (i.e., during the 1984-85 and 1985-86 fiscal years), the subsidies granted to volunteer and community agencies by the Ministry of Social Affairs continued to increase significantly, so much so that in 1985-86, a budget of $25 million was earmarked for this sector. The four branches thus receiving support were: a) community organizations offering home care services (approximately $5 million); community organizations offering services to women in difficulty (more than $5 million); community youth organizations (more than $5 million); and other types of community organizations (more than $5 million). The various subsidies provided by Social Affairs and the Health and Social Services (MAS/MSSS) affected no less than 1,000 private nonprofit organizations in 1985-86.[67]

Since the Liberals' return to power, some ambivalence in government intentions may be detected on the matter of support for volunteer and community organizations. This ambivalence is a source of concern for the organizations in question, in terms of long-term perspectives; not knowing what to expect in the future, the climate of uncertainty leads them to fear the worst. For the short term, however, the Liberal government has made the commitment to maintain the former year's level of budget support, granting $25.7 million in credits.[68] Still, given the previous government's pattern of authorizing substantial increases in budgets over the preceding years, the 1986-87 budget freeze is experienced and interpreted as a setback by the agencies which depend on Quebec government assistance.[69]

Commercial Types of Privatization

Our hypothesis here is that Quebec is currently experiencing an intensification of commercial types of privatization practices in social services. This intensification is not occurring at a breakneck speed, nor is it surrounded by a lot of fanfare. It is a current phenomenon nonetheless, one which represents something new in the circumstances forming the 1986 juncture. Commercial types of social services, after undergoing a fifteen-year period of relative stagnation or outright decline, seem to be making a comeback in the past few years. Moreover, they would appear to enjoy a more positive image in certain circles. Some high-ranking civil servants in the Ministry of Health and Social Services (MSSS) and certain management directors of public services seem less reluctant than before to speak out in favour of commercialization. They let it be known, for instance, that private commercial social services have their rightful place, and call for the development of such services with more consistent support from the state. Both the Ministry of Health and Social Services and the regional councils (CRSSS) are being flooded with requests and proposals from individuals and organizations interested in going into business in the field of social services.

The framework of the present text does not allow us to systematically demonstrate, with data relevant for the whole of Quebec, the hypothesis that an upsurge of commercialization in social services is currently underway. We can nonetheless look at a few examples and indications which point our thoughts in this direction, while awaiting the necessary means to conduct a more exhaustive study in subsequent research.

1) At the strictly governmental level, it is important to recall the highly significant commitment to billing for services, made by Finance Minister Gérald D. Levesque in the spring of 1986, during a speech on the budget. After a reminder that "billing is an undertapped source of revenue in Quebec" in terms of services delivered directly by the government or indirectly via public institutions, the Finance minister announced that he intended "to increase billing for government-provided services by $75,000,000" in the 1986-87 fiscal year, without any details as to the types of services for which billing would be introduced or increased.[70] In its implementation, such a measure might well involve social services. If so, we would be dealing with a concrete practice of commercial privatization in the broad sense of the term, as billing for services involves both state withdrawal from financing, and increased responsibility taken on by private users of the services in question.

2) Commercialization seems to be advancing rapidly in the social service area of nursing homes and rehabilitation centres for elderly and

handicapped people, and may well continue at an even greater pace in the next few years. The factors contributing to this development are fairly straightforward. If we look at the elderly community, for instance, we see the same phenomenon of an aging population in Quebec as we do elsewhere: in 1981, there were 569,380 people in the age bracket of 65 years and over, representing 8.8% of the population; in the year 2001, there will be 872,600 people in this age bracket, representing 12% of the population.[71] At the same time, we see that the era of building new nursing homes for the elderly has come and gone, relegated to the past since the early 1980s; little growth can be expected in a context of fiscal restraint and crisis, with deinstitutionalization as its watchword. But requests for admittance into nursing homes and rehabilitation centres have continued to mount as the population gets older. By the end of the 1970s, there was already a list of 10,000 elderly people waiting to be admitted into nursing homes, and the problem has not gone away. As a result, the regional councils (CRSSS), centres for social services (CSS), and local centres for community services (CLSC) do not know which way to turn to meet the growing demands. Since facilities in public nursing homes are inadequate, these public institutions make referrals, in one form or another, to private institutions: private state-subsidized nursing homes, self-financing residences, and even boarding houses or "clandestine residences" which abound in the large urban centres.[72] It is in this context that the private self-financed nursing homes and private unlicensed residences exert pressure on the network of public establishments, and on the government, to gain greater state recognition and support. This is also the setting in which we find the Champlain Group actively devoting itself to opening up new private nursing homes, enjoying the sympathy and collaboration of some public-sector managers. In the area of mental health, with pressure for deinstitutionalization in psychiatric units and rehabilitation centres for intellectually handicapped young people, and with the shortage of alternative community resources to accommodate people who were formerly in institutions, we find another factor impelling public institutions to make referrals to unlicensed private commercial institutions, and to otherwise avail themselves of such resources.

3) Home care services for elderly or handicapped people constitutes another important area of social services in which commercial private involvement has escalated. Here once again, we encounter a move toward privatization which is easy to explain. As we saw in an earlier section, at the level of government discourse, the policy of home care has become a very important one in Quebec since the end of the 1970s. In terms of concrete policies and specific programs, however, the actual practices do not

match the rhetoric. Granted, budgets targeted by the Ministry of Health and Social Services for home care programs have increased significantly in the past ten years, rising from $25 million in 1976-77 to $53 million in 1980-81, and to $100 million in 1986-87.[73] In principle, this money (which is distributed by the Ministry of Social Affairs and the Ministry of Health and Social Services, via the regional councils on health services and social services), is mainly to be used to finance public services provided by CLSC's in the home, and to support volunteer home services. But as these budgets prove to be clearly insufficient in the face of overwhelming demands, the regional councils and CLSC's, especially in the Montreal area, have learned in recent years to transfer a significant portion of the requests and budgets to the commercial private sector.[74] Thus, the CRSSS and CLSC's increasingly favour the purchase of home services delivered by traditional private agencies, or by service cooperatives such as Auxi Plus in Montreal. In other words, public budgets are utilised in such a way as to have the commercial private sector provide services which are more costly when given by workers in the public sector. Consequently, we find no less than four categories of family auxiliaries providing home care services in Quebec today: family auxiliaries in the public sector, paid at about $10.00/hour; those working for cooperatives, earning about $6.00/hour; those working for private agencies, earning about $4.30/hour; and finally, those who work on a volunteer basis for various organizations. Moreover, we seem to be presently witnessing an increase in the volume of home services provided in one form or another by the commercial private sector.

4) Since budget restraints were imposed on public social services in the 1970s and 1980s, there would appear to be a rise in commercial private practice involving the services of psychotherapists of all kinds, and social workers in particular. In 1984, the Professional Corporation of Social Workers in Quebec counted 190 social workers engaged in private practice, and re-established a specific task force on the question.[75]

5) Commercial types of privatization in public social services do not only involve the delivery of direct professional services to users; it may also involve auxiliary services and administrative services. In the latter case, there is a great deal of activity now underway. It is becoming a habit for a growing number of public institutions to contract for paid services of consultants or consulting firms. This practice has been developing over the last ten years in the Montreal Metropolitan Council on Social Services (CSSMM), for instance, and contracts for more than $500,000 were undertaken with consulting firms or private consultants in the 1984-85 and 1985-86 fiscal years. [76] This is the context framing the recent appearance

of a firm of private consultants in which we find former management directors of public services specializing in administrative services for public institutions (services which include the provision of trustees, strategic planning, expertise in grievance management, etc.).[77]

Conclusion

We set out in this chapter to do some initial spadework, in rather descriptive terms, on what is presently occurring in Quebec in the area of both voluntary and commercial privatization of social services. This is indeed the ground we have covered, taking care to introduce an approach in which the historical parameters hold a position of strategic importance. Such historical points of reference are, in our view, indispensable in examining contemporary developments in arguments and practices concerning the privatization of social services.

By taking into account the historical legacy of our distant and more recent past, thus gaining a better understanding of the predominantly private organization of social services which prevailed before the 1970s, and the predominantly public organization of such services which held sway throughout the 1970s, we were able to identify a double wave of privatization coursing through the 1980s. The first wave, dating from 1979, involved voluntary types of privatization. This was followed by a second wave, which began to appear in 1985 in particular, involving commercial forms of privatization. We began to fill out the two types of privatization, and found, through examples and indications rather than systematic demonstration, that the two co-exist under the present circumstances. Our effort thus has consisted of clearing a path to be followed up with more systematic and exhaustive studies and research. We hope to be able to pursue this research with others in the near future.

As for a critical assessment of what is presently taking place in Quebec, we prefer, for this time being, to reserve judgement until we have had a chance to pursue our study further and make a careful assessment on the basis of more solid research data.

But despite our desire for caution in evaluating the current situation, we have one comment in particular which begs to be made. Considering the historical legacy of relationships worked out between the public and private sector, under the system of social services which prevailed until 1970 in Quebec, it is very tempting to be sympathetic and receptive in our approach to certain forms of voluntary privatization, while feeling rather uneasy and reluctant about the current rise of various forms of commercial privatization. We'll no doubt come back to this![78]

Acknowledgement

This paper was translated from my original French version by Jody Freeman.

Notes

1. Gouvernement du Québec, Decree no. 2653-85 (Québec: Gouvernement du Québec, December 13, 1985) quoted in Ministre délégué à la privatisation, *Privatisation de sociétés d'etat: Orientations et perspectives* (Québec: Gouvernement du Québec, Ministère des finances, February 1986), p.13. [Quotations from French publications not available in English have been translated specifically for this paper.]
2. In addition to the above-mentioned text of February 1986 by the minister for Privatization, the following document, identified as one of the three reports of the "sages" published early in the summer of 1986, also deserves mention: Comité gouvernemental sur la privatisation des sociétés d'etat, *Rapport du comité sur la privatisation des sociétés d'etat: De la Révolution tranquille . . . à l'an deux mille* (Québec: Gouvernement du Québec, Ministère des Finances, Ministre délégué à la privatisation, June 1986).
3. In the "Fortier Report" on privatization, published in July 1986 (see note 2), it was announced that about ten crown corporations would be privatized in the eighteen months which followed. By autumn, half a dozen of these privatization operations had been completed, not counting the one involving the sale of the Manoir Richelieu to Raymond Malenfant. The latter gave rise to a very important union battle which, throughout 1986, continued to highlight the social issues involved in certain privatization operations.
4. Granted, there have been a few research projects on the privatization of health services undertaken in Quebec in the last few years. For example, some work has been done by researchers from the University of Montreal's health administration department: André-Pierre Contandriopoulos and Anne Lemay, *L'evolution de la structure des coûts du système de santé et des services sociaux au Québec* (Montréal: La Fédération des CLSC du Québec, Etude et analyse, April 1986), pp. 147-57; André-Pierre Contandriopoulos and Geneviève Tessier, "Un système privatisé, une solution?", in *Artère* (Montréal: Chronique du département d'administration de la santé, U. de M., March 1986), pp. 14-15. But on the question of privatization of social services, we are not aware of any current or completed research activities. It appears that Quebec

research on this question is in a less advanced state than that of Ontario and British Columbia, where researchers can ground their investigations in a fair number of studies carried out over the last few years.

5. *The Castonguay-Nepveu Report*, Vol. VI: *Social Services*, Tome II, English edition (Quebec: Gouvernement du Quebec, 1972), pp. 100-144.
6. The Castonguay-Nepveu Report specifies that in 1970, "the financing of private social services was assumed on an average of 87.6 per cent by the Quebec State." Ibid., Vol. VI, Tome I (English edition), p. 166. We might add a further detail on the public funding of social services: by the end of the 1960s, part of the budget which the provincial government spent on social services was nonetheless financed straight out of funds which were indirectly supplied by the federal government, through fiscal agreements (transferring four tax points on the income of private individuals) reached between Quebec and Ottawa regarding the Canada Assistance Plan. See ibid., Vol. VI, Tome II, pp. 293-94.
7. Ibid., Vol. VI, Tome I, pp. 44-47.
8. See ibid., Vol. VI, Tome I, p. 65. For a more in-depth analysis, see Donald McGraw, *Le développement des groupes populaires à Montréal (1963-1973)* (Montréal: Editions Saint-Martin, 1978); Jean-Pierre Collin and Jacques Godbout, *Les organismes populaires en milieu urbain* (Montréal: INRS-Urbanisation, 1975).
9. *The Castonguay-Nepveu Report*, Vol. VII, Tome II: *For-Profit Institutions* (Québec, Gouvernement du Québec, 1970), pp. 27-29.
10. Ibid., pp. 33-34.
11. We present a more in-depth analysis of the Quebec public assistance plan in Chapter 5 of *L'evolution des politiques sociales au Québec 1940-1960* (Montréal: Les Presse de l'Université de Montréal, 1988). See also *Santé Société: La santé et l'assistance publique au Québec 1886-1986* (Québec: Gouvernement du Québec, Ministère de la santé et des services sociaux, 1986), p. 55 onwards.
12. *The Castonguay-Nepveu Report*, Vol. VII, Tome II, pp. 28-31.
13. Ibid., pp. 33-34.
14. Ibid.
15. Ibid., Vol. VI, Tome I, p. 82.
16. *Rapport du Comité d'étude sur l'assistance publique* (also called the *Boucher Report*) (Québec: Gouvernement du Québec, 1963). In particular, see Chapter IV on "the role of the State," pp. 107-27, and Chapter VI on "collaboration between the public and private welfare sectors," pp. 153-65. For the *Boucher Report*'s contribution in historical terms, see the first of our series of articles on "L'Etat et le social au Québec" in *Le Devoir*, August 2, 1986.
17. On this subject, see *Santé Société*, ibid., p. 102.
18. Claude Castonguay left the chairmanship of the commission of inquiry on March 12, 1970. He became an elected Liberal deputy on April 29, 1970, and was appointed minister of Health, Family Affairs and Social Welfare on May 12, 1970. See *The Castonguay-Nepveu Report*, Vol. VI, Tome II, p. 5. This information leads us to believe that at the time Mr. Castonguay joined the ministry in 1970, he was aware of the contents of Vol. VII, Tome II, concerning commercial institutions, but not of what was to become Volume VI.

Moreover, legislation involving reforms in both social services and health services was beginning to be passed as early as December 1971, even before publication of the two parts of Volume VI on social services. This shows the extent to which the issue of social services was subordinated to that of health services at the time.
19. *The Castonguay-Nepveu Report*, Vol. VII, Tome II, pp. 43-44. We might further specify that the Commission's harsh assessment of commercial services in the private sector closely follows the critique developed by Jean-Marie Martin in Appendix 17 of the Report: *Pour une politique de la vieillesse* (Québec: Gouvernement du Québec, 1970), pp. 71-72.
20. *The Castonguay-Nepveu Report*, Vol. VII, Tome II, pp. 44-46.
21. Ibid., pp. 46-47.
22. Ibid., p. 47.
23. Ibid., Vol. IV, Tome I, pp. 109, 116; Vol. VI, Tome II, pp. 118-21 and 139-44.
24. Ibid., Vol. VI, Tome I, p. 167.
25. See, for example, ibid., pp. 116, 166 and Vol. VI, Tome II, pp. 122 and 293.
26. Ibid., Vol. VI, Tome I, pp. 217 and 238.
27. The following excerpt from the Report on this subject is revealing: "[. . .] the organization of a system of public social services involves a fundamental re-examination of private social services agencies. Certain of those we know must be integrated within the public sector. Others, certainly, must disappear because they have become unworkable in present society." Ibid., Vol. VI, Tome I, p. 237.
28. Ibid., Vol. VI, Tome II, p. 388.
29. Ibid.
30. *Loi sur les services de santé et les services sociaux*, in *Statuts du Québec*, Québec, 1971, Chapter 48. This act was later amended on several occasions. Quotes are taken and translated for this paper from an updated French edition published on September 1, 1984, by l'Editeur officiel du Québec.
31. Direction générale des programmes de services sociaux du Ministère des affaires sociales, *Etude et recommandations concernant le développement des C.A. privés autofinancés et des pavillons* (Québec: Gouvernement du Québec, August 1979), p. 16. This source does not give precise figures on the number of beds available in private self-financed nursing homes and rehabilitation centres.
32. Unprofessional practices encountered in institutions belonging to the ANBAR network had often made headlines in the preceding years. We believe that *The Castonguay-Nepveu Report* is referring to the ANBAR network when it mentions a private commercial enterprise with eight establishments and 1,156 beds at its disposal, representing 38.7% of the facilities for "mentally handicapped persons who can be supervised, trained and educated, and 44.4% of the beds in commercial establishments for the same categories." Vol. VII, Tome II, p. 36.
33. Author's conversation with Mr. Denis Lazure, August 12, 1986.
34. Ministère des affaires sociales du gouvernement du Québec, *Le système de santé et de services sociaux au Québec, Annexe Statistique* (Québec: Direction des communications, 1985), pp. 20-21.
35. Ibid.
36. Ibid., p. 24.

37. Ibid.
38. Ibid., p. 25.
39. Ibid.
40. Ibid., p. 29.
41. ACAPA, *Mémoire à la Commission Rochon*, March 1986.
42. See the round-table discussion on volunteer work, and the ideas expressed by Michel Giroux in particular, in *Carrefour des affaires sociales*, Vol. 2, No. 3 (Québec: Ministère des affaires sociales, May 1980), pp. 20-32; and, for a rereading of public/private relations, see the brief presented by Centraide-Montreal to the Rochon Commission in March 1986, pp. 6-14.
43. Ministère des affaires sociales (MAS), *Les services à domicile: Politique du ministère des affaires sociales* (Québec: MAS, November 1979), 30 pp.
44. Ibid., p. 13. See also p. 24.
45. Ibid.
46. Ibid., p. 14.
47. MAS, *Le réseau des CLSC au Québec: un parachèvement qui s'impose, Politique du ministère des affaires sociales* (Québec: MAS, April 1981), 26 pp.
48. Ibid., p. 1. In this document, CLSC's (centres for local community services) are distinguished from other institutions in the government network in that their responsibilities are defined not only in terms of persons, "but also in terms of families, groups, and communities at the same time." Ibid., p. 4.
49. See, for instance, MAS, *Le partage des responsabilités CSS-CLSC en matière de services sociaux* (Québec: MAS, June 1984), 59 pp. The first edition of this important document was published in December 1983.
50. See, for example, la Fédération des CLSC du Québec (FCLSCQ), *Les mutations de l'etat-providence et le devenir des CLSC* (Montréal: FCLSCQ, May 1983), 60 pp. See also Carole Lalonde, *Les CLSC face aux enjeux des années '90* (Montréal: FCLSCQ, 1986), pp. 25-26 and 34.
51. Peter M. Barclay, *Social Workers, Their Role & Tasks* (London: Bedbord Square Press, 1982), 283 pp. This report made the rounds very quickly in some circles in Quebec. For example, by autumn, 1983, Mr. Hector Ouellet of the Federation of CLSC's had already published an article on the subject, entitled "Filet de secours ou support communautaire" in *Le Devoir*, October 22, 1983, p. 15. This also explains why, in the same context, the following work by Jérôme Guay was so popular with the MAS and the FCLSCQ: *L'intervenant professionel face à l'aide naturelle* (Chicoutimi: Gaëtan Morin éditeur, 1984), 237 pp.
52. MAS, *Pour une réflexion sur la santé mentale, La santé mentale à nous de décider, Proposition d'un plan d'action* (Québec: MAS, 1985), 142 pp.; *Une politique d'aide aux femmes violentées* (Québec: MAS, 1985), 59 pp.; *Un nouvel âge à partager, Politique du ministère des affaires sociales à l'égard des personnes âgées* (Québec: MAS, 1985), 61 pp.
53. See, for example: La Commission nationale du programme du Parti Québécois, *L'Etat et la social-démocratie, Document de réflexion* (Montréal: photocopied text, 1986), 53 pp. This document asserts (p. 20) that "having seen the limitations and negative effects of institutional assistance, we should now be experiencing a renewal of individual or community initiative. There are numerous examples in Quebec which point in this direction." See also pp. 28-33.

54. Groupe de travail sur la révision des fonctions et des organisations gouvernementales (the committee chaired by Paul Gobeil, president of the Treasury Board), *Rapports* (Québec: July, 1986), pp. 31-35. See our article on the Gobeil Report in *Le Devoir*, August 4, 1986.
55. *Rapport Gobeil*, p. 34.
56. Ibid.
57. Ibid., p. 35.
58. Ibid., p. 39.
59. Claude Castonguay, "L'universalité des programmes sociaux," in *Le Devoir*, April 22 & 23, 1985.
60. The ideological course traced by Mr. Claude Castonguay over the last fifteen years is not unlike that of Mr. Brooke Claxton, the first person to hold the title of minister of National Health and Welfare in Ottawa. Claxton was known throughout the 1940s as an ardent social reformer within the federal Liberal Party and the Cabinet of Mackenzie King, and at the end of World War II, defended the need for public health insurance. But by the middle of the 1950s, he had quietened down and was defending much more conservative positions on social policy. It should also be added that he too has in the meantime left active politics to head an important private insurance company, Metropolitan Life. On the career of Brooke Claxton, consult the index in Reginald Whitaker, *The Government Party: Organizing and Financing the Liberal Party of Canada 1930-58* (Toronto: University of Toronto Press, 1977).
61. The present text was prepared on the basis of data collected in exploratory research undertaken in the spring and early summer of 1986, with the help of a research grant from the dean's office of advanced studies at UQAM. Towards the end of that summer, thanks to a separate research grant from the Rochon Commission, we were able to undertake a more in-depth study of the current process of privatization in the area of social services in Quebec. Readers can thus expect subsequent work which should enable us to verify and back up the hypotheses presented here.
62. Our arguments here are based on data collected by Edith Ouellet, who worked with me as research assistant in May and June of 1986.
63. "Un an après son arrivée, le sous-ministre Deschênes rompt le silence . . ." Statements gathered by Michel Pilon in *Carrefour des affaires sociales*, Vol. I, No. 2 (Québec: MAS, February 1979), p. 19.
64. *Rapports annuels du ministère des affaires sociales*, Québec, for the years 1975-76 to 1983-84; and MAS, *Un nouvel âge à partager*, pp. 23-24.
65. *Rapports annuels du MAS*, from 1978-79 to 1983-84; and MAS, *Le système de santé et de services sociaux au Québec* (Québec: MAS, 1985), p. 36.
66. Ibid.
67. *Les organismes communautaires: Réflexion sur les enjeux actuels et à venir.* Brief by staff members of the ministerial branch responsible for support to community organizations, Ministry of Health and Social Services (MSSS) presented before the Rochon Commission ("la Commission d'enquête sur les services de santé et les services sociaux"), Québec, October 3, 1986, p. 17.
68. Gouvernement du Québec, *Budget 1986-1987, Renseignements supplémentaires, Crédits* (Québec: Conseil du trésor, March 25, 1986), p. 56.

69. Community organizations subsidized by the MSSS in Quebec City frequently depend on federal grants as well, from Health and Welfare, Secretary for Youth, and Employment and Immigration. But as a result of cutbacks in several of these federal grants in 1985-86, the overall funds which community organizations receive in subsidies from both Ottawa and Quebec City are diminishing, while demands for their services in many cases continue to rise. This explains the especially precarious financial situation faced by community groups since 1985-1986.
70. Gouvernement du Québec, Ministère des finances, *Budget 1986-1987, Discours sur le budget et renseignements supplémentaires* (Québec: Gouvernement du Québec, May 1, 1986), pp. 17-18.
71. MAS, *Un nouvel âge à partager*, p. 8.
72. Several organizations called attention to the growth of unlicensed nursing homes for the elderly, in briefs presented before the Rochon Commission. See, for instance: l'Association des CSS du Québec, *Les services sociaux au Québec: problèmes spécifiques et pistes de solution* (Montréal: ACSS, June 1986), pp. 70-71, 128-31 and 206; CSN, *La santé pour tous: un choix de société* (Montréal: CSN, March 12, 1986), pp. 45-47; Fédération des CLSC du Québec, *Quelques pistes de solution aux problèmes du système de services de santé et de services sociaux au Québec-Document de réflexion* (Montréal: FCLSCQ, April 1986), pp. 64-66.
73. "On ne peut plus tout se permettre parce que c'est l'état qui paie," interview with Thérèse Lavoie-Roux in the journal *RND*, no. 68 (Sillery: September 1986), pp. 22-23.
74. In 1985, the MAS itself clearly acknowledged the inadequacy of public resources (both financial and human) set aside for home care services. See *Un nouvel âge à partager*, pp. 27-29.
75. See Diane Walker, "Private Practice in Quebec," in *Intervention*, no. 68 (May 1984), pp. 89-102. See also Frank McGilly, "Markets for Private Practice in Social Work", in ibid., pp. 107-11.
76. This information was passed on to us by Mr. Jean-Pierre Chicoine, then acting director of the Montreal Metropolitan Council on Social Services (CSSMM), in response to a question we raised at a public assembly organized by the CSSMM in Montreal, May 29, 1986.
77. The firm in question was founded by Mr. Jean-Pierre Chicoine, former executive director of the Ste. Justine Hospital. Mr. Chicoine recruited Mr. Aucoin, a former trustee of the Louis H. Lafontaine Hospital. Two conversations in particular helped us grasp the issues involved in the development of private firms and private consultations: one with Madame Hélène Caron Gaulin (a social worker from the CSSMM and once member of its Board of Administration), on May 9, 1986; and the other with Mr. Denis Lazure, on August 12, 1986.
78. See Yves Vaillancourt, Denis Bourque, Françoise David, et Edith Ouellet, *La privatisation des services sociaux*, research report presented to the Rochon Commission, Département de travail social de l'UQAM, Montréal, September 1987, 398 pp. This research report has been published at the same time as the Commission's report, in early 1988, by "Les Publications du Québec."

8 New Brunswick

ROBERT MULLALY

NÉRÉ ST-AMAND

> Poverty is caused by centralizing policies and practices which have put profit above all else and which concentrate wealth and employment in specific regions and in the hands of specific groups. [. . .] if there were any profits to be made in the areas of social services and social assistance, Eaton's and Simpson's would have been involved therein a long time ago.
> A senior civil servant, New Brunswick Department of Social Services, 1980

A Historical Perspective

To properly appreciate the present situation in New Brunswick, it is essential to have at least some understanding of the system of distribution of goods and services in the province of New Brunswick since its foundation. This has had enormous repercussions not only on the policy orientation of social services but also on the situation today.

Over two hundred years ago, in 1786, the system of Elizabethan poor laws was formally extended to the province of New Brunswick. It should be recalled that under these laws, each municipality or county had the responsibility to support its poor and indigent population with respect to social assistance, education, child welfare and institutional services. This resulted in unequal development of "social" resources based on the ability of the various regions to organize these services and provide support to indigents. As a result, the more economically thriving counties and municipalities (in particular in the south, which was largely inhabited by the English-speaking) were able to afford a better system of care and services. In addition, the number of persons using the system was limited since the economic situation was brighter. In fact, the process of industrialization helped some towns to attain a high level of economic and social growth.

The predominantly Acadian counties of the north, northeast and southeast of the province were not able to develop a comparable system as a result of a series of historical and political disparities—families were larger, the economy underdeveloped and these counties had practically no political leverage. This situation went back to the deportation of the Acadians, and to the control of the province by Loyalist groups. By the time of Confederation, these historico-political factors were contributing to a very different pattern of evolution.

To illustrate these differences, one may look at the rate of illiteracy in the various counties of the province. Table 8-1 shows that the rate of illiteracy is much higher in those counties in which the percentage of Francophones is higher (Gloucester, Kent and Victoria in particular). We also see that the lower the proportion of Francophones, the higher the level of education.

This situation of increasing and cumulative inequalities lasted until 1960, when the Liberal Party took power with Louis Robichaud, an Acadian, as its leader. It was hoped that the situation would change. Premier Louis J. Robichaud's promises of reform created a lot of hope among the disadvantaged that equality would be achieved at last. By the same token, the industrial sector led by the Irving empire rose against this new provincial policy.

The first significant action taken was the appointment in 1963 of the Royal Commission on Finance and Municipal Taxation (commonly known as the Bryne Commission). The task of the commission was to undertake a complete study of the impact of the problem and make appropriate recommendations. The lengthy report of the commission denounced the flagrant inequalities which helped to perpetuate and accentuate socio-economic disparities within the province. For example, while English-speaking families had relatively few children, Acadian and French-speaking families had more children (about twice the number of children in English-speaking families), but provincial grants from the Department of Education were

Table 8-1 Rate of Illiteracy and Education in the Various Counties of New Brunswick and in the Four "Canadian" Provinces, 1871*

County and Province	French-speaking %**	Rate of illiteracy %***	Rate of education %****
Albert	0.7	16	40
Carleton	2	8	42
Charlotte	0.8	9	48
Gloucester	67	53	19
Kent	56	49	23
Kings	1	10	31
Northumberland	6	21	41
Queens	0.9	8	40
Restigouche	19	17	23
St. John	0.6	14	46
City of St. John	0.6	13	51
Sunbury	2	17	35
Victoria*****	61	53	18
Westmorland	31	30	34
York	2	11	35
New Brunswick	15	21	36
Nova Scotia	NA	25	57
Quebec	NA	45	41
Ontario	NA	13	61
The four provinces	NA	26	52

SOURCE: Jean-Claude Vernex, *Les francophones du Nouveau-Brunswick*, thesis, Université de Lyon II, November 1975, page 116.

* *Department of Agriculture:* "Canada Census 1871," Vol. 7, table 3; Vol. 2, table 10.
** In comparison with the total population in each county or province.
*** In comparison with the total population in each county or province.
**** In comparison with the total population in each county or province between 5 and 20 years old.
***** At the time of Confederation, Victoria County comprised Madawaska County as well.

Table 8–2   Expenditures per pupil per county, 1960

County	Expenditure per pupil (1960)	Percentage of French-speaking
Albert	$176	1.2
Carleton	196	1.2
Charlotte	191	3.1
Gloucester	136	85.2
Kent	132	81.6
Kings	216	0.8
Madawaska	191	94.2
Northumberland	146	26.7
Queens	223	4.8
Restigouche	141	61.0
St. John	279	6.7
Sunbury	331	10.5
Victoria	224	37.5
Westmorland	191	40.5
York	225	2.8
Mean	200	

SOURCE: Report of the Royal Commission on Finance and Municipal Taxation in New Brunswick, Fredericton, 1963, p. 131.

based on the number of family units rather than the number of pupils. As such, poorer counties received less in grants if the number of pupils is taken into account, as shown by Table 8-2.

It should be pointed out that at that time, 83% of teachers with local permits (i.e., unqualified teachers) in the province were in four French-speaking counties (Kent, Gloucester, Restigouche, Madawaska), where the number of pupils totaled 12,000.

With respect to social services, the inequalities were as pronounced. While the annual family income in Saint John County was $3,604, it fell to $1,853 in Kent County which was predominantly French-speaking. The average monthly rate of financial assistance was $25 per person in Chatham, but in nearby Gloucester County, it fell to $6 per person.

The Bryne Report recommended the adoption of an equitable system of taxation and redistribution of goods and services. In 1967, Premier Robichaud launched a program known as the Equal Opportunity Program (EOP). Counties and municipalities lost their financial autonomy in favour of a uniform system of assessment for the whole province. As a result, the organization and delivery of the following services were centralized: Education, Health, Social Services, Justice and Youth Services. Implementation of the EOP was made possible by the Canada Assistance Plan signed between Ottawa and New Brunswick in 1966.

Since the federal government had undertaken to refund 50% of all expenses in the health-social services areas, the provincial government was able to implement comprehensive and universal programs and services.

Growth of the Bureaucracy

Since then, New Brunswick has witnessed a rapid increase in the role of the state in social service areas and in many related departments. For example, the social services budget (Department of Social Services at the time) went from $10.5 million in 1966 to $275,711,000 in 1984-85.[1] For its part, the number of provincial civil servants also reflects this new state control of social services. Numerous institutions were created especially in the fields of health and education. This reform has been compared to the one which took place in the province of Quebec during the same period and it should be pointed out as well that several of the architects of that reform came from Saskatchewan and Manitoba; provinces run at that time by New Democratic governments.

In terms of concrete results, this program cannot be deemed to have succeeded. The Robichaud government was in power for ten years but only had three years to implement the EOP; indeed, in 1970, the population rejected the Liberals in favour of a Conservative government which, however, generally maintained the policy until well into the 1980s.

A Need for Reform

In the early 1980s, the western economy went into a general decline; the ballooning of the budget, manpower and state responsibilities began to bear heavily on the provincial treasury. In the area of social services, entire sectors, such as social development, were abolished; reform was spoken about more and more, particularly deinstitutionalization, volunteerism and privatization. To concretize this new direction, Conservative Premier Richard Hatfield set up the Office of Government Reform in 1980 with the mandate to recommend alternatives to the state's involvement in social matters.

Consequently, one of the first decisions of the government, under its new mandate, was to establish a comprehensive review of all provincial economic and social programs, both as to their objectives and whether they were being delivered in the most efficient manner possible. An Office of Government Reform, under the direction of two senior ministers, was created with the mandate to assess whether programs were meeting the needs for which they were established, and to recommend organizational changes required to improve their effectiveness. A major benefit of this approach is that it called for full ministerial involvement and leadership.[2]

It should be pointed out that according to Mr. Hatfield, this reform was "the most comprehensive and revolutionary in recent Canadian political history."[3]

In justifying the creation of this commission, officials went out of their way to present the negative and highly critical aspects of the bureaucratic machine and the delivery of services in previous years. Here is just a sampling of the comments found in speeches made by leaders at the time:

"This reform will eliminate service duplication and overlap."

"To facilitate easier access to government programs" (Richard Hatfield).

"Improve productivity and effectiveness."

"Government is exhausting itself."

"Simplify government."

"Minimum state intervention."

"Revitalization of our network of services" (Brenda Robertson*).

"The government is losing touch with its people."

Furthermore, it must be acknowledged that the reduction of disparities promised throughout the 1960s and 1970s has not been totally achieved; others have actually been created by the state itself:

Of all civil servants earning less than $5000 per year in 1974 in New Brunswick, 90% were women; of all civil servants earning $20,000 or more per year, 4% were women. Furthermore, in each category of employment, the average salary for women was less than that for men.[4]

---

* Ms. Robertson was one of the senior members of OGR and has since been appointed to the Senate.

Whether it be from a geographic or ethnic point of view or on the basis of the relationship between the sexes, the Equal Opportunity Program did not fulfill its promise of abolishing structural disparities, as was suggested by the Liberal government in the 1960s.[5]

Commencement of Privatization in New Brunswick

In the fall of 1982, the provincial Progressive Conservative Party under the leadership of Premier Hatfield was re-elected to office in one of the largest landslide victories in New Brunswick's political history. A prominent plank in the Conservative Party platform during the election campaign was to "make every effort to maintain existing levels of essential services" and to advance "a carefully selected range of programs to improve the quality of life in New Brunswick."[6]

Soon after the election, the Conservative government began to privatize[7] the social welfare system in New Brunswick which had taken nearly 200 years to develop. Nineteen eighty-three represents the logical starting point for examining the privatization of social services in New Brunswick because it was then that the provincial government brought down its restraint budget, and established the Office of Government Reform. These two events set the stage for the policy and practices of privatization that are to date in existence in New Brunswick.

The government, in its first budget after its landslide victory at the polls, reneged on its election promises to maintain existing services and to advance a carefully selected range of new services.[8] Cutbacks were made in the areas of health, education and social services which, in effect, placed a greater load on the nongovernmental sector than it had already been carrying.

In its terms of reference, the Office of Government Reform was given the following reform objectives: efficiency, equity, public involvement, coordination, effectiveness, *privatization* [emphasis added], volunteerism, economy and accessibility. These objectives are of course consistent with retrenchment and, although the Office of Government Reform (OGR) held consultations with many organizations, groups and individuals in New Brunswick, it was the belief of many that the consultations were actually exercises in tokenism and subterfuge because it had already decided that it would embark upon a policy for delivering social services based on privatization. Evidence to support this claim lies in the fact that many of the recommended reforms which were contained in OGR's final report had already been implemented in a systematic manner throughout the consultation and study process. It appears that the reform process was used partially as a smokescreen to deflect attention away from changes which were already occurring.[9]

Although there had been some privatization occurring before the May 1983 budget (largely in the area of community-based services for senior citizens such as homemakers, meals-on-wheels and friendly visitors), it was the 1983 budget that initiated the process of privatization in New Brunswick, and it was the Office of Government Reform which formalized privatization as a goal of government.

New Brunswick's Definition and Model of Privatization

The government of New Brunswick does not have a formal policy on privatization of social services, but it has indicated in its Office of Government Reform documents that privatization is one of its reform goals. It does not specify a particular concept or definition of privatization.

The ministry which is most affected by the government's privatization thrust is the Department of Health and Community Services. Because of the freeze on the growth of the public sector in terms of manpower and programs, the department has had to turn to the private sector. Although there is no money to hire new people in the public sector and very little money for program development, there are considerable monies for purchase of service contracts. And while there has been some growth in the public sector, the purchase of services contracts has grown exponentially. For example, one program manager of community based services for senior citizens in a particular municipality said that five years ago he was dealing with two purchases of service contracts and today he has twenty-six, most of which came about in the past three years.

Thus, out of necessity the Department of Health and Community Services has attempted to meet New Brunswick's social service needs by turning to the private sector over the past five years. Today there are a substantial number of grant programs and purchase of service contracts with voluntary and other nongovernmental organizations. This growth in privatization has occurred in an ad hoc and fragmented fashion with no overall plan, framework or guidelines. The extent and the form of privatization vary from region to region.

It has only been in 1986 that the deputy minister, who recently assumed responsibility for social services under her Health Ministry, identified the need to bring some kind of order to the whole area of privatized services.

(The department's 1986/87 Work Program on privatization will be discussed later in this chapter.) Although there are no official definitions of privatization held by the department, the senior administration tends to equate privatization with purchase of service contracts. Support to nongovernmental organizations (NGO's) is viewed by them as a collaborative relationship with the community through the boards of directors of NGO's.

The senior administration of the Department of Health and Community Services does not use the term privatization because in its view, it is a term which is "overused, abused and misused" and it is too "emotive."[10] The term adopted by the department is "alternate services" which, in the department's 1986-87 Work Program, means contracted services.

The department is unequivocal in its denial that it is dismantling the social welfare sector in New Brunswick and from the investigations of the authors, this denial is justified. Rather, the department insists that it is seeking a mixed system where the government and the community (meaning the private sector) are full partners in the delivery of social services. By interchanging the terms "community" and "private," the department is hoping that this version of privatization will receive more widespread approval than the dismantling mode of British Columbia. The senior administrators insisted that no programs have been taken away from government and given to the nongovernmental sector as yet. But by withdrawing in certain areas, such as services to children with special needs, space has opened up for nongovernmental activity of both the for-profit and the nonprofit variety. And, according to Mishra, this is a characteristic of the retrenchment mode of privatization.[11]

Rationale for Privatization

Three major reasons have been presented at both the political and the administrative levels for the increased privatization of social services in New Brunswick:
1) concern with the public perception that government is too large and too costly;
2) government is inherently inefficient; and
3) local communities should be more involved with the delivery of social services.

1) *Government is too large and too costly.* As with all provincial governments, New Brunswick has been preoccupied in recent years with its deficit

and like most other provincial governments, one of the ways it has attempted to reduce the deficit is to cut government spending. There is a public perception in New Brunswick that government is too large and too costly. It is constantly reinforced by the province's English-language daily newspapers which are owned by the Irving empire (along with major radio and television stations). Everyone in the public sector who was interviewed for this chapter on privatization in New Brunswick stated that the major reason for the government's restraint policy was the public perception of a large and costly government.

As part of the government's restraint package contained in the May 1983 budget, cuts were made in a few social services, growth of old programs and development of new ones were forestalled, a hiring freeze was imposed and public sector wage increases were frozen. However, these restraint measures are largely illusionary in that the cost of social services has not been reduced. Everyone interviewed for this chapter reported that privatization, to date, has been more expensive than public delivery of services.[12] And, although the freeze on new public sector positions still exists, program managers have found ingenious ways of circumventing this policy by using the private sector.

2) *Government is inherently inefficient.* Efficiency was a term used repeatedly in the Office of Government Reform documents as a goal of government services. And, when inquiring about the rationale for privatization of social services in New Brunswick, a few senior officials alluded to efficiency as being one of the reasons. However, when asked what the basis was for this claim, these officials had no hard evidence but once again talked about public perceptions. In other words, it seems that the provincial government of New Brunswick is responding to the perception, as one official put it, "of government operating like it has a bottomless pit of money." Rather than trying to confirm or refute this claim of government inefficiency, the government apparently subscribes to it, or it wants to appear to the public that it is taking corrective action on this unsubstantiated inefficiency.

3) *Community involvement in the delivery of services.* The Progressive Conservative government contends that one of its goals for privatization is to involve the communities once again in the delivery of social services. One of the drawbacks of the Equal Opportunity Program of 1967, implemented by the former Liberal government, was that through its centralization policies it excluded local community involvement in the delivery of social services: prior to 1967, social services were delivered on a local basis with minimal provincial involvement.

The Equal Opportunity Program centralized control of all social services to the capital city, Fredericton, thus making the many community agency boards of directors superfluous; this, in turn, caused considerable resentment toward the government and its public delivery of social services.

The present Conservative government is now presenting the idea of privatization as a means of redressing the exclusionary program of the previous Liberal government. However, since the Conservatives have been in office for seventeen years and have done little during this time to involve the community in the delivery of social services, it seems that community involvement is really an afterthought rather than a driving force for privatization.

In sum, the present government has presented three major reasons for its privatization of social services: concern about a large and costly bureaucracy; public sector inefficiency; and the desire for community involvement. On the surface there appears to be both economic and ideological motivations underpinning the government's policy of privatization. However, the economic argument breaks down under closer scrutiny. No one in government would allege that the privatization activities to date were costing the government less money. There does appear to be an ideological belief that somehow the private sector will be more efficient. The main motivating factor, however, appears to be political pragmatism. That is, it does not matter if something is more expensive, more efficient or not. What matters is public perception. If the public perceives privatization or retrenchment as a good thing, then the politically expedient policy is one which is in accordance with this public perception. In fact, the provincial Conservative government has mastered a trial balloon methodology of gauging public opinion to such an extent that much of the province's social policy is now being based as much on trial balloons as on human need.[13] It is this attribute of political pragmatism that most political observers in New Brunswick believe accounts for Premier Richard Hatfield's perennial success at the polls.

Mechanisms of Privatization

The major mechanisms used by the provincial government over the past few years which have encouraged privatization are:
1) freezes on staff hirings and new programs;
2) development of volunteer programs and recruitment of church groups to replace growth in social services;

3) grant programs to nongovernmental organizations to provide complementary and/or supplementary social services; and
4) contracting with the nongovernmental (both profit and nonprofit) sector to provide social services.

1) *Freezes on staff hirings and new programs.* Because the government has imposed a freeze on the growth of the civil service and on new public sector programs, area administrators have been forced to turn to nongovernmental organizations to purchase services. In other words, while there has been no money to establish new programs or to extend old programs within the public sector, there has been money available to administrators to purchase services. Also, an interesting practice has developed within the Department of Health and Community Services which shows how far the government will actually go in wanting to prove to the public that it is serious about not expanding the size of the bureaucracy. Although there is a freeze on public sector hirings, area administrators within the Department of Health and Community Services have been able to obtain additional staff by giving money to a private agency to hire a social worker who will actually work for the area administrator. In other words, the area administrator will give a private agency sufficient money to pay the salary of a social worker, plus give the agency a three percent administration fee for carrying the social worker as an agency employee, although the agency may never see this person. On paper, the social worker is not included as a public sector employee because s/he is technically an employee of a private agency, and the government can report that the size of the bureaucracy has not increased, though there may be dozens of additional social workers hired through private agencies but financed by and working for the provincial government.

2) *Development of volunteer programs and recruitment of church groups to supplement basic social assistance.* The provincial government has been actively involved in recruiting the volunteer sector over the past few years. It established in 1983, within the Department of Health and Community Services, a "Community Volunteer Action" program which, according to the 1984-85 Departmental Annual Report,

> assists voluntary organizations and self-help client groups interested in providing clients and the working poor with a low-cost service network which supplements basic social assistance.[14]

In its first year of operation (1983-84), it assisted 17 groups and the next year, it assisted 26 groups.

Through this program, assistance from the government is given to local volunteer groups to start or expand projects such as food banks, soup kitchens, used clothing exchanges and furniture repair depots. In other words, local voluntary groups are being encouraged to assist poor people in meeting their basic survival needs which, of course, means that there is no guarantee that these basic needs will be satisfied.

3) *Grant programs to nongovernmental organizations to provide complementary and/or supplemental social services.* The Department of Health and Community Services has an "External Agency Support" program which provides assistance to "provincial and community agencies delivering services supplementary and complementary to the mandate of the Department." Whereas the Community Voluntary Action program mentioned above supplements basic financial assistance, the External Agency Support program supplements the personal social services delivered by the provincial government.

4) *Contracting with the nongovernmental sector to provide social services.* By far, the biggest growth in the area of privatization has occurred in the purchase of service contracts. The provincial government's "no growth" policy has increased the number of contracts. As well, the closure in 1985 of the only provincial residential hospital school for children with special needs (William F. Roberts Hospital School) contributed to the growth in the number of purchases of service contracts, as it was left to the nongovernmental sector to respond to the needs of these children.

Effects of Privatization on the Social Services Sector

Since New Brunswick only embarked upon privatization four years ago, the ultimate effects are not yet evident. However, it is informative to look at the short term effects which privatization has had on the government sector, on the nongovernmental sector and on the relationship between the two sectors.

1) *Effects on public sector.* Within the public sector there was a realignment of ministries in late 1985, whereby the previous Department of Social Services was split into two parts, with the income maintenance section joining with the Department of Student Aid, and the social services section joining the Department of Health to form the Department of Health and Community Services. This change came about because of a recommendation by the Office of Government Reform. With respect to social services, the rationale for putting health and social services together is that health services

in New Brunswick are relatively privatized (for example, all nursing homes are privately owned and all hospitals are managed by boards of directors), and the provincial government wishes to use the privatized health services as a model for social services.

Since there has been no plan or formal policy with respect to privatization of social services in New Brunswick, each regional manager has purchased services on an ad hoc basis according to the needs or demands of his or her particular region. Consequently, no one in government has a complete picture of what presently exists, which is why the deputy minister has recently ordered that an inventory be carried out of all purchased services in the province. The Department of Health and Community Services has included, for the first time in its annual Work Program, a section on privatization or what the department terms "alternate services." The following goals which were taken from the 1986-87 Work Program[15] are revealing in terms of showing how the department is just beginning to attempt to make sense of the product of a process that has been going on for three years:

GOAL #1: To develop objective criteria to determine which programs/services may be contracted out to the private sector.

GOAL #2: To complete a review of all programs/services or components of programs or services that shall be or *may* be contracted out privately.

GOAL #3: To develop criteria for approval of service provider agencies.

GOAL #4: To prepare a written contractual model that describes the contractual models that are available for service delivery.

In addition to having a chaotic system owing to the absence of policies or guidelines, there is a concern on the part of field personnel that for many contracted-out services there are no service standards, and for services which have standards there is very little monitoring being carried out. As well, there is no one evaluating many of the programs carried out by private agencies and no one checking the qualifications of private agency employees.

A concern with privatization in New Brunswick that has not been addressed by the provincial government, but which is beginning to manifest itself, is that of a two-tiered social services system. That is, in urban areas where there exists a population base from which to draw boards of directors, privatized services are being developed. However, in rural areas this development does not exist. In time, it appears that the rural areas will have an inferior social services system to that of urban areas. Furthermore, predominantly francophone areas do not have the same system of services enjoyed by anglophone communities. Indeed, it must be pointed out that private services in francophone areas were primarily organized by religious communities, whereas the English population was able to count on a secular system. With the decrease in church influence, especially the Catholic church, during the 1960s, the francophone communities were caught off guard; only the government had taken the responsibility for delivering social and community services. Also, it seems reasonable to assume that various communities will eventually compete with each other for government dollars to develop services in their respective loyalties and that with this pluralistic system, other criteria than need (such as political power) may determine which community will be successful in obtaining government assistance.

2) *Effects on private (for-profit and nonprofit) sector.* A concern expressed by private nonprofit agencies is that the provincial government is expecting more from them in terms of fiscal responsibility and accounting standards. However, the province has done nothing to assist or strengthen these agencies which are usually managed by a voluntary board of directors. It has been reported by both public sector workers and private nonprofit agency personnel that there has been little monitoring of services to date, but excessive audits have occurred. One public sector manager observed that in his region, because many small private nonprofit agencies do not have the resources to carry out the elaborate accounting systems forced on them, that the Department of Health and Community Services is turning more to the private for-profit sector which does have the fiscal management resources.

Some services which were originally assigned to private nonprofit agencies are now being sought after by private for-profit agencies. For example, Red Cross was originally given the contract by the Department of Social Services for homemakers services. This contract led to an incredible expansion of Red Cross involvement in New Brunswick and it reached a point where the agency was able to negotiate that 30 percent of its overhead was to be covered by the province, in addition to paying for the homemakers and other purchased services. Recently, an American based private for-profit franchised corporation, Upjohn, made a sales pitch to take over homemakers services at a lesser cost than Red Cross. Qualifications of the homemakers or personnel practices of Upjohn were not included in the sales pitch. So, it seems that a trend may be emerging in New Brunswick whereby services are initially assigned by the province to the private nonprofit sector, but that the private for-profit companies move in subsequently.

One other area in the private sector that has grown exponentially is the use of private contracted professionals. With the staff freezes, the field offices of the Department of Health and Community Services have had to contract with private professionals for services that previously were provided by the public sector. Most of these contracts have been made with psychologists for diagnostic testing and with various counsellors for counselling and psychotherapy. To date, there have been very few social workers who have contracted their services to the government. The concerns expressed by departmental managers are that the rates charged by these private contractors appear exorbitant, and that there is no accountability of work because it is carried out under the banner of professional expertise and autonomy. Social services managers claim that these contracts are much more costly than when the public sector provided the same services.

3) *Effects on voluntary sector.* Immediately after the May 1983 provincial budget which initiated privatization in New Brunswick, the Department of Social Services made several attempts to involve the voluntary sector in the provision of social services for low-income persons. In June 1983, the department initiated the Community Voluntary Action Program to assist voluntary organizations in providing goods and services to supplement basic social assistance. However, after a series of meetings between the minister of Social Services and the voluntary sector, the voluntary organizations unanimously opposed the cutbacks that had come out of the 1983 budget and stated that they were already doing all they possibly could for the poor under difficult circumstances. They also stated that they did not possess the administrative set-up, the expertise or the financial resources to do any more.[16] Many voluntary organizations remain resentful today for being in the position of supplementing inadequate social assistance benefits, as they feel it is a return to a system based on charity. It should be noted, however, that there are a few exceptions which have praised the government for placing more emphasis on the voluntary sector (e.g., The Salvation Army).

To show how far the Department of Social Services was willing to go with its attempts to enlist volunteers, it is worth noting that accompanying the February 1984 welfare cheques was a letter from the minister of Social Services exhorting the recipient to volunteer "in assisting the department." Although it did not say in the letter what they would volunteer for, it did state that "Each and every one of us has a responsibility to help ourselves and volunteerism is a good way to start." The question for many welfare recipients was that if they did not or could not volunteer, what would happen to their assistance? The coercive nature of this letter was of course in clear violation of the nature and spirit of volunteerism.

To date, although there has been much attention and activity directed toward recruiting volunteers, there is no policy stating which services cannot. Also, the provincial government has not provided much in the way of resources to train volunteers or even to cover out-of-pocket expenses that volunteers often incur. Again, the rationale for volunteerism seems to be to downsize government, as the place of volunteers in the system has not been identified or defined.

4) *Changing relationships between public and private sectors.* At this point, the effects of privatization on the private sector are inconclusive. More people, through the boards of private agencies, are involved with social services—a goal of government. But, at the same time, it appears that government is gaining a stranglehold over the nongovernmental organizations because all contracts between the two sectors contain a clause that states: ". . . The Department [of Health and Community Services] has the final say." An example of the one-sided nature of these agreements or contracts became apparent on October 1, 1985, when the department increased Adult Day Care participation fees to $5 per diem in the middle of a one-year agreement that set the fee at $3. Because the Day Care Centres had budgeted for the $3 fee, most of them incurred a deficit for that fiscal year. Field personnel of the province report that this unilateral action undid the trustful and collaborative relationships they were trying to build with the private agencies.

There is unquestionably a closer working relationship developing between the public and private sectors in New Brunswick, although it appears that this relationship is not an equal one. As might be expected, the sector with money—the government—is tightening its control over the sector with limited resources. One of the logical outcomes of this developing relationship is that as private agencies devote more time working with the public sector, it will diminish the time and attention that private agencies have historically devoted to developing innovative services, such as rape crisis centres and transition houses. In other words, as the private agencies in New Brunswick become more tied into the government sector, it is only reasonable to assume that over time they will adopt more of government's agenda and devote less time to their historical role of advocating for innovative services.

Effects of Privatization on Social Workers

One of the effects of privatizing social services has been the implementation of some questionable labour practices by the provincial government. Much more use is being made of part-time workers than even three years ago, because the province finds they represent a more flexible and cheaper labour force and require less commitment from government. As well, social workers have had their wages frozen and/or suppressed over the past three years, which has caused considerable morale problems. One other questionable practice has been to hire personnel on a six-month contract and not renew the contract after the six months expire. This enables the provincial government to evade paying fringe benefits or making a long-term commitment to the employee. It is now common practice for workers to be employed for six months, laid off for six months (the required time period under the Civil Service Act so that government has no commitment to the worker) and hired again at the end of that period for a further six months. This practice is rationalized by the government as another means of maintaining a flexible work force.

One of the more dramatic effects of privatization on public sector social workers in New Brunswick is that it is changing the nature of social work practice. Traditionally, social workers have been employed by the province principally to deliver services directly to clients. This meant that the nature of social work practice comprised mainly various modes of direct interventions such as crisis intervention, personal counselling and family therapy. Because caseloads are much higher due to hiring freezes, and because many services that public social workers used to carry out are now being contracted out, it has changed the nature of public sector social work from case work to case management. This case management function has been officially adopted as the primary function of social workers in the Department of Health and Community Services. This function assumes that no single social worker at the client interface has sufficient time, resources, expertise, discretion, or information to respond to a case situation. The role of the case manager is to ensure that contracted services get to the client at the right time and in the right amount. Rather than direct intervenors, case managers are diagnosticians, negotiators and facilitators.

Front-line supervisors of social workers have also been affected by privatization. Whereas, prior to 1983, their main responsibility was to supervise social workers carrying out social service functions, most of their time is now being spent in negotiating contracts for services and programs at the field level. Although final approval for these contracts rests with the central office, the actual negotiations have been decentralized to the field level which has added a new role to front-line supervisors.

Effects of Privatization on Service Users

Although privatization of social services has been a policy of government for only five years, a number of negative effects have already been felt by service users. Nowhere are the effects more apparent or more devastating than in the Community Voluntary Action Program which provides goods and services to supplement basic social assistance. Local organizations which receive assistance under the Community Voluntary Action Program are soup kitchens, food depots, clothing banks and emergency shelters. Negative effects respecting these services which have been experienced by consumers are access, availability, quality and stigma.[17]

The soup kitchens and food banks which are located in the larger municipalities serve both the municipality and its surrounding area. Obviously, people who live considerable distances from the soup kitchen or food bank and who are without transportation (which is usually the case) have a major problem of access, and many do not have their basic food requirements supplemented. In addition, the food banks have restricted hours of service. For example, the Fredericton food bank is open from 10 A.M. until 2 P.M. two days a week, which makes it inaccessible for many needy families and individuals who are receiving inadequate levels of basic financial assistance. With respect to the emergency shelter, often it is used as permanent housing for single persons on assistance (who only receive $188 per month) and it is not open during the day. This is especially devastating in the winter months. Increasingly, the burden for provision of food, clothing and emergency shelter is falling upon the community. And, generally, the community is responding kindly and charitably and is doing its best with what little it has. However, the need is too great and it is not uncommon to hear public appeals from soup kitchens and food banks to help them replenish their depleted resources. New Brunswick's experience shows clearly that charity does not guarantee availability of the basic necessities of life for those in need.

With respect to food banks, there are times when the health of service users may be compromised because of the questionable quality of the food. Cans of baby milk with no labels or past their expiry date, fruit so old that there is mould growing on it, and potatoes that turn black when cooked are some of the problems experienced by users of food banks.

No matter how much effort these local organizations spend trying to put the service users at ease, the fact that people have to line up in public for a meal or for a hamper of food or for a place to sleep at night is a public declaration of poverty, dependence and, in the view of many, of failure.

The use of these facilities, in the words of one worker, "is so destructive to the human spirit that I cannot find words to describe [it] . . . ."

The freeze on the growth of the public sector has also had negative effects on service users. With the freeze has come an increase in caseloads of social workers and, although this may be partially offset by purchasing services from the private sector, social workers in the child protection area report that they are spending much less time on each case than before the hiring freeze occurred. As well, the practice of hiring social workers for six-month periods only has led to a large turnover in service users' workers. The quality of service is bound to suffer when a new social worker takes over a caseload every six months. Nowhere is this more apparent than in the province's only residential care facility for children who have run into conflict with the law. Child care personnel work in the dormitories in three shifts over a 24-hour period, which makes it difficult enough for some children to establish meaningful relationships. With the six-month hiring policy in effect, it means that many of the child care workers are gone in six months and new workers hired which, according to officials at the centre, is devastating to some of the children and their treatment process.

Another concern with respect to the effects of privatization on service users is that, to date, most of the private agencies tend to have paraprofessionals on staff rather than professional social workers. Although it is too early in the process yet to assess the effects of this on service users, it is a reasonable fear that they may not receive the same quality of service as they would from a professional.

An example where quality of service is being compromised by privatization is in the area of Adult Day Care. Recently, the government has been paying to private agencies a per diem rate of $5; the private agencies have demonstrated to the Department of Health and Community Services that this fee does not meet expenses. Rather than increasing the fee, the department has suggested to the agencies that they increase the volume of people they are caring for. It is this sort of response which reinforces the worst fears concerning privatization.

Regional Disparities

At the beginning of this chapter, we referred to certain disparities which existed in the province. Briefly, we pointed out that the southern areas of the province, where the majority of the population is English-speaking, experienced a higher level of economic development and expansion than the northeast and northwest areas of New Brunswick. The Equal Opportunity Program created the hope that the situation would be rectified.

However, a few figures allow us to see that the situation remains unchanged, at least in several sectors:
- Whereas 34% of the New Brunswick population is French-speaking, francophones hold only 15% of management positions in the government.[18]
- In the area of specialized care, French hospitals in New Brunswick receive 12.3% of the budget whereas English hospitals receive 87.2%.[19]
- Examination of the population/physician/language ratio leads to the same conclusions: the English-speaking population is served by two and a half times more physicians than the French-speaking population.
- Here briefly are a number of findings made by an extensive study conducted recently on regional disparities in our province.[20]
  — The level of dependence is higher in the north of the province (88%) than in the south (81%); the Canadian average is 71.5%.
  — People in the north are poorer and the level of unemployment was higher, 62% in the north in 1981 (17.8% vs. 11%).
  — The aggregate per capita income in 1980 was 50% higher in the south.
  — The proportion of the population in the south with a university degree is 51% higher than in the north.

Conclusion

After reviewing privatization of social services in New Brunswick, it appears that the role played by the state over the past few years has contributed towards deluding, if not destabilizing, service users and towards putting certain classes of New Brunswickers at a disadvantage. We are convinced that the next few years will be characterized by a preservation, if not an increase, in regional disparities and that certain groups will be particularly hard hit. In particular:
- the disadvantaged in rural areas: redistribution through nongovernmental agencies implies that a service infrastructure exists in all the regions concerned; rural areas often do not have any alternatives in terms of organization of social services. Palliative service agencies are rarely found there; these areas often have little power or political clout which would even allow them to ask government for grants so as to set up alternative resources. In this respect, the northern part of the province will be particularly affected, whereas, in general, the southern part of the province benefits from a better network of services.

- minority groups, and especially single mothers and Acadians: given that these groups have had little influence on the present political system, other more articulate and influential groups will be in a better position to channel their demands. In a period of deregulation of social services, we believe that the situation of the disadvantaged will only deteriorate in the years to come.
- the less-informed persons: with the present policy of privatization, grants will be made first and foremost to those who are better informed and to more influential persons in the political and social arena. The role of lobbying will be paramount; in this respect, the population must be made aware of the services. Certain classes of people will be excluded because they are not aware of social developments, directions and policies in the province.

Furthermore, we believe that the current philosophy of privatization, while maintaining the illusion of the welfare state, will contribute towards destabilizing the system of services on many levels. For example:

- service users: they will be unable to rely on continued contributions from the state and will probably have to depend on private agencies, which themselves are dependent on subsidies which are always granted on a short-term basis.
- volunteer agencies which will have to negotiate their subsidies on an annual basis; this will limit opportunity for short and long-term planning and force them to undertake political lobbying, something they were not necessarily used to beforehand.
- professionals working for the state: not knowing when their service sector will be transferred to a private agency, they become worried and sometimes paralyzed; this leads to a considerable degree of frustration or apathy, or even burn-out.

Moreover, the new direction with respect to services makes them administrators rather than service suppliers, whereas their professional training had prepared them for an interventionist role.

Summary

New Brunswick is one of two provinces which originally adopted the system of Elizabethan poor laws as a means of dealing with the social welfare needs of its people in 1786. This method, which placed the responsibility for meeting social welfare needs with the local municipalities, remained in effect until 1967 when the provincial government assumed responsibility for health, education and welfare programs and services. Since that time, there has been rapid growth of the public social welfare sector in New Brunswick, so that by 1980 the discrepancies between the province and most of the others, with respect to quality of services and level of benefits, was not substantial although New Brunswick still lagged behind.

After approximately 15 years of steady growth of the public social welfare sector, the provincial government has embarked upon a policy of restricting the scope of this sector, leaving the private sector to pick up the slack. The government is quietly and almost passively abdicating its role as the primary provider of social services. It is carrying this out using a variety of restraint mechanisms. The rationale appears to be a combination of conservative ideology and electoral pragmatism.

Although New Brunswick is only in its fifth year of privatization, there are already indications that this policy is having a number of negative unanticipated consequences. Although government provision of services has been curtailed, there appears to be a tightening of its control over the private sector which depends on the state for funding. As well, the nature of public social work practice is changing; the issue of service standards is problematic and many service users who now must rely on privatized services are suffering—especially those in need of basic life-sustaining goods and services.

To date, there has not been a serious attempt to monitor the effects of privatization in New Brunswick. From the investigations carried out for this chapter, it seems that the vagaries of a system based partially on charity, community goodwill and private benevolence have returned to New Brunswick. The great irony is that the province established a public social welfare sector in 1967 to eliminate these vagaries. One can only hope that the provincial government will remove its ideological blinders and engage in some proactive rational social planning before the gains of the past are completely undone.[21]

Acknowledgements

Since there are very few written documents that describe or analyse the New Brunswick social situation, the authors of this chapter had to resort to personal interviews with civil service administrators and practitioners in preparing this text. The authors wish to thank them for their excellent cooperation.

Notes

1. Information from the 1966 and 1984-85 annual reports of the Department of Social Services.
2. Statement by the Honourable Richard B. Hatfield on the Re-structuring of the Government of New Brunswick, October 2, 1985, introducing the statement of the results on reform.
3. *Telegraph Journal*, July 3, 1984, p. 3.
4. Departmental Committee Report on the Role of Women in New Brunswick Society and Economy, presented in April, 1985, by Raymond P. Campbell, p. 46.
5. See, in this regard: Isabelle McKee-Allain and Huguette Clavette, *Portrait socio-économique des femmes du Nouveau-Brunswick*, Tome I (Moncton: 1983); Jean-Bernard Robichaud, *La Santé des francophones*, Tome I (Moncton: Editions d'Acadie, 1985) and Tome II (Moncton: Editions d'Acadie, 1986); Néré St-Amand, *Folie et Oppression* (Moncton: Editions d'Acadie, 1985).
6. "Meeting the Challenge of the 80's," the Platform of the Progressive Conservative Party of New Brunswick for the October 12, 1982 Election (Fredericton: 1982).
7. New Brunswick's form of privatization is what Ramesh Mishra in his chapter on the Ontario experience refers to as retrenchment, which means a policy whereby the mixed economy and the welfare state are not rejected outright (if they were, the policy would dismantle the welfare state). A policy of retrenchment seeks to tilt the balance from the state to the private sector; to restrict the growth of the welfare state rather than abolishing it.
8. See Robert Mullaly, "Social Welfare in New Brunswick Vigilante Style," *Perception* 8, no. 2 (November/December 1984), pp. 23-25 for an elaboration of reneged promises and cutbacks.
9. For an analysis of the whole process carried out by OGR, see Robert Mullaly, "Supply Side Social Policy: Government Reform in New Brunswick," *Perception* 9, no. 5 (May-August 1986), pp. 28-31.
10. In conversation with three senior administrators of the Department of Health and Community Services, May 16, 1986.
11. Ramesh Mishra, "Public Policy and Social Welfare," mimeographed copy, 1986.
12. Peter Faid, in his article "Privatization: eroding the social safety net?" confirms this statement that privatized services are not less costly nor less bureaucratic. The more contracting out, the more consumers pay, in terms of kickbacks, overcharge and poor service, *Perception* 9, no. 2, p. 8.
13. Mullaly, "Supply Side Social Policy."
14. New Brunswick Department of Social Services, "1984-85 Annual Report," p. 16.
15. Department of Health and Community Services, "Work Program, Community Social Services Division, 1986-87" (Fredericton: March 24, 1986).
16. Presentation to the minister of Social Services made at the "Forum on Community Support," held at the University of New Brunswick, June 27-28, 1983 and sponsored by the Department of Social Services.

17. These problems have been documented by public sector social workers in certain areas of the province.
18. Néré St-Amand, *Folie et Oppression* (Moncton: Editions d'Acadie, 1985), p. 75.
19. André Braen, *La Santé au Nouveau-Brunswick* (Moncton: La Société des Acadiens du N.-B., 1981), p. 107.
20. See, in this regard: Jean-Bernard Robichaud, *La santé des francophones*, Tome I, (Moncton: Editions d'Acadie, 1985).
21. Since this chapter was written, a new landslide victory gave the political leadership of the province to Frank McKenna and his Liberal government. From the author's observations, nothing does indicate more liberal social policies; to the contrary, in terms of social programs this Liberal government seems to adopt a very conservative approach.

9 Federal Policies and the Privatization of Provincial Social Services

ANDREW F. JOHNSON

Privatization is a catchword of the 1980s. It is a catchword which has fascinated the current federal government but Conservatives tend to be most reluctant to use the concept of privatization in relation to social welfare functions. Instead, they have subjected welfare service programs to a global policy of "deficit reduction" in word and in deed just as their Liberal predecessors have addressed the same programs with "expenditure restraint." However, "deficit reduction" and "expenditure restraint" are two sides of the same coin which has the same overall effect as privatization. Broad cutbacks in federal welfare expenditure shift financial responsibilities for social services to the provinces; provinces which are sufficiently hard-pressed for funds or unfavorably disposed towards public financial support for social services or both, are, in turn, likely to pass on the financial burden of their programs to the voluntary sector and, ultimately, to individuals themselves.

According to the provinces, this is just what they are being forced to do because Conservative and Liberal governments have encouraged them to privatize social services indirectly via the federal expenditure-budgetary process. However, Conservative and Liberal governments have also reacted strongly to thwart provincial support for privatization in the field of health care. At the same time, they have not acted at all to either promote or prevent privatization with respect to the Canada Assistance Plan which has a major impact on the administration and delivery of provincial social assistance services, notwithstanding its modest costs. In short, the financial policies of Conservative and Liberal governments in regard to the privatization of provincial social services in the 1980s, have been similar insofar as both have been characterized by action, reaction, and inaction.

Thus, the purpose of this chapter is to assess the effects of similar Conservative and Liberal approaches to social spending on the ability of the provinces to administer and deliver publicly-funded social services in the 1980s. The next section analyzes the principles endemic to the Conservative-Liberal approach to the financing of social services. Subsequent sections evaluate its general impact on the phenomena of privatizing social services in the province.

Liberals and Conservatives: Towards a Common Social Services Strategy for the 1980s

Spending power—the ability to grant or to withhold funds to promote particular social objectives—enables the federal government to exercise a general but substantial influence in regard to the administration and delivery of social services in Canada for which the provinces are almost entirely responsible.[1] It is generally understood that spending power has enabled the federal government to spread among the provinces as a whole, social service innovations that have been pioneered by individual provinces; spending power has also enabled the federal government to impose national standards on provincial programs.[2] And federal spending power has, by its very existence, greatly affected the direction of privatization in relation to provincial social services.

Governing parties at the federal level have not presented specific objectives with respect to the privatization of social services, except in regard to health care services. However, the objectives of both parties, as governing parties, are apparent if understood in the context of the general principles underlying their financial approaches to social security as a whole.

The social security objectives of the two major parties have not differed significantly throughout the 1960s and 1970s, according to observers of Canadian political parties.[3] Thus, it should come as no surprise that during the 1980s, Conservatives and Liberals have also displayed similar policies towards the financing of social security and, concomitantly, towards the privatization of provincial social services. Their respective policies are similar inasmuch as they are similarly inconsistent in their approaches to social expenditure and to privatization. The inconsistencies are due to basic ideological distinctions that were involved in the process by which Conservatives and Liberals reached a similar perspective on the financing of social security during the 1980s.

The distinctions are primarily based upon two fundamental but antagonistic perspectives of social and economic life in Canada. Bryden speaks of a "market ethos," the cultural expression of the market economy "whose unifying principle was what Macpherson called 'possessive individualism'."[4] But, Lipset and others allude to a general predisposition towards state interventionism.[5] While the Progressive Conservative Party is widely regarded as the expression of the market ethos, the Liberal Party has been viewed as an embodiment of interventionism. These predispositions rise and fall from time-to-time within the Canadian electorate and party fortunes rise or wane in accordance with their abilities to capture and articulate the dominant mood of the electorate in general policy strategies.[6]

During the latter part of the 1960s, the Canadian economy was growing, if not by leaps and bounds, at least gradually. The prosperity of the majority brought the poverty of the few into sharp relief. A groundswell of interventionism emerged concomitantly with this relative prosperity and was articulated by the Liberals in terms of a "social security strategy." The social security strategy largely consisted of institutional welfare; it was mainly designed to prevent rather than to alleviate poverty, but the bottom line was that the strategy required greater government financial involvement in social security. As is well known, the interventionist-oriented Liberals implemented a pension scheme and universal medicare, announced a Social Security Review by the early 1970s, and, simultaneously, implemented a revamped—and very costly—scheme of unemployment insurance.

The costliness of the revised unemployment insurance program was the primary, but not the only, catalyst to activate an antithetical Conservative response founded on a market ethos. Recession and inflation plagued Canada in the 1970s. Slumpflation was widely attributed to the spendthrift policies of the Liberals since the mid-1960s. A retrenchment of interventionism accompanied by a return to a market ethos, that is, an attitude of restraint towards public activity, was generally held to be the solution to Canada's economic malaise.

The Conservatives aptly captured this public mood through an "economic strategy" which essentially contained two major principles: tax reductions and the removal of obstacles that ostensibly prevent labour from responding to the demands of the market or disincentives to work. The Conservatives' counterproposal relied on business, unobstructed by direct or indirect taxes (such as higher old age pension, medicare, and unemployment insurance premiums), and labour, unimpeded by social security "disincentives," to generate expansion in the economy, to create jobs, to reduce unemployment, and, in the final analysis, to reduce poverty. In short, the Conservative economic strategy demanded reduced government spending especially on social security or as one prominent Conservative MP put the case: "The philosophy of my party is that the government should not move until it is actually and really required. In other words, the individual should be able to help himself."[7]

Hence, towards the end of the 1970s the Liberal government began to sense that a mood, best characterized as a market ethos, had begun to dominate the electorate. In addition, economic strategists, especially those in the ranks of the Progressive Conservatives but also the electorally sensitive within the ranks of the Liberals, were perceived as threatening because they spoke for this mood. The Liberal government had to undercut the appeal of the Conservative and a minority of Liberal economic strategists by partially satisfying their demands, that is, by reducing social security expenditures. However, the Liberal government also had to maintain the support of social security strategists within its own ranks and offset the appeal of the New Democratic Party which, traditionally, was squarely within that camp. What better way to maintain that support than by retaining the basic financial structure of the welfare system albeit with some of the supposed excesses eliminated?

The Conservatives also came to realize that their economic strategy would have to be modified in order to placate dissension within the rank and file and to appeal to the electorate at large. Red Tories, and especially Tories from economically depressed constituencies and regions, had already begun to disassociate themselves from the economic strategy prior to 1979. But it took the hard experience of a brief tenure in office to dramatically demonstrate to Conservatives that electoral support can hardly be sustained by taking away public goods. So when the Tories returned to power they maintained the support of economic strategists by reducing social security expenditure. What better way to assuage the fears of those inclined towards a social security strategy than to provide assurances that the basic system should be held in trust and then, at worst, that the system would remain intact but that certain funds dispersed to those not in need would be redirected to those in need?

Thus, by the beginning of the 1980s Conservatives and Liberals had begun to share a common approach, a "social security cum economic" approach, to the financing of social security. On the basis of this ideological predisposition, basic funding has not been withdrawn from existing programs but funding for social security as a whole has been eroded. However, this rather vague and somewhat contradictory predisposition has not been converted into an articulate and consistent policy towards the privatization of social services.

Nevertheless, as a result of this predisposition, the federal government has acted—perhaps, inadvertently—to promote the privatization of some provincial social service programs by decreasing social spending. It has also reacted via its spending power to prevent privatization initiatives in regard to provincial health care services; and it has left well enough alone in the area of provincial social assistance services. At least that is what is suggested by the behaviour of the two governing parties since the late 1970s.

Action: Reducing Transfers, Equalization, and the Budget

The market ethos that was stamped into the October 1980 budget heralded an inauspicious future for social services in the 1980s. In the budget speech, Liberal Finance Minister Alan MacEachen declared his government's intention to "achieve significant savings in the large element of expenditures in the social affairs envelope which consists of transfers to the provincial governments."[8] His statement triggered a panic in provincial capitals. The provinces were quick to realize that they had more to worry about than the $1.5 billion MacEachen intended to shave from the $18.5 billion in cash and tax transfers for fiscal 1980-81; they were also very much concerned about the forthcoming renegotiations for the Established Programs Financing (EPF) arrangements which were to expire in March 1982. Eventually, provincial health ministers launched a counter attack by means of a joint comminiqué which, in effect, threatened a reduction in the quality of national health care services if the federal government enacted cutbacks.[9]

The Liberal government, however, was undaunted in its first major attempt to pursue a broad social security cum economic approach to social services.[10] After all, federal Liberals did not necessarily view reductions in transfer payments as a threat to social services but as a way of controlling expenditure and as a way of ensuring that transfers would be spent for the purposes that were originally intended.[11] However, for the sake of a quiet life, a parliamentary task force was struck to examine transfers and related fiscal arrangements within the context of the government's expenditure plan as set out in the October 28 budget.

Clearly, the federal government was determined to chop transfers whatever the outcome of the task force deliberations. The prime minister sent a cryptic but ominous letter to provincial premiers before the task force report was tabled in which he remarked that since the October budget "there have been developments at the international, national and provincial levels which inevitably will have an impact on our future course .... Mr. MacEachen will be consulting again in the early fall to discuss in detail what adjustments in policy might be required."[12]

As it turned out, the task force reported before the fall budget was presented. The report concluded that funding for the established programs and the Canada Assistance Plan was adequate but that there had been some erosion since the EPF had been transformed into a block fund in 1977. It was claimed that "there is now, for the most part, no fat left in the system—no fat in post-secondary education, no excess spending in social assistance, little redundancy on social services ... serious cuts in program funding would cut in to muscle and sinew, not fat."[13] Despite the warning, MacEachen promised that he would press on with the cuts announced in the October 1980 budget. And he made good his promise in the November 1981 budget.

In all fairness to MacEachen, he was not asking the provinces to do something that the federal government would not do itself. The budget, in effect, limited federal expenditures just as it restrained provincial spending inasmuch as transfers to the provinces over a five year period were expected "to grow at least as fast as the rest of our (federal) expenditures."[14] However, MacEachen was overly, if not ridiculously, optimistic to expect the provinces to find his proposals desireable because tax changes in the budget were expected to automatically increase provincial revenues. The point is that even by his own accounting, the provinces could only make up to $1.9 billion from the tax changes over a five year period while sustaining $5.7 billion in losses.

There was no agreement between the federal government and the provinces about the magnitude of projected losses. There was, however, substantial agreement among the provinces themselves that the reductions would exert considerable financial pressure on their social services programs. Of course, again they brought the issue before the electorate with a straightforward, albeit somewhat misleading, claim that the financial strain would culminate in a significant deterioration of the health care system.

The 1981 budget resulted in more than just an erosion of health care services in Canada; it exacerbated the deepening recession which was rapidly eroding the economic well-being of Canadians in general. Eventually, the federal government chose to assist in the process of economic recovery or, at least, to alleviate some of the hardships of the recession by pumping funds into job creation. Thus, in the 1982 and 1983 budgets, the Liberals managed to channel funds to labour and manpower projects by way of a fiscal sleight of hand which enabled the government to maintain its twin virtues of restraint and equity: social programs, such as family allowances and old age security, fell victim to the "six and five" program of restraint while increased expenditures on job creation were financed from savings accrued from these new austerity measures. Hence, restraint was maintained by shuffling funds from one program to another within the social sector.

Thus, Liberal budgets were a double indemnity for the provinces and a powerful justification for their growing fascination with the notion of privatizing social services. Liberal budgets reduced transfer payments thereby forcing the provinces to either make up the shortfall from their revenues or to shift social responsibilities to the private sector. Liberal budgets also reduced federal social spending thereby placing additional pressure on provincial services to take up the slack. Moreover, the Conservatives decided to continue the double indemnity tradition, despite their good intentions to re-establish co-operative relations with the provinces.

The first Conservative budgetary statement indicated that the finance minister was greatly concerned about a rising deficit.[15] As a result, major expenditure reductions of $4.2 billion for 1985-86 were announced. However, social programs were to be largely left as they were for the worst news was simply that "the state of our finances will not support the costs of many new initiatives."[16] Transfers were also left as they were so that, despite the widespread vote for "change," the broad outlines of economic and fiscal policy remained pretty much the same as they had been during the Liberal regime.

The 1985 budget, however, did introduce the Conservative changes to social welfare policy.[17] Old age security and family allowances were to be partially de-indexed once again so that benefits could be "targeted to those most in need and funds . . . freed for other social priorities."[18]

Of course, the policy bore a striking resemblance to earlier Liberal budgets in which funds were simply shuffled within the social affairs envelope. However, the Conservatives were ill-prepared for the public ire that was stirred over the "universal-selective" debate and thus withdrew their selective initiatives in respect to old age security payments. Hence, the 1986 and 1987 budgets were designed so that interventionist sentiment would not be provoked a second time. Both budgets have provided the usual mixture of restraint and moderate tax increases but have not fundamentally altered existing social programs.

This is not to say that Conservatives have ceased to promote privatization indirectly through the heavy-handed use of fiscal levers. The universal-selective debate was something of a "red herring" which drew attention away from the Conservatives' determination to continue the Liberal policy of reducing transfer payments to the provinces. In 1985 the Conservative finance minister, Michael Wilson, further limited the growth of transfers in order to generate $2 billion in annual savings by the end of the decade. In his 1986 budget speech, he boasted about the government's success in having reduced these payments.[19] Furthermore, the government, in the context of its fiscal plan, has changed the formula used to determine EPF arrangements so that beginning in fiscal 1986-87 the indexation factor was reduced by two percentage points a year.[20] In April of 1986, federal Conservatives unilaterally tabled legislation to this effect, Bill C-96, and, as a consequence, a recent estimate holds that all provinces stand to lose over $8 billion between 1986-92.[21] Table 9-1 dramatically demonstrates the estimated cumulative effect of this and other recent federal measures to trim transfers to the provinces between 1982 and 1992.

However, the federal government has not entirely abandoned the provinces to their own fiscal devices to maintain social services. There was some consternation among the provinces, especially among the poorer provinces, when the governing Liberals decided to recalculate the equalization formula in 1981. In the end, the federal government followed the recommendations of the Parliamentary Task Force on Federal-Provincial Fiscal Arrangements (the Breau Report) which urged authorities to remove certain inequities from the formula. More importantly, the Liberal government agreed to adhere to the principle advanced by the task force that these direct, unconditional payments to provincial governments should be "designed to be sufficient to guarantee that all provincial governments have the fiscal capacity to ensure comparable levels of public service at comparable levels of taxation."[22] Thus, the Liberal government provided transitional or supplementary equalization payments to provinces whose benefits were to be appreciably reduced by the new formula. The Conservative government has stuck to this principle and, in fact, proudly indicated in its 1986 budget that it had "provided supplementary equalization payments for all six equalization-receiving provinces in 1985-86 and for Manitoba in 1986-87."[23]

Table 9-1 Impact of Cuts in EPF (in millions of dollars)—All Provinces

	Total 1982–87	Total 1987–92	Total 1982–92
Cuts made by previous Liberal government			
Withdrawal of compensation for revenue guarantee (1982–83),	−4,970.7	−7,088.8	−12,059.5
6% and 5% (1983–84 and 1984–85),	−983.6	−1,885.1	−2,868.7
Canada Health Act (1983–84)	−192.9	—	−192.9
Total	−6,147.3	−8,973.8	−15,121.1
Cuts planned by the Conservative government			
Bill C-96 (1986–87)	−317.4	−7,816.4	−8,133.8
Total Cuts			
Compensation for revenue guarantee, 6% and 5%, Canada Health Act, Bill C-96	−6,464.6	−16,790.2	−23,254.9

- Indications to the contrary, it is assumed that all provinces will comply with the Canada Health Act as of 1986–87.
- Figures include cuts to the post-secondary education component of the EPF.

SOURCE: Ministère des Finances, "Fiscal Arrangements: Contracting-out by the Federal Government?" Appendix F in Ministère des Finances, *1986–1987 Budget: Budget Speech and Additional Information* (Québec: Governement du Québec, 1986), p. 21.

Despite the federal government's declared intentions to sustain their fiscal capacity to provide services, the poorer provinces have every reason to be concerned about the future of equalization payments. As of April 1, 1987, supplementary equalization payments were withdrawn and now all the provinces will bear the impact of the formula introduced in 1982.[24] The Government of Quebec estimates that it will incur losses of about $200 million per annum alone compared to what it would have received under the formula in effect prior to 1982. Quebec concludes that "this will even further accentuate the disparity in fiscal capacities between Ontario and Quebec."[25] In other words, fiscal capacity to maintain social services between rich and poor provinces as a whole is likely to widen if the current equalization formula is not modified.

In sum, Liberal and Conservative budgets have reduced transfers to persons and transfers to the provinces and equalization payments are only being maintained at levels intended to ensure that some provinces will be able to deliver a uniform standard of social services. However, a uniform standard of social services does not necessarily imply the highest standard. Federal spending cutbacks have placed a considerable strain on provincial social services and have, consequently, provided a boost for privatization.

All of this is entirely consistent with a social security cum economic strategy for social services. The strategy favours a withdrawal of government from the social services sector, but not a complete withdrawal. Clearly, the strategy is disposed towards an erosion, but not a dismantling, of social services. As a matter of fact, Liberal and Conservative governments have been stridently defensive of certain programs that have been perceived as not interfering with individual initiative. Health care services are a case in point.

Reaction: Defending Health Care Services

All in all, public health care programs are avidly supported by federal Liberals and Conservatives because they are enthusiastically supported by the electorate at large. In his report on health services for the 1980s, Justice Emmett Hall put the case another way: "I found no one, not any Government or individual, not the Medical Profession nor any organization, not in favour of Medicare."[26] He added that "there were differences of opinion, it is true, on how it should be organized and provided, but no one wanted it terminated."

Justice Hall also identified issues related to privatization as the main issues that had haunted governments in Canada since the late 1970s; these are, first, "the growing practice by physicians to extra-bill" and, second, "the controversies that flow from the conflicts between the Medical Profession and the scale of fees payable to physicians."[27] He claimed that the two issues are "inextricably interrelated" but he did not extend a connection between them and the more basic issue of underfunding. Instead, he recommended that extra-billing be banned outright by stricter legislation; and he also recommended that doctors' salary disputes be resolved by binding arbitration.

The federal minster of Health and Welfare, Monique Bégin, also refused to draw a connection between direct charges and underfunding, although her provincial counterparts, spurred by provincial medical associations, did so. More importantly, she threatened the provinces with the legislation recommended by Justice Hall when they began to grumble about the renegotiation of the EPF arrangements and a potential erosion of health care. Her case had been bolstered by the Breau task force which also recommended that extra-billing and user-fees be prohibited by legislation. Moreover, the provinces' case had been weakened and Bégin's case strengthened by the task force's conclusion that "in aggregate, and in present circumstances, federal government funding for health care services in Canada appears to be generally adequate."[28] With right on her side coupled with favourable public opinion polls, Mme. Bégin decided to prevent the provinces from encouraging privatization by introducing the Canada Health Act in December 1983. The Conservatives, also influenced by the exigencies of electoral politics, fully supported the legislation as did the New Democratic Party.[29]

The Canada Health Act, 1984, reaffirms the federal government's responsibility to ensure the original five principles of the health care system: universality of benefits; comprehensiveness of services; accessibility to services; portability throughout Canada; and public administration. However, the act essentially focuses on the criteria of universality and accessibility. The entire population is entitled to health care services according to the provisions of the act. More importantly, provincial medicare programs, which limit access via user-charges and/or extra-billing, are meted financial penalties. The act permits the federal government to withhold $1 in transfer payments for every dollar directly paid by patients for health services. The money is held in escrow and is to be released if direct charges are eliminated within three years.

However, the act constitutes a rather weak defense of the health care system. First, the penalties imposed by the act place offending provinces in a "no win" situation. Health economist Lee Sonderstrom points out that a province has two options to avoid the tax penalty.[30] A province can attempt to persuade doctors to forego extra-billing voluntarily but must do so by raising medicare fees in the long-term. Alternatively, a province can ban the practice outright but would probably still require higher fees to satisfy wage demands of doctors. Either way the provinces face higher costs, unless they can convince the medical profession to accept reduced incomes, a most unlikely possibility. These are costs that provinces can ill-afford without trimming spending elsewhere in their health care budgets.

Second, the act fails to address the underfunding issue. Bégin justified the act by pointing out that health care spending, as a portion of national income, had been nearly constant over the decade prior to the introduction of the Canada Health Act.[31] Furthermore, she reminded her provincial counterparts that their governments had received more funds from block-funding financial arrangements than they would have from previous cost-sharing arrangements.[32] Mme. Bégin's contention was borne out by subsequent studies.³³ However, studies have also demonstrated that the costs of provincial health care services have risen—about 14% per annum—and should continue to rise largely due to investments required for new medical technology and the increasing needs of an aging population. Hence, the Canada Health Act has been successful in reducing extra-billing but it has done nothing to alleviate the strain of rising health care costs on provincial treasuries.

The Conservatives were compelled to recognize this during the 1984 electoral campaign. Their longstanding Conservative allies in Alberta, New Brunswick, and Ontario were most adversely affected by the act because of extra-billing practices permitted in those provinces. But federal Conservatives were also wary of public opinion which was overwhelmingly opposed to extra-billing.³⁴ They, therefore, chose the relatively safe course of not raising the act along with the privatization debate as an election issue. Instead, they promised to repair the financial damage inflicted on their provincial stalwarts by the penalties imposed under the act. Mr. Mulroney agreed to provide an extra $100 million for provincial health care programs in the forthcoming fiscal year, an amount roughly equal to the losses incurred by the three provinces not complying at that time, and an additional $150 million in the following year.

The Conservatives as a government neglected to fulfill the promise for extra funds. However, they carefully—very carefully in the aftermath of the universal-selective debacle—initiated a study of privatization in relation to health care services. Bud Sherman, a former Manitoba Health minister, reported that the publicly-funded health care system works well and that there is no need to consider full-scale privatization.³⁵ At most, he recommended that governments consider contracting-out nonmedical services such as housekeeping, dietary and laundry services. More importantly, he sidestepped the underfunding issue. However, he did note provincial dissatisfaction with the current funding formula and diplomatically opened the door to further negotiations by recommending "an exchange to consider the proposed changes in federal health financing legislation, agreeable to the provinces, to encourage wider address of current needs."³⁶ Sherman was not to have the last word on this, although Conservative Health and Welfare minister, Jake Epp, claimed that he thought that the report would have "put privatization to a large extent to bed."³⁷ A statement similar to Sherman's was issued six months later by A Study Team Report to the Task Force on Program Review (the Nielsen Report).³⁸

The study team report concludes that it found no evidence to prove that the health care system is either underfunded or overfunded; it contends that "a balance overall appears to have been achieved at the present time."[39] Yet the report recognizes that cost pressures are building up and these are cost pressures that the provinces may not be fully equipped to handle due to the current terms of the EPF Act and the Canada Health Act. The report emphasizes that the two acts are "inextricably linked to each other" and, in so many words, implies that they are "the two pillars" which anchor the case for privatization.[40] Thus, the report promotes an "evolution option," a restatement of the Sherman recommendation, as a means of maintaining the present funding balance. The evolution option simply urges both levels of government to define and establish a new and more appropriate relationship in regard to the two acts.

Has the issue of privatizing health care services been finally put to bed as a result of these similar recommendations? Not quite. Epp steadfastly adheres to the principles of a social security cum economic strategy while discussing the future financing of health care services. In the first instance, he has recently begun to promote volunteer services—individual initiative— as a means to slow the growth in health care costs.[41] In the second instance, he holds the system inviolable but he also stresses that the entire system is based on one condition: economic growth. According to the minister, "we cannot maintain the system as Canadians, if we don't get the economy generated. It is as simple as that."[42] And the minister does not hesitate to point out that the same applies to services provided under the federal regime of social assistance.

Inaction: Maintaining Services Under the Canada Assistance Plan

The Canada Assistance Plan (CAP) only constitutes slightly less than 10% of federal spending on social assistance. However, CAP has a considerable direct impact on provincial social assistance services. It represents a substantial source of revenue for the provinces which would otherwise lack the fiscal wherewithal to maintain the current range and levels of social services. Yet CAP has escaped the acrimonious feuding which has typified federal-provincial relations in regard to the application of the social security cum economic strategy, and especially the economic aspect of the strategy, to other programs in the social affairs envelope.

Nevertheless, CAP has been a centrepiece of federal-provincial discussions on social assistance since 1973, although less so since the collapse of the Social Security Review. Of the various themes that have dominated these talks, the funding theme bears the closest relationship to the privatization issue.[43] But the privatization of CAP *per se* has rarely been raised as an issue essentially because the program legislation prohibits delivery of services for profit. In addition, the provinces, which administer CAP expenditures, use public agencies to deliver the welfare component but permit a mixture of public and private agencies to deliver the social services component. Still privatization is not entirely a dormant issue. The provinces, and especially the poorer provinces, contend that they cannot afford to meet their financial obligations under CAP. This may force them to let individuals fend for themselves or to leave the provision of many social services to the voluntary sector.

CAP's funding problem is much like the funding problem which has emerged within the health care system; the plan is neither underfunded nor overfunded in terms of its current parameters. Under CAP legislation, the federal government cost-shares provincial welfare payments to individuals and families; it also shares the costs of a plethora of provincial social services provided for those in need and those likely to be in need. Hence, conditional cost-sharing, conditional grants, and direct funding, which has increased from a total of $343 million in 1967-68 to $4.033 billion in 1984-85, enables the federal government to exercise a major influence over CAP-sponsored programs.[44] However, CAP spending is expected to rise to $8.45 billion by 1989-90 because the costs are fueled by demand which cannot legally be denied to persons in need. The Nielsen Task Force remarks that "some degree of (spending) discretion does exist and restraint measures are exercised by the provinces, not by the federal government."[45] In other words, if CAP expenditures are to be curtailed, then, according to the terms of the legislation, the provinces must take the initiative by reducing the number of programs and program costs.

However, in the late 1970s federal Liberals did not see fit to leave restraint initiatives to the province. They considered various ways, including a Social Services Financing Act, to reduce CAP expenditures without fundamentally altering the plan.[46] Eventually, Health and Welfare officials were asked to seek ways to limit growth in the social services component to 11% but not in the welfare payment component of CAP. This was set aside during the brief Tory interregnum and eventually the Breau Task Force was left to make the first major recommendation on CAP financing.

The Breau Task Force unequivocally recommended that the federal government not reduce its fiscal commitment to CAP. The figures demonstrate that Liberals and Conservatives alike have heeded that advice;

they have not only maintained CAP expenditures but have actually sustained considerable increases. However, the Nielsen Task Force, reporting four years later, implies that the government may soon be compelled to reconsider that advice.

The Nielsen Task Force claims that CAP funds are well-spent but recognizes that rapidly increasing costs coupled with present economic trends may force a change in the open-ended character of funding arrangements. The task force puts the case bluntly: "if the cost of CAP becomes intolerable, the federal government might limit its expenditures."[47] Moreover, it is quick to point out the main negative implication which is that "the burden would be shifted to the provinces or simply ignored."

Just as the provinces are unable to shoulder the burden of expanding costs in health care services, they, and especially the poorer provinces, can ill-afford to support rising costs in social assistance for several reasons. First, the provinces have already absorbed much of the costs resulting from federal cutbacks to other social security programs. A series of amendments to the Unemployment Insurance Act, beginning in 1976, transferred much of the financial responsibility for supporting the unemployed to provincial social assistance schemes. Moreover, provincial social assistance programs may be required to sustain the impact of additional cuts, in light of the recommendation of the Forget Commission to slash $3 billion from unemployment insurance expenditures.[48]

In addition, spending on job creation programs—programs that have traditionally reduced provincial welfare caseloads—apparently peaked in 1984-85 and has since declined.[49] Indeed, it has been argued that present spending on the Canadian Jobs Strategy program, the centrepiece of current federal jobs creation projects, would have to be increased from $1.7 billion to $2.5 billion just to maintain 1984 funding levels.[50]

It is not surprising that the Nielsen Task Force acknowledges that CAP is highly sensitive to unemployment rates in light of the effects of unemployment insurance amendments during the last decade. Yet there are no apparent signs that unemployment will be significantly reduced in the foreseeable future. Furthermore, the six and five program has reduced incomes of those in receipt of welfare payments and placed pressure on the provinces to make up the shortfall. In short, cutbacks to federal social security programs have lengthened provincial welfare rolls and have strained the provinces' capacity to fulfill their financial obligations under CAP as a whole.

Second, CAP funding cannot be considered in isolation from funding changes to the EPF and to equalization payments. Actual and intended cutbacks to both have added an enormous burden to provincial social budgets. It is estimated that these cutbacks combined with the financial implications of the Canada Health Act will result in over $23 billion in revenue losses for all provinces between 1982-92.[51] Thus, if an upper threshold were to be placed on federal spending on CAP, the provinces would be hard-pressed to deliver the social services required to meet increasing demands.

Finally, in the future the poorer provinces will not be able to absorb reductions in transfer payments as easily as the richer provinces especially because of the unsatisfactory role that equalization is expected to perform. The richer provinces will continue to possess a higher fiscal capacity which gives them more latitude to levy taxes. Yet the richer provinces have less social service needs to support than poor provinces. If CAP transfers were to be limited, the poorer provinces would have the most difficulty in maintaining social assistance services.

All of this anticipates the worst. In the meantime, the federal government has more than maintained its financial obligations in satisfying provincial needs for social assistance services. Federal Liberals and federal Conservatives have spared CAP the scalpel that has been wielded on other social welfare programs via the application of a social security cum economic strategy for two reasons: first, CAP is too small to count in the context of total federal disbursements on social security. Second, CAP has effectively cushioned much of the impact of cuts to other programs. However, the costs of the plan are rising. And the close adherence of federal Liberals and Conservatives to a social security cum economic strategy suggests that measures could be taken which would exert considerable financial pressure on the provinces to experiment with privatization alternatives in the sphere of social assistance services.

Conclusion: Eluding Privatization

In his 1986 budget speech, the minister of Finance clearly stated that Conservatives as a governing party are not likely to stray from a social security cum economic strategy:

> This government is not prepared to dismantle social programs. The best ways to reduce the cost of social measures are to make sure that spending and tax assistance are targeted effectively and to reduce the need for such support—by keeping the economy growing and creating jobs so

that greater opportunities are provided, to those Canadians now in need.[52]

The minister's remarks suggest that for the time being the Conservative response to privatization will remain a continuation of the Liberal response—action, reaction, and inaction. But why should the response be otherwise? It enables the governing party to elude responsibility for privatization, a contentious issue which any party seeking to retain electoral popularity must try to avoid.

The complex host of mechanisms that federal Liberals and Conservatives have employed to trim transfer payments are, for the most part, far too confusing to capture the undivided attention of the electorate. In any event, the federal parties possess an effective device to dramatically demonstrate to electors of a interventionist disposition that they are fully committed to publicly funded social services: a balance sheet which reveals that the federal government spends a staggering $40 billion annually on social programs. It is also an effective device to legitimize cutbacks to those oriented towards a market ethos. Moreover, federal parties can appeal to both social security strategists and economic strategists by pointing out that social expenditures have not decreased or increased, since the late 1970s; expenditures have grown in proportion to the growth of the economy.

As if that were not enough, Liberals and Conservatives can appease both camps of strategists by justifiably arguing that they have done their utmost to protect health care services, the jewel of Canada's social security network. Health care expenditures have likewise increased in proportion to growth in the economy. Finally, CAP expenditures should create no controversy. Interventionists are likely to appreciate increases in CAP spending while advocates of a market ethos are inclined to accede to public disbursements for those in need as long as spending is not excessive.

Nevertheless, both federal parties have been eluding responsibility for the privatization of social services. They have failed to fully contribute to their share of rising costs for social services. As governing parties, both have continued to suggest that social expenditures are enlarging the deficit despite evidence which shows that increased spending on other policy sectors and on debt servicing are primarily responsible.[53] Finally, both have failed to generate significant economic growth, the raison d'être of containing social spending. In short, Liberals and Conservatives are largely responsible for creating financial and economic circumstances that are encouraging the privatization of social services.

Be that as it may, the application of a social security cum economic strategy to social issues cannot continue indefinitely. A new mood of interventionism has recently emerged within the electorate. The mood is apparent in a general dissatisfaction with federal Conservatives and Liberals and with the policies that have been developed within the context of the strategy. More importantly, the mood is expressed in widespread demands for governments to redress problems related to child abuse, to provide homemakers' pensions and, especially, to establish a system of universal day care centres.

If federal Conservatives and Liberals wish to remain serious contenders for office, they will be required to modify their current strategy by absorbing the essentials of this new mood. In the meantime, federal Conservatives recently created a somewhat modest program to prevent child abuse; the provision of homemakers' pensions is still under consideration; and while Liberals have yet to present their program, Conservatives have begun to prepare a policy on a national system of child care facilities in conjunction with provincial governments. To date, the government has baulked at the costs involved, which, according to the Cooke task force, would amount to $2.9 billion annually in the "medium term" and an additional $6.3 billion spread over the "longer term."[54] At any rate, the government has not found more comfort in a House of Commons committee report which estimates that a national day care system could cost between $767 million and $966 million annually by 1989.[55]

When and if adequate financing is made available, hard choices will have to be made about the public and private mix in the administration and delivery of day care services. But the program will be cost-shared with the provinces and the governing party will, therefore, be able to elude much of the responsibility for whatever the degree of privatization.

Of course, this is just what governing parties have done in the past with respect to social services as a whole. In the end, the provinces administer and deliver health and social services. Thus, for better or for worse, the provinces will continue to shoulder much of the responsibility for privatization. It may be for better or it may be for worse, but that is what the authors of the other chapters must decide.

Notes

1. The federal government administers and delivers job creation, retraining and placement programs often in conjunction with provincial governments and/or the private sector. The provinces are responsible for administering and delivering other social services.
2. See Claude E. Forget, "The Harmonization of Social Policy" in Mark Krasnick (research coordinator), *Fiscal Federalism* (Toronto: University of Toronto Press, 1985), pp. 97-148, for a detailed explanation of these two functions and for a thorough historical analysis of the federal spending power.
3. See, for instance, F.C. Englemann and M.A. Schwartz, *Canadian Political Parties: Origin, Character, Impact* (Toronto: Prentice-Hall, 1975), p. 211; and Douglas McCready and Conrad Winn, "Redistributive Policy" in C. Winn and J. McMenemy, editors, *Political Parties in Canada* (Toronto: McGraw-Hill Ryerson, 1976), pp. 206-27.
4. Kenneth Bryden, *Old Age Pensions and Policy-Making in Canada* (Montreal: McGill-Queen's Press, 1974), p. 19.
5. S.M. Lipset, *Revolution and Counterrevolution* (New York: Anchor Books, 1970), pp. 52-53. For a thorough and perceptive discussion of broad ideological currents in Canada. Also see David Bell and Lorne Tepperman, *The Roots of Disunity: A Look at Canadian Political Culture* (Toronto: McClelland and Stewart, 1979), pp. 1-71.
6. J.R. Mallory, *The Structure of Canadian Government (Revised Edition)*, (Toronto: Gage, 1984), p. 219, effectively makes this point.
7. See the remarks of Lincoln Alexander in Canada, *House of Commons Debates*, April 2, 1971, p. 6583.
8. Hon. Allan J. MacEachen, *The Budget* (Ottawa: Department of Finance, October 28, 1980), p. 13.
9. *Globe and Mail*, December 17, 1980.
10. The 1980 budget was a first major attempt to reduce federal transfers for social services. However, Allan Moscovitch, "L'Etat-providence au Canada depuis 1975" in Diane Bellemare et Céline St. Pierre, editors, *Les stratégies de reprise* (Montréal: Editions Saint Martin, 1984), pp. 26-29, points out that a decline in social security spending, as a portion of total federal expenditure, began as early as 1975. Moscovitch argues that this was largely due to the influence of neoconservative ideology, originating in the United States and Britain. In addition, he demonstrates that the federal share of social security spending during that period was considerably reduced while provincial and municipal shares increased significantly.
11. Several provinces were alleged to have diverted funds transferred for the established programs to other programs. See *Globe and Mail*, February 19, 1981.
12. Canada, *Report of the Parliamentary Task Force on Federal-Provincial Fiscal Arrangements (Fiscal Federalism in Canada)* (Ottawa: Minister of Supply and Services, 1981), p. 1.
13. *Globe and Mail*, September 1, 1981.
14. Hon. Allan J. MacEachen, *Budget Speech* (Ottawa: Department of Finance, November 12, 1981), p. 6.

15. Hon. Michael H. Wilson, *Economic and Fiscal Statement* (Ottawa: House of Commons, November 8, 1984).
16. Ibid., p. 13.
17. For a comprehensive analysis of social policy and the 1985 budget, see Michael J. Prince, "Social Policy in PC Year One," *Perception* 9, no. 1 (September/October 1985), pp. 7-9.
18. Hon. Michael H. Wilson, *Securing Economic Renewal: The Budget Speech* (Ottawa: Department of Finance, May 23, 1985), p. 12.
19. Hon. Michael H. Wilson, *Securing Economic Renewal: The Budget Speech* (Ottawa: Department of Finance, February 26, 1986), p. 11.
20. Hon. Michael H. Wilson, *The Fiscal Plan* (Ottawa: Department of Finance, February 1986), p. 28.
21. Ministère des Finances, "Fiscal Arrangements: Contracting-out by the Federal Government?" Appendix F in Ministère des Finances, *1986-1987 Budget: Budget Speech and Additional Information* (Québec: Gouvernement du Québec, 1986), p. 11.
22. Canada, *Report of the Parliamentary Task Force*, p. 158.
23. Hon. Michael H. Wilson, *Securing Economic Renewal: The Budget Speech* (Ottawa: Department of Finance, February 26, 1986), p. 11.
24. In March 1987, the federal government introduced Bill C-44 which, like Bill C-96, is an amendment to the *Federal-Provincial Fiscal Arrangements and Post-Secondary Education and Health Contributions Act, 1977*. Bill C-44 permits the federal government to provide $175 million or approximately a 5% increase in equalization payments over a two-year period. These funds hardly make up for provincial loses incurred under Bill C-96, especially for several provinces. Hence, the provinces have begun to bear the impact of Bill C-96 but not the *full* impact.
25. Ministère des Finances, "Fiscal Arrangements," p. 5.
26. Hon. Emmett M. Hall, C.C., Q.C., Special Commissioner, *Canada's National-Provincial Health Program for the 1980's* (Ottawa: Health and Welfare Canada, 1980), p. 2.
27. Ibid., p. 23
28. Canada, *Report of the Parliamentary Task Force*, p. 114.
29. Dennis Guest, *The Emergence of Social Security in Canada*, second edition (Vancouver: University of British Columbia Press, 1985), pp. 227-28, provides a succinct summary of The Canada Health Act and of the events related to its passage.
30. Lee Sonderstrom, "Does Extra-Billing Erode Health of Medicare?" in *Montreal Gazette*, December 22, 1983. Sonderstrom's arguments against extra-billing and other elements of privatization related to Canadian health care services are fully presented in Lee Sonderstrom, *Taxing the Sick: Health Policy at a Crossroad*, Publication No. 11 (Ottawa: Canadian Centre for Policy Alternatives, no date).
31. Hon. Monique Bégin, *Preserving Universal Medicare: A Government of Canada Position Paper* (Ottawa: Minister of Supply and Services, 1983), p. 13.
32. Hon. Monique Bégin, *Statement by the Hon. Monique Bégin, Minister of Health and Welfare, to the Conference of Provincial Ministers of Health* (Halifax: September 7, 1983), p. 6.

33. See Gilles Grenier, "Health Care Costs in Canada: Past and Future Trends" in François Vaillancourt (research coordinator), *Income Distribution and Economic Security in Canada* (Toronto: University of Toronto Press, 1985), pp. 264-74.
34. In May of 1984 a Gallup Poll reported that 83% of Canadians were opposed to extra-billing. See *Montreal Gazette*, May 10, 1984.
35. Association Health Planners, *Management by Private Contract: A Study for the Minister of Health and Welfare Canada* (Winnipeg: A.H.P., June 1985)
36. Ibid., p. 14.
37. *The Ottawa Citizen*, February 20, 1986.
38. A Study Team Report to the Task Force on Program Review, *Improved Program Delivery: Health and Sports* (Ottawa: Supply and Services Canada, 1985), p. 13.
39. Ibid., p. 33. The report identifies ideology as the primary source of the privatization debate. However, it adds that "the two pillars anchoring the privatization argument appear to be supplements for financing and the management of institutional care."
40. Ibid., p. 45.
41. Hon. Jake Epp, Minister of Health and Welfare, *Achieving Health for All: A Framework for Health Promotion* (Ottawa: Supply and Services Canada, November, 1986). He takes the position that community and volunteer groups should take the initiative to educate the public in order to prevent various illnesses.
42. *The Ottawa Citizen*, February 20, 1986.
43. A Study Team Report to the Task Force on Program Review, *Service to the Public: Canada Assistance Plan* (Ottawa: Supply and Services Canada, 1985), pp. 81-90 identifies and discusses in detail three themes that have dominated developments in the social assistance field: the plight of "unemployed employables," fiscal restraint, and federal-provincial friction. However, the report does not draw a specific connection between fiscal restraint or funding and privatization.
44. Ibid., p. 5. However, federal influence via CAP disbursements on provincial social assistance expenditure may be more apparent than real. At least this is implied by Philip Hepworth "Trends in Provincial Social Service Department Expenditures, 1963-1982" in Jacqueline S. Ismael, editor, *Canadian Social Welfare Policy: Federal and Provincial Dimensions* (Montreal: McGill-Queen's Press, 1985), pp. 139-72. Hepworth persuasively argues that the spending of individual provinces is primarily related to the demand and resources for services in each province.
45. Ibid., p. 5.
46. Duncan Matheson, "Clarifying Social Welfare Policy" *Policy Options* 4, no. 4 (July/August 1983), pp. 26-29, identifies and evaluates the various options.
47. A Study Team Report to the Task Force on Program Review, *Service to the Public*, p. 14.
48. Canada, *Report of the Commission of Inquiry on Unemployment Insurance* (Ottawa: Supply and Services Canada, November 1986). As of July 1987, the employment minister had reserved judgement on the Forget Report. He was

also considering the recommendations of a *First Report: Unemployment Insurance* submitted by the Standing Committee on Labour, Employment and Immigration to the House of Commons on March 19, 1987.
49. Leslie A. Pal, "Tools for the Job: Canada's Evolution from Public Works to Mandated Employment" in Jacqueline S. Ismael, editor, *The Canadian Welfare State: Evolution and Transition* (Edmonton: University of Alberta Press, 1987), pp. 33-62, argues that "job creation strategies have been in stasis since 1980" and that Ottawa has begun to focus its job creation energies on "mandated employment" or affirmative action employment.

Furthermore, the *Forget Report*, pp. 87-91, and A Study Team Report to the Task Force on Program Review, *Job Creation, Training and Employment Services* (Ottawa: Supply and Services Canada, 1985), pp. 9-20, do not recommend increased funding for job creation. Rather, their recommendations advocate the better use of funds already in the system.
50. Canada, *House of Commons Debates*, March 19, 1987, p. 4352.
51. Ministère des Finances, "Fiscal Arrangements," p. 21.
52. Hon. Michael H. Wilson, *Securing Economic Renewal: The Budget Speech* (Ottawa: Department of Finance, February 26, 1986), p. 12.
53. Ministère des Finances, "Fiscal Arrangements," pp. 8-9, discusses this point and indicates that federal transfers as a portion of the GNP have remained constant since the late 1970s but that federal expenditure as a portion of GNP has risen.
54. Canada, *Report of the Task Force on Child Care* (Ottawa: Supply and Services Canada, November, 1986), p. 339.
55. Canada, *Report of the Special Committee on Child Care (Sharing the Responsibility)* (Ottawa: House of Commons, March 1987), p. 133.

10 Conclusion
Privatization in Comparative Provincial Perspective

JACQUELINE S. ISMAEL

YVES VAILLANCOURT

The introductory chapter of this volume raised issues about privatization as a process and as part of a broader trend. Each of the case studies explored these issues in a different political unit and from a different perspective. This chapter will provide a comparative overview of the case studies, highlighting both the similarities and differences that emerge from them.

Privatization as a Process

One of the most striking similarities to emerge from the seven provincial case studies is the pervasive commitment to privatization. Six of the seven provinces have made explicit commitments to the process of privatization of social service delivery. Manitoba is the only province that has not adopted such a policy. Furthermore, while federal policy remained noncommital and apparently neutral on the issue of privatization of social service delivery, it has at the same time effectively encouraged provincial movements in this direction through the advancement of a "social security cum economic strategy" to social services.

The process of privatization of social service delivery began in all provinces studied here as a response to fiscal restraint; but in all these cases, except Manitoba, it has progressed from a response to economic crisis to a means of paring down the welfare state and revitalizing the private sector. In British Columbia, Alberta and New Brunswick, privatization has been pronounced as an explicit objective of public policy. But whether declared or not, in six of the seven provinces, it is the manifest objective of government actions vis-a-vis the social services.

The evolution of social service delivery systems varies from province to province, as reflected in the case studies. In all provinces, a form of welfare pluralism developed historically, with social service delivery provided through a mix of public and private nonprofit agencies. The introduction or increase of proprietary agencies into this model is a recent phenomenon, generally concentrated and growing in specific service areas—primarily care and custodial facilities. While the welfare pluralist model is a common feature of provincial service delivery systems, its form varies from province to province, being a product of the unique demographic history, economic and social development and political culture of a province.

A striking similarity across the provinces, however, is the strong preference for nonprofit, community based social service delivery systems. This preference has historically cut across political, social and economic differences among and within the provinces, and seems in some provinces to be based in a kind of self help or populist cultural tradition that has rooted itself in Canadian social administration. Much of the rhetoric of privatization draws upon and appeals directly to this tradition.

Thus, in all of the provincial case studies examined here, the historical and contemporary organization of social services relies heavily on private nonprofit social services of one kind or another. The degree and nature of the state's responsibility in the organization of social services in these provinces is an important variation across the provinces. In the 1980s, for example, the state's involvement in the delivery and administration of social services has been greater in some provinces (such as Quebec and New Brunswick), and less in others (such as Ontario and British Columbia). The point is that the rate at which public services are privatized is directly related to the degree of public involvement in social service delivery.

As a result of the variation in the provinces and their social service delivery systems, provincial privatization policies vary in their style, form and scope. British Columbia represents the most comprehensive and conspicuous privatization package, where every mechanism to foster downsizing of the welfare state has been employed—from divestment and disentitlement to contracting out and underfunding. While the other five provinces that have adopted privatization strategies for social services have not appeared to be so blatant or bold in their attack on the welfare state, they have all, nonetheless, pursued downsizing through a more selective package of the same kinds of mechanisms and more selective targeting of programs. For example, while British Columbia is perhaps the most flamboyant model of privatization, Ontario has been deliberately and systematically implementing the policy longer than any of the other five provinces. It has used underfunding of services and contracting out as primary mechanisms.

In the introductory chapter, privatization was identified as both a means of rationalizing social spending in a market economy and of restraining the rate of growth of the public social sector in a period of increasing demand for services—demand generated by the hardships of high unemployment, slow economic growth, fiscal restraint, and demographic transition. With the failure of the Social Security Review and the introduction by the federal government of wage and price controls in 1975, federal policy has been an important stimulant to provincial privatization. The Saskatchewan case reflects how Prime Minister Trudeau's wage and price controls exerted pressure on provinces to freeze the development of provincial social expenses. Changes in federal fiscal and equalization policies in the late 1970s and the 1980s have been "largely responsible for creating financial and economic circumstances that are encouraging the privatization of social services" in many provinces. This was done in the last ten years both by Liberal and Conservative governments in spite of the differences of their rhetoric and their common tendency to elude responsibility for privatization, as demonstrated in the federal case study. Dr. Johnson's chapter shows, for example, that the changes introduced, mainly in 1982, in the Established Programs Financing (EPF) formula have meant, for many provinces, a dramatic reduction in the amount of transfer payments previously received from the federal government. This forced "the provinces to either make up the shortfall from their revenues or to shift social responsibilities to the private sector."

Paradoxically, one of the case studies which strongly demonstrates this is that of Manitoba. In this province, the only one in which we have not found practices of privatization, the reduction of transfer payments has created a strong pressure on the province to move towards cutbacks of social programs and to dismantle the provincial welfare state. However, Manitoba, led by an NDP government, was able to overcome this pressure toward privatization and maintained the proportion of provincial revenues dedicated to social programs and services. This achievement, however, has been an exception. In other provinces (New Brunswick, Quebec, etc.), the reduction of federal funding became a push, or a pretext, to move toward privatization.

On the other hand, the Canada Assistance Plan (CAP) has played a limited role. To some extent, it has limited the ability of those provinces that have declared privatization to be an objective of social policy to take bolder steps toward the commercialization of social services. The very fact that CAP regulations do not allow cost-sharing of provincial social services delivered by for-profit agencies (in day care or in homemakers services, for example), represents a pressure toward forms of privatization in which delivery of social services is done by nonprofit voluntary agencies. In other words, CAP rules and tradition may have so far restrained the commercialization drive in some provinces. But the very selective nature of CAP represents another federal factor stimulating provincial privatization. CAP's record, in other words, is less impressive than CAP's image, in terms of its contribution to the financing of provincial social services. Indeed, CAP is far from financing 50 percent, or even 30 percent, of the provincial social services in Canada. Recently, for example, the Rochon Commission argued that CAP's contribution to the funding of Quebec social services represented 23 percent of their total costs. Under this kind of cost-sharing arrangement, it is not surprising that provinces may be reluctant to get involved in the delivery of social services, and prefer to contract out with private agencies or community organizations.

Privatization as a means of rationalizing social spending is more clearly associated with forestalling growth in the size of the public social service sector and circulating program funding through the private sector (profit and nonprofit) to stimulate growth there than with cutbacks in overall social expenditures, at least in the short-term. In all of the provinces, significant portions of the social expenditure budgets are locked into statutory programs. While the state must maintain funding responsibility for such programs, the case studies suggest that increasingly such programs and/or ancillary services related to them, are contracted out to the private sector on a fee for service basis. At the same time, fiscal restraint policies curb the rate of increase in the costs of these programs, in effect producing underfunding, but the contracting out mechanism places the private sector between the state and the populace as an administrative buffer against service accountability. While the dynamics of this vary from province to province and are related to the particular mix of public and private delivery in each province, the process converges at the point of devolving administrative responsibility for service delivery onto the private sector.

Though the case studies are more suggestive of this than documentary, the dynamic is evidenced in the case of child welfare services in British Columbia and corrections services in Ontario. In Alberta, decentralization/regionalization has served a similar function.

Privatization as a means of rationalizing social spending in a market economy is part of a larger social security cum economic strategy which restricts social policy to a handmaiden role vis-a-vis economic policy formulated on the principle of privatization. The relationship between privatization of social services and economic policy is highlighted in the various provincial reports examined in the case studies. Privatization as a broad economic policy at the federal level, and cutbacks in benefit levels in federal social programs, are mirrored at the provincial level, and reflected in collapsing benefit levels to social allowance recipients, restrictions on eligibility to social programs, and contracting out of service delivery to the private sector.

While examined directly in only one chapter (Saskatchewan), and indirectly in the chapter on federal policy, the changing relationship between income security policies and job creation policies is directly related to privatization and has profound implications for social services. The Saskatchewan chapter revealed the distinction between deserving poor (the young, the old and the handicapped) and the undeserving poor (unemployed employables) that is emerging in terms of differential program access and benefits. The linkage between cutbacks in social assistance and increases in privatization are evident. On the one hand, the province is limiting the availability and amount of social assistance benefits, through the "welfare reform" introduced by the Devine government in 1983. On the other hand, the role of food banks and other traditional charity initiatives run by private nonprofit organizations has been increasing since 1983 and many of the food bank clients are individuals and families touched by the cuts in social assistance benefits.

This illustrates the point that the devolution of state responsibility at stake in the privatization process is not necessarily done in the domain of in-kind programs. It can take place in income security programs, obliging the recipients receiving less public support in cash to rely more heavily on private support in kind (food banks, soup kitchens, homeless shelters, etc.). These phenomena are related to privatization of social services.

Privatization as an economic strategy may be identified with the objective of promoting private-sector led economic recovery by decreasing government involvement in the economy and stimulating private market activity. Privatization of social service delivery must be understood as an

Table 10–1   Provincial Services in the 1980s Examined in These Case Studies

Province	Services
British Columbia	child welfare services family support services day care services young offender services
Alberta	social allowance child welfare
Saskatchewan	social allowance child welfare vocational rehabilitation services for the handicapped
Manitoba	child welfare home care services day care
Ontario	children's services: group homes, day care services for the handicapped homes for the aged home care services young offender services correctional services health related social services
Quebec	home care services youth services services for battered women nursing homes rehabilitation services
New Brunswick	social services provided under the auspices of the Department of Health and Community Services

integral part of this broader economic strategy if it is to be distinguished from the policies promoting private nonprofit community based social welfare services that dominated the heyday of expansion of the Canadian welfare state. Viewed only as a set of policies aimed at stimulating private sector provision of social services, privatization policies may appeal to the grassroots tradition in Canadian social administration for these policies do serve to promote and support community based nonprofit provision, and there has not been the wholesale development of profiteering agencies—as the case studies here have demonstrated. Considered in the broader context of state policies aimed at rolling back the rate of growth or absolute amount of state activity in the social service delivery system—the approach taken in this volume—privatization of social service delivery addresses the changing role of the state in social welfare provision, as well as the changing role of the social welfare institution in relation to the market economy. It is in this context that privatization may be identified as part of a broader trend.

Privatization as Part of a Broader Trend

The distinction between privatization as a means of maintaining an institutional model of services—community based and responsive to local needs (the ideal of the Canadian welfare state)—under conditions of fiscal restraint, and privatization as a means of devolving unto the private sector (profit and nonprofit, formal and informal) responsibility for service provision to the needy is highlighted in the contrast between the Manitoba case and the other six provincial cases examined in this volume. The services examined are summarized in the Table 10-1.

While the case studies contrast in the services examined and the issues focused on, two major themes emerge that help to clarify the trend. Fundamentally, it is a distinction based upon where responsibility for need rests and where accountability for service provision consequently resides. This distinction is primarily a qualitative one at this stage in the process of devolution. It certainly derives from the rhetoric of privatization. The very incentive of the privatization drive is not so much to permit individuals and local communities to assume more responsibilities; it is more to allow provincial governments to reduce their social program responsibilities in order to limit the financial resources of the state committed to the empowerment of individuals and local communities to assume responsibilities. In this sense, the rhetoric of privatization of social services sounds like a regeneration of the old residual model of social provision.

In practice, this is evident in the imposition of a treatment model of service delivery unto the nonprofit sector through contracting out on a fee for service basis. It is also evident in the empowerment of the for-profit sector through public legitimation of its role in social service delivery and the contracting out mechanism. Growth of the proprietary sector has been observed primarily in care and custodial services. Thus, the combination of contracting out to the nonprofit sector for treatment services and empowerment of the proprietary sector appear to be central characteristics in devolution.

This study set out to assess the scope and magnitude of privatization of social service delivery across the provinces. We may conclude that it is substantial, and is a provincial policy response in six of the seven provinces to the changing pattern of social welfare needs—changing patterns generated by demographic change as our population ages, by structural change in the labour market as our economy adjusts to slower economic growth in a more competitive world economy, and by changing federal social policies (e.g., the Young Offenders' Act and cutbacks in federal social programs). The changing patterns of social need constitute challenges to our social safety net as more senior Canadians become socially dependent, younger Canadians fail to find permanent full-time employment in the labour force and provinces absorb more of the financial burdens of social programs. What the case studies identify is that privatization as a response to structural changes in the economy and demography of society constitutes the investment of public funds into the private market for service delivery. Nonprofit social service agencies are being drawn into the expanding market framework for established services, while proprietary agencies are rapidly expanding in new service areas. The case studies could only allude to the impact of these changes on the social service delivery system since this was not our primary focus. In particular, the British Columbia and New Brunswick chapters address the effects of the privatization trend on the quality of services in the service delivery domain and on the identity of nonprofit agencies and community groups. In other cases, many of these issues were identified as issues in need of further study. We would encourage this in an inter-provincial comparative framework, and hope that the challenge will be picked up, especially in light of the free trade agreement which may well have profound repercussions on both the patterns of social need and service delivery.

LEWIS AND CLARK COLLEGE LIBRARY

Lewis and Clark College - Watzek Library
HV108 .P75 1988   wmain
/Privatization and provincial social ser

3 5209 00358 9948